GW00982583

SIMON HILL

JUST A GOB ON A STICK

SIMON HILL

JUST A GOB ON A STICK

THE VOICE
BEHIND THE MIC

CONTENTS

CONTENTS

FOREWORD

Simon Hill's voice has been part of just about every big moment in Australian football for more than ten years. To many fans, Simon's commentary has become an integral part of their memories of those events. They don't just remember John Aloisi hitting the penalty to send us to the 2006 World Cup, they remember it with 'He's scored! Australia have done it!'

The first time I met Simon was when I was playing for Millwall. He interviewed me around the time that I was trying to get clearance to represent Australia. Ever since, it seems as though our careers have run side by side – from that penalty shootout against Uruguay in 2005, through the 2006 World Cup...and both still going strong today!

Simon has been a constant in Australian football through a period of massive change. Starting with the NSL, he was there through the A-League's inception and his voice has become synonymous with the league. All of the experiences that you will read about in this book have helped Simon to educate the Australian public, especially those new to football, about the beauty of our game. Simon's fair, knowledgeable and insightful comments have made him popular throughout the football community – no small achievement!

Football breeds passion. One of the best aspects of the Australian game is the way that it captures so many cultures and brings them together. Simon not only understands that, he's a part of it. When John scored the winning penalty against Uruguay in 2005, it's hard to tell who was more excited, us on the pitch or Simon in the commentary box!

Both Simon and I have a strong passion for football, and we haven't always agreed with everything that the other person has said, but Simon has a great talent of being able to listen and consider a different point of view. This is one reason why he is such a great asset to Australian football; he can see the viewpoints of all the different groups who come together in the game, from the fans to the administrators, to the players and coaches, to those who have a commercial interest, and he will genuinely listen to what they have to say before coming to his own conclusion.

I won't forget, and I doubt that Sanitarium will, what he said after I scored against Japan in 2006: 'He did have his Weet-bix this morning!' I should really be sending him royalties!

I want to thank Simon for letting me write these few words. Thanks for being 'the voice' for nearly all of my career with the Socceroos. And continue to do what you do so well – educate, challenge, promote and bring colour to those who love our beautiful game, so that it will continue to develop until, as Ange says, we win the World Cup!

Tim Cahill

CHAPTER ONE

STORY OF THE BLUES

I knew at 12 years of age that I was never going to be good enough to play for Manchester City. Twelve is far too young an age for that dose of adult reality – and I wasn't ready for it. But that's where it all started. On a muddy field in north-western England, walking disconsolately towards a shoddy prefab dressing room on a freezing Sunday morning.

It was supposed to be my day.

Oughtrington Rovers under 13s were a good little junior side, finishing third in the league, and I was their ever-so-average left winger (or on occasion, centre forward). Good enough for 10 or 12 goals a season, a decent passer, a bit of pace and an unselfish provider for our prolific striker, Derek Hampson, who must have netted at least 40 goals that particular season.

Hampson may have caught the attention of the grey-haired man stood silently watching that particular afternoon. But it was our goalkeeper the Manchester City scout, Eric Mallender, was really interested in. Steve Crompton went on to star for City's all-conquering FA Youth Cup winning team in 1986, playing alongside Paul Lake, Andy Hinchcliffe, David White and Steve Redmond – all of whom went on to become City first-teamers, with two of them going on to win full England honours.

Crompton, though, never made it at City, and had only a short career in the lower leagues with Stockport and Carlisle before his professional playing days fizzled out. And he was our top player by a mile!

Me? I wasn't even good enough for that, and try as I did that day, the scout never gave me a second glance, and I knew it was over. Dreams shattered, even before the onset of puberty. It's a cruel game, football.

But already, the seed had been sown. Football was my life – and not just playing it either.

Even at that young age, I was obsessed with the minutiae of the sport. I filled pages and pages of notebooks, scribbling down every team's line-up, 1 through to 11. Not just the Arsenals or Liverpools either, but the Crewes, the Halifaxes and Chesterfields. I played Subbuteo (the forerunner of today's video games) for hours on end, collecting different team-coloured kits, and forming my own league with schoolmates. I even got to the quarterfinals of the North West of England Championships one year, receiving my certificate from Manchester United legend, Sir Bobby Charlton.

Dad, a former copper, sports fanatic, and a football tragic since childhood, took his son's anorak-like fascination with Bury's back four all in good humour. But Mum, not much interested in football (perhaps her ex-boyfriend, a former pro at Southport and Mansfield had something to do with that), was less impressed.

'What are you bothering writing all those out for? That won't get you a job when you get older!'

It's a quote I still get a chuckle out of all these years later.

Mum, while not against sport as a hobby, would have preferred me to direct my energies towards studying, and learning to play the piano, like my sister, Fiona. Mum taught piano to various school pupils, and the tinkle of ivories being plinked and plonked reverberated throughout our house for years.

But I was never much interested in learning notes and keys when I could be discovering why Aston Villa's Chris Nicholl played for Northern Ireland, even though he was born just up the road from me, in Wilmslow. Football had already begun giving me an education.

My childhood asthma also played a part in my newfound obsession. As a baby, I was so wheezy I could barely walk upstairs. Dad tells me he used to have to carry me, as my underdeveloped lungs struggled with the affliction. But aged five, Dad had brought out a football, and I began to kick it around our back garden. My asthma improved, almost immediately, through exercise.

Aged six, he took me to my first ever game of live football. Manchester City was his team, and his dad's (my grandad's) team too. In fact, the family lineage went back even further. Nanna Hill told me stories of her father, Fred Taylor, who had played for City back in the 1890s, when they were known as Ardwick FC. She had a photo of him in long baggy shorts, hobnail Victorian boots and a woolly jersey, all topped off by the obligatory handlebar moustache. It's a photo that, to my lifelong regret, went missing after she died, and I've never been able to trace any details of his career.

The game itself was instantly forgettable. It was Manchester City versus Ipswich Town on Saturday, 6 April 1974. City, who'd just been to Wembley, losing the League Cup Final to Wolves, lost again 3–1, or at least that was what I found out, many years later. I wasn't much interested in the game, preferring to play with my toy cars on the hard wooden benches of the old Platt Lane End. I was so clueless that when City went in trailing at the interval, apparently I asked my dad whether they started again at 0–0 after half-time.

But there must have been something about the experience I liked, because when the next season came around (1974/75), and Dad asked me whether I'd like to go again – to the opening match of the season against West Ham – I readily agreed. So, with Grandad in tow as well, the three generations of Hills trooped off to Maine Road, in unison for the first time.

This time it was different. City won 4–0, and I came home sporting a brand new sky blue and white rosette from the souvenir shop. Whether it was the result, the atmosphere (I'd actually watched the game properly this time), or just those beautiful sky blue jerseys, I was hooked.

From that moment on, football, City and I became inseparable. I was enrolled as a member of the Junior Blues, City's young supporters club (membership number 596), and, clad in my awful tracksuit (which had the words 'Manchester City' emblazoned all over it in a headache-inducing, pinstripe effect) I went to regular branch meetings, occasionally grabbing an autograph from first-teamers like Tommy Booth, Joe Corrigan and Peter Barnes. I became a regular at Maine Road, even venturing across the Pennines for a special birthday treat to see my first ever away game in 1975, as City met Sheffield United at Bramall Lane.

The City stars of the era became my heroes. Francis Lee and Mike Summerbee were coming towards the end of their time at the club, but the third member of City's holy trinity, Colin Bell, was at his peak.

Bell was my idol. I had a huge cardboard poster of him on my wall, and eagerly devoured every morsel of information to be found on this sublimely talented midfielder, which wasn't much, as the title of his later autobiography *Reluctant Hero* suggested.

Bell's talents were supplemented by a new generation of City stars such as Dennis Tueart, Dave Watson, Joe Royle, Asa Hartford and Willie Donachie, who had taken over the mantle from the successful team of the late 1960s (perhaps it was apt I was born during season 1967/8, the last time City were champions). It seemed only a matter of time before the trophies began rolling in again.

An opportunity came in the 1975/76 season when the team reached the League Cup Final again. Sadly, neither myself, nor Colin Bell, would be at Wembley. Despite being regular attendees at Maine Road, my dad and I were not yet season ticket holders, so when City won through to the final to play Newcastle, we were unable to secure tickets. I was crestfallen – nonplussed by my dad's cheery assertion that City regularly took part in such occasions, and we could go the next time (though the 'regular' part of the sentence was clearly a fib, as I later found out).

City won 2–1 thanks to a brilliant overhead kick from Dennis Tueart, but I had to content myself with waiting for the final score to come through on BBC's *Grandstand* programme, these being the days before the internet or any live coverage. So obsessed was I with the game at this point, that I had been banned from writing about football in my weekly 'news diary' at junior school. I'm pleased to say my teacher, knowing how important this game was to me, made an exception the Monday after the final, even though she must have been bored stiff by reading my match analysis.

Bell, meantime, had sustained an horrific injury en route to that final, damaging his knee so badly in the 4–0 win over rivals United in the fourth round that he didn't play again in nearly two years. In truth, he was never the same player again. When he did return, in December 1977, ironically against Newcastle, the ovation given to him by the Kippax (the huge standing terrace that ran the entire length of one of the touchlines at Maine Road) almost took the roof off. But it wasn't the Colin Bell I had worshipped; he looked awkward, his leg seemed to be locked in a strange position, and he ended up playing in the centre of defence to accommodate his declining mobility. Such a waste of talent.

By then though, there were other players I admired – and not just wearing the blue of Manchester City. Liverpool were THE team of my childhood generation. Bob Paisley had fashioned a side capable of mopping up not just domestic trophies, but European Cups too. Kenny Dalglish was rightly nicknamed 'The King' by the adoring Kop, and many times he came to Maine Road and simply destroyed City. Lots of my schoolmates were Liverpool fans and so I came to appreciate the goalkeeping abilities of Ray Clemence, the defensive toughness of Tommy Smith, and the wonderful wing play of Steve Heighway. Even their super-sub, David Fairclough, who I was to later work with for ITV, and who caused me no end of childhood tears when he damaged our title charge by scoring an equaliser on an icy night at Maine Road in December 1977.

Other big clubs of the day included Leeds and QPR. A trip to Yorkshire for a Leeds-supporting school friend's birthday gave me my first glimpse of Tony Currie, Peter Lorimer and Eddie Gray, the latter pair, remnants of Leeds' glory days in the late sixties and early seventies. Queen's Park Rangers had Gerry Francis (the first England captain I remember), and winger Dave Thomas, who played with his socks rolled down to his ankles, spawning a generation of primary school imitators.

My steep learning curve of life through football was accelerating. All sorts of questions filled my young mind. Where exactly WAS Queen's Park for example? And, more importantly, who were these strange sounding foreign teams Liverpool (and, on occasion, City) went off to play in Europe?

There was something special about European nights. Games under floodlights were always a thrill for a child, but when my dad told me we were going to see City against Juventus in the UEFA Cup in September 1976, I had no idea just how different this was going to be.

I had no clue who Juventus were, nor where they came from, but what I saw that night was captivating. Sat high in the Main Stand (special treat from Dad to sit in the 'posh' seats), we witnessed a quite brutal display of what would now be called cynical gamesmanship. Juventus were a team full of (what I later learned were) world-class stars – Dino Zoff, Roberto Bettega, Romeo Benetti, Franco Causio, Roberto Boninsegna, Marco Tardelli – but they also had a ruthless streak about them. In particular, their central defender, Claudio Gentile, belying his name, kicked anything that moved that night, including one particular 'tackle' that caught our skipper, Mike Doyle, flush in the chest. He sank to his knees as though he'd been hit by a sniper. All around, fans booed and gesticulated angrily but I just sat agog. This was something I'd never witnessed before, and that, along with the very different theatre a night game provides, mesmerised me.

City won that night 1–0, but lost the return leg in Turin 2–0 to go out on aggregate, and, only then did it dawn on me, the reason why Juve had played that way in the first leg, disrupting the game to stifle City's home advantage, and thus minimise the margin of defeat. From that moment on, football took on a whole new meaning.

This new passion of mine wasn't just about City, or England, this was about other people, living in strange lands with different looks, surnames, upbringings and attitudes too. The people who, more than most, brought all those fabulous images of far-off lands into my head were Peter Jones and Bryon Butler, two BBC commentators who seemed (to my childish mind) to spend all their time travelling across Europe, watching football. What a way to earn a living! I'm pretty sure it was they who first put the thought of a career in sports broadcasting into my head.

Midweek Sports Special on BBC Radio 2, replete with its funky seventies style title music – featured commentary on the European games involving English clubs (invariably Liverpool), plus reports from the others. It was compulsive listening in the days before live football on television and the chemistry between Jones and Butler in particular was irresistible.

Jones was the classic mixture of a Welsh upbringing combined with a career at the BBC. His tones on radio tended towards the clipped, but his Celtic background gave his voice a beautiful rhythm, and his earnest delivery always portrayed the importance of the occasion. Tragically, he was to die on duty while commentating on the Boat Race for the Beeb in 1990.

Butler though was my favourite. His chocolatey voice betrayed just a hint of west country burr, and set against the buzz of a European crowd, on a crackly line in the days before modern satellite hook-ups, he was intoxicating.

In 1986, he brilliantly called Diego Maradona's sublime second goal against England by describing his turn in the centre circle as akin to that 'of a little eel' before rounding off his call of the goal by saying 'and that's why Maradona is the greatest player in the world'. His rhythm and cadence were superb. You can still find it on YouTube.

Many years later, I had the pleasure of meeting the great man while covering a Blackburn Rovers game at Swindon Town's County Ground. He was a perfect gentleman, even allowing me, a rookie reporter, to ask the first question in an 'all-in' interview with Rovers' then up-and-coming star, Alan Shearer. Butler subsequently asked another, rather straightforward question, which Shearer dismissed as being irrelevant. I was angry at his impertinence towards one of my heroes. Butler was unperturbed; he smiled at me when we'd switched our tape recorders off and said, 'They give such bland answers, you'd think they'd welcome bland questions!' A lovely man, and without doubt, my broadcasting hero.

I also listened to Manchester's Piccadilly Radio religiously, particularly their sports coverage. Whenever a goal had been scored involving one of the local teams, they'd play what I later learned was called a 'sting' – a short five-second burst of crowd noise, with a 'commentator' shouting 'It's a goal!' That immediately grabbed your attention, even if you'd wandered off to do something else. Had City scored? Or had our opponents scored against us? It was captivating stuff, and something mimicked at Fox Sports during our FFA Cup coverage, many years later.

That coverage was complemented by the Saturday *Manchester Evening News* 'Pink Final', the paper that (before the computer age) was the only way to satisfy every adolescent's fascination with football. Often, after a City home game, we'd rush back from Maine Road to the local newsagents, where at 6 pm, the distribution vans would drop off the precious newspapers, containing every result from the English leagues that day, plus reports, features and updated tables.

I used to marvel at how they could gather that information so quickly, when the games themselves had only finished just over an hour ago. The print was still fresh on the paper, and the copies would literally fly off the shelves. I would devour every scrap of information, and my fingers were often black by the time I'd finished.

I would also wait anxiously for the weekly delivery of *Shoot!,* the magazine that was a staple of every football-loving kid in England in the seventies and eighties. Every year, they would give away free 'league ladders' with each team having their own 'tab' which could be moved up and down the various divisions through specially serrated slots. It's hard now to imagine just how much pleasure this – pretty basic – giveaway provided. The magic of childhood!

I was starting to play football properly too, earning my first call-up to the Thelwall County Junior School first team in 1977 at the age of nine (a year younger than the regulars).

I only played the one game that season, but even now, I can remember the pride at pulling on the school's dark blue and yellow jersey. To top it off, I scored my first-ever competitive goal, a hooked shot with my left foot that crept inside the post.

But it wasn't to be the start of a glittering career. Although I became a regular for both school, and my two Sunday League clubs – first, Grappenhall Sports and then, the aforementioned Oughtrington Rovers – the nearest I got to taking it to another level was a trial for the town team. The only trophy I ever won was a runners-up medal in the 1981 Auxiliary Cup Final, a competition for teams knocked out in the first round of the proper Cup.

As luck would have it, my club, Oughtrington Rovers, were playing my old team, Grappenhall Sports in the final. The venue was the nearest thing to a proper stadium in the Hilden League (so named after Warrington's twin town in Germany) – Victoria Park, which had a single stand leading out on to the pitch, via a running track.

My grandad and dad were both in attendance, but despite dominating, we lost to a late goal, and I was hugely disappointed. My misery was further compounded by a cursory flick of the hand wafted in my direction by Grandad, as I went up to collect my runners-up trophy. Grandad, typical of many northerners, was never backward in expressing an opinion, and his message was one I'd seen many times when watching City on their off days. Rubbish! He was right.

In fact, I was rather better at other sports. I represented the northern part of the county in athletics (discus), broke the school record in the high jump, and was captain of the school basketball team. But in particular, I had a bit of talent for cricket.

Like many English kids, I had been thrilled by England's Ashes victory in 1981. Ian Botham and Bob Willis had almost single-handedly dismantled the Australians, and, in the summer months, I'd spend hours imagining myself steaming in like Willis, hair akimbo, before hurling a tennis ball down towards the old wooden garage doors at the end of our driveway. It drove my parents mad.

A year or two earlier, I had discovered I had a bit of ability, not for fast bowling, but for leg spin. What started as a request to 'try something different' during a school match by the sports teacher Mr Gould, ended with me flipping the ball out of the back of my hand and making it turn sharply upon impact with the ground.

Mr Gould was as amazed as I was. He asked me to do it again. I obliged, and he puffed out his cheeks before exclaiming, 'You're going to go a long way with that skill son!'

Before long, I was taking wickets down at Grappenhall Cricket Club, a well-respected local outfit, that had already nurtured Neil Fairbrother, the Lancashire, and later, England batsman.

My big school mate, Stephen Titchard, was already there, and with the two of us in tandem, Grappenhall started to make their way towards the latter stages of the prestigious Cheshire Junior Cup. The pair of us were also invited to trial with the county team, and to my astonishment, I was selected, receiving my county cap at the age of 13.

'Titch' was a superb batsman who went on to play for Lancashire (and later Derbyshire) for many years. In one school game, we were all out for 85, and Titch scored 49 of them! He was an outstanding talent, although he never managed to play for England, which shows just how supremely gifted you have to be to make it to the very top.

As for me, well, I loved playing the game, and for a time, I convinced myself that this was what I wanted to do with my life. I was competing against, and with, excellent junior sportsmen – Michael Atherton, Graham Lloyd and Stephen Bramall, who all went into the pro ranks, and Andy Kilner, who, like me, was clearly more interested in football, as he was to play for Burnley and Stockport County.

But cricket wasn't my passion, and matters came to a head in May 1981, when I made a couple of decisions that would kill off any potential future as a cricketer.

In the run up to the Cheshire Junior Cup semifinal, I'd been training (along with Titch) with Lancashire, who clearly thought I had a bit of promise that could see me move into the pro ranks. My coach was Geoff Trim, a former batsman with the Red Rose county, and much to my chagrin, he'd been trying to alter my bowling style. I'd always flipped the ball through the back of my hand, Shane Warne-style, but Trim wanted me to develop a method of finger spinning. As a headstrong kid, I was having none of it. I decided I wasn't going back to the weekly sessions at Old Trafford.

Then, with the Cup semi looming for Grappenhall, Manchester City won through to the FA Cup Final by defeating Ipswich Town. The date of the final, 9 May 1981, was scheduled to be on the same day as the cricket semi. This time, there would be no problem in acquiring tickets; we'd been season ticket holders for the best part of four years, and when Dad confirmed we'd got our precious pieces of paper, I had a big decision to make. In the end, it was no decision at all – I was going to Wembley to watch my boys.

The fates conspired against me that year – City would lose the Cup Final to Spurs in a replay and Grappenhall would go on to win the Cheshire Junior Cup, without me.

Quite reasonably, as I'd opted out of the semifinal, I wasn't considered for the final itself – I understood that. But what irritated me was the team photo that hung proudly in the clubhouse the following season. Underneath the victorious picture was a list of the players that had also contributed by playing in the other matches. My name wasn't among them, despite having played in every round up until the semi. That was typical of the blazer brigade, even at a local club, to treat a kid like that.

I'd experienced similar modes of behaviour during my county days too. During my brief Cheshire career, I was looked down upon by the other members of the team, as I wasn't from the right school. Most of those selected were at elite private establishments – I was from a scummy comprehensive, and didn't fit in. To cope with being ostracised, I resorted to humour. With my old mate Steve Crompton in tow in my second season, we'd take the micky out of the posh boys in the team, and laugh at our on-field failures. It was childish, but that's what we were – kids – and the coaches had no concept as to why we were acting in such a way. Instead of healing the divisions and encouraging us 'outsiders' they marginalised us further, by singling us out for criticism.

Matters came to a head, and after one particularly fractious game our coach made it clear where I stood, and told me that I 'hadn't really developed' as a player. He may have been right, but the environment certainly hadn't helped. From that moment on, I was finished with cricket – at least as a player.

It wasn't going to be too long before I was finished as a footballer at junior level too. Two character flaws saw to that – one a personality trait, the other self-inflicted. I'd always been a sensitive kid, taking criticism very much to heart, and reacted by getting angry, although thankfully, never in a physical sense.

I'd also had a bit of a personal trauma, which may have had an influence on my emotional nature. In 1983, Nanna Lomas (Mum's mum) was making one of her regular visits to our house to stay overnight. I was never really close to Nanna, she being rather old-fashioned to my mind, living in a terraced house in Leigh that seemed positively archaic. I hated staying there, not least because there was no proper bathroom, no colour television, and, worst of all, an outside toilet. Getting up in the middle of the night to relieve yourself meant putting an overcoat and shoes on then battling it out with the spiders in the yard. It wasn't a pleasant experience.

Nanna Lomas had a much closer relationship with Fiona than me. Still, she was family, and towards the end of her life I felt sorry for her, as she started suffering from what we'd now call dementia. To me then, it just seemed like forgetfulness. For example, she'd quite often forget she was a widow. Her husband, Robert, from where I get my middle name, had died all the way back in 1947 – my mum was only 12 at the time. Sometimes she'd ask when 'Bob' was coming back from his round – my grandfather had delivered bread back in the day. Other times, she'd get mixed up with other family members, once asking my mum (her daughter) whether her husband was still alive – when my dad was sat next to her. 'Yes he damn well is!' my dad would reply, only half-joking!

But the night she died, I was unfortunate enough to be the one who found her. Sound asleep one night in my bed, I was awoken by a thud which sounded like a sideboard falling over – it was a tremendous noise. Stirred from my slumbers, I nervously went to investigate, fearing burglars. My nanna was at the bottom of the stairs, having fallen, perhaps all the way from the top. I ran down the stairs, and tried asking her if she was alright, but there was no sound. I presumed she'd knocked herself out.

My mum and dad of course, were almost as quick on the scene, having also been awoken by the noise, but when my dad felt for her pulse, he shot me a glance that told me this was more serious than a mere concussion. Within minutes, an ambulance was at the house, and she was rushed off to hospital. We later learned she'd had a massive heart attack, probably before she even fell. She was dead by the time she hit the floor. She was 81, a good age, yet even so, the manner of her passing seemed too horrific for words.

That was a fairly profound experience for a youngster. Death was a new, and horrible, reality and it haunted me for months afterwards.

I was snappy, irritable and more than a little insecure, so when my coach at Oughtrington Rovers (who I'd joined after leaving Grappenhall in a similar fit of pique), left me as a 15-year-old on the subs bench for what seemed like the umpteenth time, I reacted truculently. Taking the snub personally, I went back into the prefabricated hut next to the pitch – where my dreams of becoming a pro had been smashed just a year or two earlier – threw my kit on the floor, and walked out.

Half-heartedly, I joined up with another club for the next season, Rylands FC, but played just two games. The last match was a preseason friendly against my old mates at Oughtrington. I made my point by scoring all four goals in our 4–2 win, made sure my old coach saw all my celebrations, and left that club too.

Another, self-inflicted wound would last far longer – in fact, it still haunts me today. When I was 15, I took up smoking. As kids do, it started as a dare, but before long, I was puffing my way through first three, then five, then ten fags a day. It's a habit I've never quite been able to kick since, more fool me.

Having also had that terrible asthma as a child, the dreaded weed had an effect on the sporting field too. Although the wheeziness didn't trouble me nearly as much, I was no longer one of the fitter kids, and, as I moved towards 16 and adulthood, I followed the lead of many others in my generation and started to hit the pubs as well. Always tall for my age, passing myself off as 18 was rarely an issue, and so, alcohol was added to my regular nicotine intake.

Other influences were now starting to take over too.

I'd always rejected my mum's attempts to get me interested in music, but when a school friend, Russell Reason, had played me one of his old vinyl records, Deep

Purple's 'Burn', I'd been instantly captivated, particularly with the skills of Purple's drummer, Ian Paice. So, when I had a spare half an hour away from schoolwork, football or cricket practice, or playing Subbuteo, I would grab a pair of my mum's knitting needles and hammer away on upturned waste paper bins, trying to replicate Paice's intricate stick work. I loved it, even if my parents didn't, and by age 15 I wanted a proper drum kit; particularly as by then I was massively into heavy rock, the up-and-coming British metal bands such as Saxon, Judas Priest and Motorhead, as well as AC/DC, Led Zeppelin and especially Hawkwind, the first band I ever saw, at the Liverpool Empire in 1981.

Neither Mum nor Dad were keen on the drums idea, feeling it was a phase and that I'd soon grow out of it. Mum in particular, pressed home her desire to make me learn the piano, but I was determined, and eventually got my own way. A second-hand set was purchased for the princely sum of 40 pounds, and I was away.

Two school mates were of a similar mind – Jason Arber and Mike Bearpark. Mike obtained a guitar, Jason a bass, and with the acquisition of Caroline Wright as singer, I was in my first band, called Molotov Cocktail.

Actually, it was a pretty apt moniker because the combination of our less than refined musical talents was certainly an unwanted explosion of noise. One of our first compositions was a tune (if you can call it that) called 'Corridor' which consisted of three chords, a flimsy beat, woeful lyrics and a lot of head banging. We were dreadful.

But we persevered, annoying the neighbours at Jason's parents' rather large house, and gradually, we improved. I took drum lessons (briefly, before my patience again ran out), and by the time we hit 16, the now re-styled 'Eye to Eye' were playing local gigs to only relatively mild abuse.

Football was still there – a constant presence, courtesy of my devotion to City. By then, I'd graduated from the safe Platt Lane seats into the vast Kippax terrace, where in the mid-eighties, I felt right at home among the trench coats, pixie boots and plumes of smoke that wafted over the crumbling edifice that was Maine Road.

I'd also joined the City Travel Club, meaning I got discount travel to away trips on the notorious 'Football Specials' that were running up and down the country at the time.

This was the era when football hooliganism was rife, with gangs such as the ICF, the Zulus, and, in City's case, the young governors, running rampage throughout the country. The hooliganism never interested me, nor bothered me. I was aware it took place, and on occasion I did see trouble. Blackburn fans once threw a rock at our Travel Club coach outside Ewood Park, cracking a window just a row or two behind me. Another time, at Maine Road, we had to stand flush against a wall to allow hordes of angry youths fly past us, en route to a pitched battle with Newcastle supporters. But on the whole, they were isolated incidents, and the only one that really disturbed me was seeing a City fan in the next carriage to me, staggering with blood pouring from a cut on his face, after apparently being slashed with a knife on the train home from Liverpool, one season back in the mid-eighties. I tucked my scarf away in my pocket and kept quiet.

If I seem blasé about it it's because I was. I don't know why, but I always had the feeling that unless you were really unlucky – or went looking for it – then trouble wouldn't find you. Perhaps it was the innocence (or the feeling of invincibility) of youth, but I always saw the animated mob of away fans as being made up of people like myself. Young blokes full of bravado (and beer), strutting and posturing, but little else. I'd have run a mile at the first sign of any real trouble – and felt my peers were pretty much the same.

In retrospect, I can see that was an unwise assumption, particularly with Heysel just around the corner, but as a result, I took chances that today seem stupid.

Back in 1985, City played a derby at Old Trafford. United were gunning for the title, while City were in their usual lower mid-table comfort zone. I went to most away matches in those days, but really struggled for a ticket for this particular game, so, in desperation I asked a United-supporting mate if he could get me one. He obliged, giving me one for the Stretford End, in amongst the home fans!

Off I went, blue-and-white scarf tucked deep into my trench coat, feeling bulletproof. That was until I got inside the stadium, and I realised (I don't know what took me so long) that I was in enemy territory, and that if City were to score, I wouldn't be able to keep up the pretence for long. So, I asked a kindly-looking steward (quietly) whether there was any chance of a switch of ends. These days in all-seater stadiums that wouldn't even be an option, but then, with open terracing on both sides, it wasn't so much of an issue.

'Are you a blue?' he whispered. I gently teased the merest hint of blue scarf out of my pocket, at which point, he nodded and escorted me out through the fencing to be marched around the pitch.

I couldn't resist; as soon as I was at a safe distance from the United fans, out came the scarf and I started waving to the Reds, now angrily spitting and hurling abuse at me!

To make my day even sweeter, City came from two goals down that day to earn an unlikely 2–all draw, thus ending United's title hopes. So, high on adrenaline, I decided to not only display my scarf around the environs of Old Trafford afterwards, but to take my coat off to reveal my sky blue shirt too, singing loudly as I went. I must have been mad.

'Eye to Eye' meantime – complete with new singer, the Bono look-a-like John Done – were starting to gig a little further afield, playing at Birmingham University for example, and the Greenbelt Rock Festival in Northampton. We'd also attracted interest from a local management agency, plus a small independent record label in Forest Gate, East London. They offered us the chance to record a single, which they would then (bizarrely) distribute throughout Scandinavia.

The hitch? They wanted us to fork out around a thousand pounds to record a track in a proper studio. That seemed a fortune at the time to four school kids, and we couldn't afford it. That was the end of that.

CHAPTER TWO 2

P&O, PORTSMOUTH & (FINALLY) A PROFESSION

All of these extra-curricular activities seriously affected my schoolwork.

In my school days, you sat your 'O' or ordinary level qualifications at 16 (today they are called GCSEs), and the results determined whether you stayed on to do 'A' or advanced level studies, or left to get a job. But at that stage, I was in no doubt as to what I wanted to do. My school career had followed my earlier sporting prowess – a good start (I was a more than capable student with a little application), followed by disinterest at the first sign of things getting a little tougher. With my exams fast approaching, I just wanted to get out of there, and get a job with enough money to pay for my beer, fags and football, and play in my band. I'm afraid I paid little attention to revision, and got the results I absolutely deserved.

With just three 'O' level passes to my name – English language, literature and German (which I quite enjoyed, having been on my first overseas trip on a school exchange to Nuremberg; the place, incidentally, where I also saw my first-ever overseas game, a dour goalless draw between FC Nürnberg and Hertha Berlin) – I didn't have anywhere near the results I needed to further my education.

Not that I cared. I'd fallen in with a guy called Andy Bramhall – the brother of cricketer Stephen. Andy was a brilliant guitarist. He'd joined our band playing lead, and with his talents, we felt we were destined for stardom.

Andy was like me: disinterested in academic work, passionate about his music, and keen to get a job – any sort of a job – to make ends meet, until the inevitable call came to appear on *Top of the Pops*. He suggested we join a YTS (Youth Training Scheme) together at one of the local factories in Warrington, Pierpoint & Bryant.

I was all for it. Twenty-five pounds a week was the going rate for a YTS employee, and to us at that time, it seemed like a tidy sum.

I obtained the application forms, filled them in, and was all ready to go and post them when the voice of sanity intervened. My dad asked me to wait a week or two. Knowing my headstrong nature, he didn't rant and rave, but he knew I had potential that was going to go to waste if I spent my days doing manual labour in a factory. Quietly, but repeatedly, he queried whether I should resit some of my exams to 'try and get something behind me.' He knew staying on at school was a non-starter, but the local sixth form college would offer a slightly different, less rigid environment. Eventually I succumbed, albeit rather begrudgingly.

Priestley Sixth Form College was where my life path changed for good. Rather bohemian in its approach, it was the 'second chance' that many a wayward student had cause to be thankful for in later life.

For me, the opportunity to resit my exams (and start 'A' level courses simultaneously) was only part of the equation. The real appeal was that Priestley treated their students as adults. There was no uniform, no assembly, no religious education – something I had grown to loathe after the slavish devotion to it at school, and my mum's insistence that I attend first Sunday School, and then church, on a weekly basis as a youngster.

Most teenagers are rebellious by nature, and I was no different. Priestley gave me the room to mature without imposing too strict a framework. If I didn't turn up to lectures, no-one checked or imposed penalties – manna from heaven for someone who, by now, was regularly out getting drunk.

Football was still a powerful draw though, and in May 1985, I was on the terraces the day Manchester City won promotion back to the top flight by defeating Charlton 5–1. There were 47,000 people at Maine Road that day, and on a hot afternoon, I remember being distinctly uncomfortable in being squashed on the mobbed Kippax – so much so, that when City scored one of their goals, someone was standing on my feet and I lost my shoes, forcing me to walk back to my dad's car (he was in the safer seats), in my socks. When we returned home, we learned of the awful carnage at Bradford City, where a stand had caught fire, killing 56 people. There but for the grace of God went all of us UK football fans in the eighties, and it wasn't until the Hillsborough disaster that something was rightfully done about the shameful treatment of football supporters on the dilapidated terraces.

Back at Priestley, gradually, my absences from lectures lessened, and my interest in my 'A' level subjects grew. I was particularly fond of politics, and, reflecting the times and generation of northern English kids, I fancied myself as a bit of a left-wing radical. I devoured the *Guardian* daily, absorbing every scrap of information of the polarised political landscape of Britain in the 1980s, which, to me, seemed a straight fight between the political right (wrong!), and the political left (right!).

Those were also the days of the Cold War, and the threat of nuclear war hung heavy over my generation. I became a passionate advocate of disarmament, briefly joining CND, the UK lobby group who objected strongly to Britain being used as a base for Trident missiles.

I also joined the Labour party, ordering election posters to be displayed in my very first car, a scruffy Vauxhall Viva, bought from a dodgy dealer in Salford, costing £400, but which was condemned as a death trap only 12 months later due to a front axle that had been fibreglassed together, and could have split at any moment.

But any political affectations I pretended to have were shattered by some news delivered by my father in 1986. Dad had worked hard all his life, and had scrapped his way up the ladder from the police force, through CID, and into an office job before moving into social services. Unfortunately, he worked on Merseyside, which in the 1980s was just about the most politically charged environment in the country. The Labour-controlled council on Merseyside was the most militant in the UK, and they wanted their own people in all the key jobs. My dad – by this time Assistant Director of Social Services for the region – was no radical. Over the course of the year, it seemed to us that his superiors tried everything they could to force him out of his post. Eventually he was moved on, although he took his employer to an industrial tribunal for unfair dismissal, and won (receiving a large settlement in return), the damage had been done – he was out of work at 52. While he continued to work in other jobs until retirement, his career as such, was over.

For me, an idealistic teenager who believed socialist policies were right and fair, it was a big shock to learn of such dealings. I began to examine my political leanings a bit more critically, and shifted towards the centre – well, a little anyway. My dad was to gain his revenge many years later, when he became a Liberal Democrat representative on the local parish council, defeating the Labour candidate along the way.

By mid-1986, I'd re-sat (and passed) the 'O' levels I'd failed, and passed two 'A' Levels as well. My metamorphosis from lazy, disinterested youth to (relatively) successful student with some kind of future ahead of him was seemingly complete.

Mum and Dad were keen on me becoming the first member of the family to go on and study for a degree, but I wasn't sure. Most British kids who go on to further education up sticks and leave home for some far flung destination, but despite my bravado, I wasn't 100 per cent sure I was ready to go. I received an offer from Teesside Polytechnic, situated in Middlesbrough, and half-heartedly accepted, but the closer the day came to leaving, the more I knew it didn't feel right.

At the last moment, Portsmouth Polytechnic came through with a similar offer – a place and course (Social Policy and Administration) that appealed far more, but by then, my mind was set on having a year off, the usual cop-out for teenagers like me who put most things into the 'too hard' basket. Portsmouth asked me if I'd like to defer their offer for 12 months – perfect.

So, with a whole year stretching out in front of me, I decided I'd go and get a job. Now, there aren't too many openings for an 18-year-old with no experience, so when a job at P&O Containers in Manchester came up, I grabbed it. My job title was Imports Clerk, and I was paid what was probably the absolute minimum sum of £5001 per annum. My duties included sorting bills of lading on the giant container ships that came up the Manchester Ship Canal, and the distribution of the cargo to various companies and individuals around the Manchester area. At first, I thought this might be the life for me – some of the senior guys were part of the sales department, they had flash suits and nice company cars. I put the idea of going to study on the backburner – but only for a few months.

Working nine to five in an office soon lost its lustre, and, typical of a restless teen, my feet started to itch. So, in October 1987, I quit the job, and took the plunge. At 19, I was leaving home to go to Portsmouth and study for a degree. Little did I know, I would never be going back home to live, at least permanently, again.

Having taken the year to fully make my mind up, now I was raring to go. The only person I was sad to be leaving behind was my girlfriend, Lisa, but that didn't last long – we broke up within two weeks of my arrival down south, after I fell madly in love (or lust, more likely) with a Londoner called Marion. What a lovely guy I was.

All of a sudden, I was in a different world. Portsmouth may only be four hours from the north-west of England, but it felt like another planet.

Just like with Priestley College, it wasn't so much the academic fare on offer (although the course was interesting in places), but the life experience. I was having a ball, partying, meeting people from different parts of the country, and learning how to live on my own for the first time. For a kid from the north (where the walls can tend to close in on you somewhat), this was the beginning of seemingly endless possibilities.

For the first time, I began to understand that this path could lead to the sort of life I wanted. The sort of existence so different to the one I'd grown up with. All of my family had worked in public service – the police force, social services, hospitals – and while they enjoyed their work, I was after something different.

I wanted adventure – travel, new experiences – and being in this sort of environment only fuelled my confidence to believe that I could do just about anything I wanted. The question though, was what?

For a while, I dabbled with the idea of working in public administration, that was, after all, the title of my course, at least in part. Politics still interested me, but I doubted I was either clever, or dedicated enough to pursue a career in that arena. The thing that really grabbed me – still – was football.

Portsmouth reinvigorated my interest in a career in the beautiful game. I got back playing in the inter-departmental football league, and better still, Fratton Park was literally five minutes' walk from my college digs in Southsea.

Pompey weren't exactly world-beaters; they were in the old Second Division, and having a tough time of things following relegation in 1988 under Alan Ball. But games at Fratton Park felt just like Maine Road, the place being antiquated, yet full of dyed in the wool fans. I began going to games regularly, and started to get quite passionate about the club's progress.

In fact, there was a brief moment that year when I felt slightly torn. City had been relegated the year before, so when Pompey dropped a division, the two were competing in the same league. Such was my commitment to Portsmouth that when City arrived in town, I wondered whether I should stand in the home, or the away section. City won eventually of course.

In fact, I saw plenty of City games during my time in Pompey. Quite how I afforded the tickets and travel on a student budget, I'm not sure, but I would regularly head up to London to see City play at the likes of Arsenal, QPR and Crystal Palace.

But one trip stands out above the others, as it was right at the height of the inflatable craze that bizarrely came into fashion in the late eighties, with City at the forefront.

I'd made the short hop to see City's game at Bournemouth, just down the road from Portsmouth, and then also a Second Division club. Many fans, including me, had the inflatable bananas that had become popular thanks to the efforts of a City fan called Frank Newton, who had started the craze. So the story goes, Newton had a friend who was a toy collector, and who had, as part of his collection, a five-foot inflatable banana. Newton thought it would be fun to parade it on the terraces at Maine Road, so his friend loaned it to him, on the condition that he provided proof he'd taken it to a game. Being a hot afternoon on the day of the game in question (City v Plymouth in August 1987), Newton took his City replica shirt off, and put it on the banana.

With the addition of a bobble hat, and a face drawn on, all of a sudden, the banana had a personality – and City fans quickly changed a tribute song to (then) striker, Imre Varadi, to be something more reminiscent of 'Imre Banana'. Others caught on, buying their own inflatables, and by October, the old Kippax was full of the things – and not just bananas.

That night at Dean Court, the craze was totally out of control. I barely saw any of the action, as all around me the terraces were a seething mass of inflatable crocodiles, paddling pools, beach balls, chickens and blow-up dolls. It was utterly ridiculous, but lots of fun, at a time when football was looked down upon by the establishment as being a game for working class, violent people. City fans knew differently, and they were determined to have fun in their own inimitable way.

Meanwhile, my studies progressed well, and although the digs I lived in were pretty awful (one house was so infested with snails in winter, the trails were all over the carpet every morning), I loved the student life. I had a new girlfriend too, after Marion had broken my heart and dumped me. Jayne was a local girl who danced on cruise ships and acted in pantomime at the Kings Theatre every year. It was a little taste of show business as she mixed with various celebrities. I liked it, and wanted more of it.

Music was still a possibility as a career. The drums had followed me south, and I'd quickly hooked up with other aspiring musicians at Polytechnic, forming another new band, bizarrely entitled Tabasco Cat (no, I've no idea either), but even then I think I realised I was destined never to be anything more than a pub musician. As with politics, I was neither talented enough, nor hard-working enough, to make the big time.

Still, the gigs were fun. Once, we were invited to play at Bristol University, so we packed the gear up into the cheapest van we could find, and set off west. The gig was split into two sets at the annual college ball to allow for speeches, and the venue was incredible – a huge ballroom, complete with winding staircases that wouldn't have looked out of place in *Gone With the Wind.*

The problem was, the hour delay between sets allowed us to get stuck into the beer; great if you were partying, not so great if you had to be coordinated behind a drum kit.

It was only when we struck up the first few bars of our second set that I realised I was too pissed to play. I couldn't find a rhythm, and the more I tried, the more I missed beats and drifted out of time. Worse still, my uncoordinated attempts to find my range led to me getting my thumb trapped between stick and snare rim as I attempted to play a beat, after which the audience was treated to the rather odd sight of blood spattering both kit, and my (white) t-shirt. I came off looking like I'd been involved in a fight.

Back in Portsmouth, I sat my final degree examinations in the summer of 1990. Without ever having been an exceptional student, I'd done enough to get by, and with two months' solid revision ahead of my finals, I was confident I'd get my degree. The question was what to do with it.

The answer came when leafing through one of the Graduate Press booklets at the Polytechnic library. Applications were being sought for the NCTJ Pre-Entry Course in Newspaper Journalism. Better still, the one-year, post-grad course was based at the nearby Highbury College of Technology in Cosham, just a couple of miles north of Portsmouth. I got the forms, filled them in, and waited.

The process was lengthy. An interview, a written exercise, then a further interview and psychometric testing. In all, over a thousand students applied for just 44 places – but I got lucky, and was accepted, on the proviso I passed my degree.

In May 1990, just in time for the World Cup in Italy that year, where Gazza's tears captured the heart of a nation, I had confirmation that I had indeed, passed my degree. A solid 2:2 (second class, second division) was the best result I could have hoped for, and, exactly what I got. My usual approach of doing just enough for a middling pass mark got me over the line. So, after a beautiful summer's day when I was presented with my scroll, dressed in gown and mortarboard at Portsmouth City

Hall, watched by a very proud Mum and Dad, I was off to Highbury College. I was going to be a journalist.

Of course there was never any doubt in my mind that I wasn't JUST going to be a journalist – I was going to be a sports journalist, to follow my football passions. I was sure I was destined for *The Guardian,* or at the very least, *The Daily Mirror.* So it was a bit of a rude shock when a lecturer (when learning of my ambitions) dismissively informed me that sports journalism wasn't really rated by newspapers, and that in any case, an apprenticeship of at least five years was required before anyone was let near the sports desk.

Bugger that. I wasn't intending to spend half a decade filing reports on local council meetings or garden fetes – I wanted to be at football stadiums. Luckily, good fortune was to smile on me, right at the outset of my journalistic course.

Highbury College in fact ran two annual journalistic post-graduate courses. The first ran from January to October, the second (the one I'd enlisted for) was the more usual UK academic term of September to June. In the college refectory, I met one of the lads on the earlier course, a Yorkshireman called Richard, who like me, was a mad football fan. He informed me that the local paper, *The Portsmouth News,* employed one of the Highbury intake each year to write match reports on Pompey's youth team. He'd been doing the job since January, but was about to leave and return back north. Would I be interested in taking over from him?

One phone call later, and I had my very first journalistic gig. I couldn't believe my luck. I still remember my very first game as a reporter. Leyton Orient youth versus Portsmouth youth at Orient's training ground in East London. Not only was I reporting, I was reporting on the road.

Portsmouth had a good relationship with the newspaper, so I was to travel on the team bus, leaving from Eastney Barracks at 8 am on the Saturday morning. I was to be paid the hardly life-changing sum of £5 per match report, although Pompey would provide me with a fish and chip lunch on the way back after the game.

I was in heaven. I filed my first report from a public pay phone back in Portsmouth when we returned, just in time for the evening 'Pink', and at 6 pm I raced to the local newsagent to pick up my copy, fresh from the presses.

There it was. On the front page (just below the first-team report), a 10-paragraph column on the 2–2 draw earlier in the day in East London, and, for the first time, I was a printed journalist with a by-line (a BY-LINE – my fellow journalism students couldn't believe it), and a beautiful Pompey badge next to it. I still have a copy of that report; it remains one of the proudest moments of my career.

That young Pompey team incidentally, were another reminder of just how tough it is to succeed. From the batch that played under Frank Burrows, only Stuart Doling and Russell Perrett made it to the first team.

However, even though the job was to continue for a few months after that, I was starting to lose interest in the journalism course itself. The course was very intense – as (I later realised) it needed to be. Every morning at 9 am we had an hour's lesson in 'Teeline' shorthand, an essential tool (then) of the journalistic trade. At first, I couldn't get my head around it; the swirls and scribbles seemed impossible to compute, and we were expected to reach 100 words per minute by the end of the course. I could barely manage more than 10 for the first few months.

Then, there was law – the rules and regulations regarding defamation and libel, all taught from the bible *McNae's Essential Law for Journalists,* of which I still have a copy. It bored me senseless, with a lot of it (to me) seeming like mere common sense.

Finally, there was 'Patch' – the practical side of the course, where we were expected to go out and fish for stories in exotic places such as Gosport, Fareham and Portchester. Wandering down the main street of a quiet town on a Monday afternoon looking for a yarn wasn't my idea of fun, and with my usual impatience, I quickly became jack of it all.

By March 1991, struggling for motivation with the course and seriously skint after four years as a student (I'd run up debts of nearly £5000), I'd decided the course, at least, wasn't for me, and left.

It was also a time of more personal trauma however, which played a part in my rather knee-jerk decision. In 1990, my sister Fiona had given birth to her first child, Beth. I was never much of a kiddie person, but she was cute enough, with a mop of red hair and an eager smile. All was normal back in the north for the first 12 months of her life, before tragedy struck.

What began with a routine infant cough quickly escalated. After two lots of antibiotics, the cough hadn't improved, so Fiona took her to the doctor again, and he decided some tests were required to rule out anything more serious. Within two weeks, Beth was dead. Killed by an acute strain of myeloid leukaemia. I was summoned back from Portsmouth with Beth critical at Alder Hey Children's Hospital in Liverpool. From my idyllic student life down south, I was thrust into the maelstrom of an intense family tragedy. My sister, in truth, was never the same again, and she was to die tragically young too.

That wasn't all. Life can play cruel tricks on people who are suffering. On the day Beth died, some local thieves stole Fiona and her husband Mike's car from the hospital car park. The baby seat, and some of Beth's clothes, were still in the back. It still appals me that anyone could steal from a hospital, but it happened, on the very day she died.

Poor Fiona and my brother-in-law, they couldn't understand what they'd done to earn such bad luck. Fiona grieved terribly.

Perhaps what struck a chord with me most of all however, was that the local paper in Liverpool, *The Echo,* wanted to run a front-page exclusive, after somehow learning of the story of the stolen car. Intrusion into private grief. Fiona and Mike turned their offer down, but it left a sour taste in my mouth as to what journalism was all about.

Back in Portsmouth after the funeral, I decided what I needed most was a job. The seriousness of life had smacked me in the face after years of carefree student excess, and I reckoned it was time to start earning some money. I was still with Jayne, and even though we were both only 23, she was keen to put things on a firmer footing. In truth, I was half-hearted about it. I knew I was far too young for marriage.

But finding work wasn't easy. Even if I'd wanted to recant my distrust of journalism and give the industry another go, it appeared impossible. This was 1991, when the recession in the UK had hit the media industry particularly hard, and at the time, journalism jobs were like finding needles in haystacks. So, when the local recruitment office in Portsmouth advertised two temporary posts at the local IBM factory, just north of Portsmouth, we both decided to take the plunge. Bad move.

Nothing prepared me for the monotony of working on a production line. I'd done it on a temporary basis once before as a teenager in Runcorn, where I'd spent hours shaping aluminium frames for gas cookers. The result? A slip on a smooth floor, a fall onto razor sharp metal, and two gashes in my chin that left a lifelong scar and required eight stitches. I clearly wasn't cut out for a life on the factory floor.

At IBM, we started at 8 am, and we had to wear 'clean' suits, covering the body and face entirely. This was because we were working in a sterile environment constructing computers, which were then probably state of the art, but would today, no doubt, be labelled prehistoric. The mind-numbing nature of the work, conducted in that sort of bizarre environment, made me feel claustrophobic, and it wasn't long before we both decided we'd had enough.

I was always willing to do whatever job was necessary to get by. In my student years to make ends meet, I'd worked as a labourer on a building site, as a furniture removal man, a litter picker in Liverpool, a kitchen porter in Chichester, an attendant guiding cars on and off the cross-channel boats at Portsmouth ferry port. But my concentration levels were miniscule, and I quickly got bored.

Unfortunately, quitting the job at IBM also meant that my time in Portsmouth was coming to an end. I really wanted to stay in the city I had grown to call home, but my money situation hadn't eased, and although Jayne wanted me to stay, I knew if I was going to get myself straightened out financially, and focus on a proper career, I had to go back home for a while.

So, in May 1991, and with a very heavy heart, I left my scruffy studio flat in Southsea, and said goodbye to Pompey. I was never to return, either to the city or Jayne, despite several abortive attempts at reconciliation. Living in different cities can do that to you when you are young, especially as we didn't have the modern tools of communication like instant messaging.

Back in the north with my parents for the first time in nearly five years, I quickly sunk into a depression of sorts. With debts now nearing £6000 (a fortune it seemed to me at the time), I was restricted as to how much socialising I could do, which, to a 23-year-old, is never an easy thing to bear.

I also couldn't make much headway in terms of trying to find a career. Scouring the graduate press for vacancies was a soul-destroying experience. Despite having a degree, I struggled, even to get to the interview stage. I must have sent off close to 200 applications in the space of three months. In return, I received precisely one offer of an interview.

The job was in Sales for Swallow Hotels, a chain of 18 establishments spread throughout the UK. I was invited to attend a two-day 'selection procedure' in Northampton. Here, my inexperience around business professionals spoke volumes. Although I did all right in the psychometric testing and the general exercises they put on during the day, I made the big mistake of assuming the friendly 'evening' function was for social purposes only, and so, I could therefore relax. Instead, as I later learnt, they were, quite rightly, still assessing our behaviour and interpersonal skills from the far side of the bar. So my being blind drunk and trying to chat up one of the female candidates didn't really help my cause.

Salvation was to come, financially at least, thanks to Mum. Despairing of my plight, and no doubt keen to get me out of the house as well, she asked around at the local hospital where she worked, and found me a temporary job as a medical secretary to an orthopaedic surgeon.

It wasn't exactly the role I'd planned for, but it was money, and I needed to pay off some of my debts. Medical secretaries were normally female, but I had good typing and shorthand skills due to my journalistic training, and the surgeon (a Mr Boot, would you believe), was so impressed he gave me extra pay for typing up notes from his private consultancy.

I became expert in the anatomical terms used to describe orthopaedic complaints – although spelling them was a different matter – and for a time, I considered making hospital life my full-time career. But deep down, I knew I didn't want to follow my parents into a career in public service. Despite my misgivings, journalism, and football in particular, was still a voice inside my head that wouldn't go away. If only I could get an opportunity.

That opportunity finally knocked in September 1991.

One of my many job applications was to a small radio station in South Wales called Red Dragon FM. The graduate press didn't carry any journalistic jobs, they usually came via word of mouth, or in specific industry papers, and normally demanded experience. But this job caught my eye because it was the nearest thing I'd seen to a media post. The job was for a writer in commercial production; in a nutshell, writing scripts for adverts to be broadcast on the station. With the British economy still in recession, that seemed a decent halfway house between what I really wanted to do, and what I could expect from the current job market, so, what the heck, I applied.

A couple of weeks later, an envelope dropped on the mat at home – and it didn't look promising. When you've received nearly 200 rejection letters, you tend to know that a thin-looking envelope isn't a good sign. This was a thin-looking envelope.

With a sigh, I opened up the envelope with the Red Dragon logo stamped on the front, and began reading. It wasn't a promising start.

'Dear Simon, thank you for your recent application for the post of commercial copy writer – unfortunately…'

Yet another rejection. Except it was, but it wasn't. The letter went on to say that, while the management didn't feel I was quite right for the commercial job, another vacancy had arisen at the station in the meantime. The role was as a sports reporter.

They had noticed my interest (and brief experience) in sports journalism, and wondered if I'd be interested in applying?

Red Dragon wanted me to demonstrate my journalistic skills by providing an article on a topic of interest from the Welsh sporting world, so I scribbled a couple of pages of foolscap on the advent of the new, semi-pro, Welsh National League, due to start in 1992.

My references to the 'poetry' of the names of the regional feeder leagues such as the 'Tanners Wines Montgomeryshire Premier League', which I described as being 'pure Dylan Thomas'. must have gone down well, because within a week or two, I was invited down for an interview. Soon after that, I had a letter of confirmation of employment.

My post as sports reporter was to pay only a pittance, and I was off to South Wales, a part of the world I knew little about, and where rugby, not football, was king. But none of that mattered; after all the traumas and doubts of the last few years as to what I'd end up doing, I had my dream job at last. I was about to become a sports journalist.

CHAPTER 3 THREE

'I'M JUST HOLDING THE PHONE FOR HIM MATE!'

Cardiff in 1991 was not a particularly happy place. In September of that year, the so-called 'Ely Bread Riots' had broken out – racially motivated violence in one of the Welsh capital's most ethnically diverse suburbs – after a dispute between two shopkeepers, one white, one Asian, when the latter had started to sell bread, which put the former out of business.

The atmosphere in the pubs and clubs of the city wasn't much better, with fights regularly spilling out into the streets, as workers from the valleys came down for their regular weekend night on the town, to get tanked up.

But for all that, I had a great time in Cardiff. My first job in sports journalism went swimmingly. At first, I was only entrusted with preparing and delivering twice-daily sports bulletins, but soon I was straining at the leash, wanting to learn how to present the weekend sports show.

Chris Moore, the regular host, was gracious enough to teach me the ropes of how a 'desk' worked – no mean feat on his part, considering it was clear I was after his gig. Fortunately, Chris wasn't dependent upon the sports show for his living, he was a regular DJ with the predominantly music-based station. Sport was one of his passions, but music was his livelihood.

For me, it was the other way around, which made Red Dragon the perfect starting post from which to launch my career. I made friends for life at Red

Dragon. Mark Collins, the drive time show presenter in particular, was, and still is, one of my best mates in the world. Like me, he loved football (Liverpool fan, sadly) and heavy rock, and we spent many nights head banging in his studio flat to Black Sabbath or AC/DC after another evening's drunken excess. Kevin Thomas hosted the mid-morning show, and his hilarious impressions had me in stitches. In the newsroom itself (where I worked), Phil Mercer and Dominic Hughes, both of whom later emigrated to Australia, were also regular attendees on nights out, particularly at 'Kiwis', our bar of choice in Wyndham Arcade, just off St David Street. Mark Threadgold, a freelance rugby reporter, is another who I've stayed in touch with; that despite him being a United fan.

I was learning the trade quickly too. These were the days before new-fangled technology, so radio production and presentation was a very 'hands-on' experience. Interviews were recorded on clunky Marantz tape machines, and the tape edited via razor blades after you'd marked your 'in and out' points with white marker pencil (called a chinagraph). I'd often finish the day with white thumbs due to the pencil, or cut fingers thanks to the blades.

Presenting the sports show involved being as dexterous with your hands as your mouth. The studio desk was a vast array of buttons, switches, faders and cart machines, into which you had to insert chunky pieces of hardware which vaguely resembled cassettes. Today, many radio hosts have studio engineers to do all the technical work for them, but then, we had to do it ourselves. It was a marvellous education, and taught me how to keep the conversation flowing, while making sure everything else was running smoothly.

But that all came crashing down around my ears one day when I was hosting a particularly busy *Saturday Sport* show. On any normal Saturday, the station would have reporters out 'at the grounds' reporting on the local rugby and football games, and this was no different, except that, on this particular Saturday, the local rugby games had an unbelievably large number of tries flying in.

Now, my regular Cardiff City reporter was Phil Suarez – a mainstay of the Dragon team for years, although he was a pension salesman by day. Phil was also the ground announcer with the Bluebirds, and being a passionate football man, he hated rugby. Perhaps that was unsurprising given the prominence the oval ball game was given in the area, so the two of us became as thick as thieves in our defence of the round ball game. We became such good friends, that he actually persuaded Cardiff City to pay for me to join him on what was to be my first ever European trip professionally

– a Cup Winners Cup tie in Austria, as Cardiff travelled to play Admira Wacker in Vienna. But on this particular day, he did me no favours.

Phil was paid to provide regular reports from home and away games involving City, and that day, Cardiff were away at Walsall, and Phil had travelled with the team to Bescot Stadium as usual. At Phil's first allotted reporting time (3.20), I called him on the phone and patched him through to the studio, telling him off air that he was number two in the running order, after a rugby game at the Arms Park. 'Bloody rugby,' he said, and I laughed.

After getting the update from the Arms Park, I had word from my producer that a try had been scored at the Pontypridd game. As the City match was still goalless, I informed Phil I was going to Sardis Road first. 'For fuck's sake, who cares about Ponty?' was his response.

As we were coming to the end of the Ponty report, wouldn't you know it, another try at the Arms Park. 'Sorry Phil…'

By the time I handed over to the Bescot, Phil had clearly lost patience. 'Let's cross live now to Bescot Stadium and get an update on Walsall v Cardiff with Phil Suarez,' I said, as I opened the fader…but there was only crowd noise at the other end.

'Hello Phil, can you hear us?' I repeated. Still nothing.

'Come in Phil Suarez. What's the latest from the Bescot?'

To which, an agitated voice replied, live to thousands listening across the region 'I'm just holding the phone for him mate – he's gone for a piss.'

I quickly forgave Phil his (and by extension, my) faux pas. He was a super guy, who never stopped telling me (without any ulterior motive of course) that I needed to update the pension plan he'd taken out on my behalf, and pay more money into it. He was fond of recounting his own experience in taking out a policy later in life. 'I'm fucked mate – that's why you have to up your payments!'

Sadly, Phil wouldn't live to see retirement, dying of cancer tragically young. He wouldn't be the only Dragon reporter I worked with who passed before his time.

Graham Evans was 30 years my senior when I started at Dragon in 1991, but he quickly became a valued friend, a father figure if you like. Graham was a passionate Rugby Union man, but he admired the intensity of my love for football, and we became each other's teachers – him educating me about Union, me him regarding football. He took me to the old Arms Park once (before it became the refurbished Millennium Stadium) and literally talked me through an international involving Wales, play-by-play. I was never a rugby fan, but I had great respect for his insight, and the way he, and 60,000 others, would belt out the Welsh national anthem 'Hen Wlad Fy Nhadau'; truly spine tingling.

Graham was also a cricket lover, and the two of us would share reporting duties in the summer season at Sophia Gardens, home of Glamorgan CCC, where I once interviewed the legendary Viv Richards, literally the coolest man alive.

We also went (briefly) into business together. I'd enjoyed playing basketball at school, and had occasionally watched matches in the old national league. So when Cardiff acquired a team in Division Two of the competition, Graham and I spotted an opportunity. I approached the fledgling club, suggesting we produce their fortnightly match programme – me writing and editing, Graham putting up the capital for the venture, and taking care of advertising and printing. They agreed.

In the end, it only lasted a season. Graham – bless him – ended up out of pocket, with his printing costs more than the club were able to pay him through a proportion of their sales on match days.

Only a year after I left Cardiff, I learnt Graham had been tragically killed in a bizarre accident on the M4 motorway. He'd pulled onto the hard shoulder after his car had broken down, and as he got out to investigate the problem, an erratic driver had veered into his path, killing him almost instantly. I wasn't able to attend the funeral due to work commitments, but I sent a wreath in honour of a lovely, lovely man.

Before leaving Cardiff, however, I had embarked upon a serious relationship.

A colleague of mine at Red Dragon told me he had a couple of (female) friends coming down to Cardiff for the weekend, and that one of them would be just my type. He told me to that I should make it my business to be in Kiwis on the Saturday night, as they were heading that way. He was right.

A blonde with a look reminiscent of a young Brigitte Bardot, we hit it off immediately, and were quickly an item. But things were about to change for me professionally, leading me to make a snap decision, which again reflected my impatient and emotional nature. It would take me four years to unpick the mess.

After two years at Red Dragon, I felt I had learned all I could, and I was anxious to progress my career. I thought I was ready, after having had a taste of what broadcasting was all about. I was presenting the sports show regularly, had reported on football and rugby matches throughout the region. I'd interviewed fascinating people such as George Best (in a pub, inevitably), Lennox Lewis (on the back of his world title fight with Frank Bruno, when I was lucky enough to have a personal audience with him, and his world championship belt), and others, like snooker star Stephen Hendry and Australian Union legend David Campese, who was in town to promote his book.

I also had an interesting night covering a WBC World Super-Middleweight title fight at the Alexandra Palace in London. Local Cardiff boxer, Nicky Piper, who I'd got to know quite well, was up against Nigel Benn, then THE big name in British boxing. He wasn't known as the Dark Destroyer for nothing, and I was at ringside for the bout.

I'd seen a few fights from the bleachers, but this was different. The brutality was scary; Benn was relentless, and while Piper tried to give as good as he got, by the time the eleventh round came around, I was almost praying he'd throw the towel in. He was taking a hell of a beating.

Eventually, the ref stopped the fight after 1.44 of that round, after a punch had landed so hard, I (and no doubt many others), got showered in Piper's blood and sweat. Afterwards, I was allowed into Nicky's dressing room for an interview, and he looked like he'd been in a war zone.

'Why didn't you stay down?' I implored him during the interview, referring to his many knockdowns, after which he'd climb back to his feet for more punishment. I genuinely liked Nicky, and with his Mensa membership and IQ of 153, he was far from your average street brawler.

'I just wanted it bad Simon…so, so bad,' he replied mournfully in his lilting Welsh accent, through mangled lips and perhaps a broken tooth or two.

Boxing gave me a few high points, in fact, during my time at Dragon – one totally unintentional.

The big local noise in the sport was a guy called Kevin Hayde. A former fighter himself (with the deformed knuckles, cauliflower ears and distorted nose to prove it), he'd set himself up as an agent, manager and promoter, and one of his charges was a nuggety little flyweight called Robbie Regan. The boy from Bargoed was aiming for the European title, held by an Italian named Salvatore Fanni. Eventually, Hayde struck up a deal for the fight to take place in Cardiff, and I nabbed an interview with him after the official press conference to announce the bout.

My opening gambit was a fairly simple one: how pleased was he (Kevin) to get this shot at the crown for his charge?

‘I’m absolutely delighted to be bringing Fanni to Cardiff,’ said Hayde, before instantly becoming aware of his unintended double entendre! We both laughed and giggled our way through the rest of the interview. Happy days.

But the role at Dragon was limited in terms of its football scope, and if I’m honest, I was also keen to improve my wages; the peanuts Dragon paid was barely enough to pay the rent on my rather damp flat in Roath Park. I even had to rent a television, as I didn’t have enough money to pay for one outright.

Many of my peers had made the move to the BBC, which, for any aspiring journalist, seemed like the ‘promised land’. So, when a job appeared in the BBC press magazine *Ariel* advertising for a sports reporter at BBC Radio Lancashire, based in Blackburn, I sent in an application.

After travelling north for the interview, I was offered the post. The station had also recruited Guy Havord from Radio City in Liverpool as sports editor, as it sought to revamp its coverage. Guy was a Londoner by birth, but in many other ways, exactly like me. He was ambitious, football-mad and rather impetuous. The two of us would butt heads many times over the next 12 months but, if I say so myself, the station benefited hugely from our youthful drive.

I was determined to make a huge success of the move; Lancashire was not only a region I knew well, but also, unlike South Wales, it was a big football area. The station covered four local teams – Blackburn Rovers, Burnley, Blackpool and Preston North End – plus a myriad of non-league outfits, and, of course, cricket in the shape of Lancashire CCC and the well-respected Lancashire League.

From day one, I loved the excitement the role offered. I was working with established professionals such as Andy Peebles, the former Radio 1 DJ who’d been the last man to interview John Lennon alive. Jim Bowen, who’d become famous presenting the tacky quiz show *Bullseye* on British TV was a regular presenter, while among the youngsters attempting to make their way in the business was a certain Richard Hammond, then a long-haired producer, now a world famous presenter on *Top Gear*. It was a heady mix for a cub reporter like me.

The workload however, was brutal. The station had a four-hour sports show every night of the week, which meant finding enough material to keep the evening sports presenter (Gary Hickson, a gruff Mancunian with a biting sense of humour and wonderfully world-weary outlook) going for each marathon session. An example of Gary’s wit came one day when we were discussing some negative feedback to one of our shows.

'You know, whatever any of us say on air, to the public we'll always be just a gob on a stick,' he said resignedly.

In addition to the shows, we had to present three main sports bulletins throughout the day, and find a live phone guest for a chat with Peebles, who loved his sport, at 1.50 pm each day (known to all of us as the '10 to 2' slot).

Peebles was a tough taskmaster. He didn't want just any old guest, nor just any old story. The bigger the star, the better, so my contacts book grew exponentially within the space of a year as we ferreted away, trying to find suitable interviewees, from Niall Quinn to Ian Botham to former rugby star, Dusty Hare – all wonderfully accommodating in offering their time, as we sought to satisfy the relentless beast, seven days a week. We did all of that with just the three of us working full-time; and Gary only appeared later in the afternoon, in readiness for his evening shift.

At weekends, the spotlight shifted onto the live action, and after a few weeks finding my feet at my new home in the summer of 1993, the new football season hove into view. It was to be my breakthrough season.

We'd had some fun in the off-season as we began our preparations. Guy was trialling some new freelance reporters, and two in particular were beyond bad. One had a stutter so pronounced, he could barely get his words out on air, while the other put in such a substandard display in a preseason friendly at Oldham, he simply packed up and went home at half-time! Needless to say, neither worked again for the station.

But now, it was down to the real business. In August of that year, Guy and I sat in the office trying to work out who would cover what in the coming campaign. With four local league clubs to cover, both of us would need to be on the road for at least one game every weekend, with freelancers covering the others. It was decided that Guy would present the sports show on Saturday (Gary didn't work weekends), while I would host the Sunday show. Guy would commentate on the Sunday matches, and I would commentate the main game on the Saturday. This was a departure for me. I'd dabbled in commentary during my time at Red Dragon, occasionally calling 'live' action during my reports when the need arose, but I'd never actually called a game in its entirety.

Guy told me my first such assignment would be on the opening day of the season – Chelsea versus Blackburn Rovers at Stamford Bridge. So, on 14 August 1993, I set off in my Nissan Micra (I'd been able to buy a car with my new, improved wages) and drove to London, nervous as hell, but excited, ahead of my commentating debut.

Guy had told me just to relax and enjoy it – and to try and rope in Colin Hendry (the Rovers defender, who was out injured) to help me with summarising. It's a sign of how things have changed in the world of football (and broadcasting), that I literally shouted out my request to Colin over the fence at Stamford Bridge, and thankfully, he readily agreed, and hopped up into the stand.

Colin was a huge help during my time in Lancashire. He always made himself available for interviews and summarising (when he wasn't playing that is), and on my big day, he was a superb analyst, filling in the gaps in my knowledge on the tactical side, and generally acting as a brilliant wing man. I was so sorry to hear of his troubles in later life, when he lost his wife after a botched cosmetic surgery procedure.

My debut passed by in a flash. The history books record that Rovers won that day 2–1 thanks to goals from Mike Newell and Stuart Ripley, but I don't remember much about either the game, or my call; but Guy seemed happy enough, and I felt I had really arrived in the big time, having called a Premiership game at such an historic venue.

Rovers were big news in the area, which led to some tension in our relations with the other local outfits, but that couldn't be helped. This was the time when Jack Walker had taken over, and was ploughing his personal fortune into reviving the famous old club. Ewood Park was being transformed into the modern stadium it is today, and the investment on the park was paying dividends. Rovers had acquired Chris Sutton, David Batty, Tim Sherwood, Tim Flowers, and, most famously, Alan Shearer. They were quickly becoming a fine side, and would finish that season (just their second back in the top flight after a long absence), as runners-up to Manchester United.

But in some ways, the transition from provincial makeweights into title contenders was happening too quickly for the infrastructure of the club. All of a sudden, Rovers were in demand, but, in common with many other top clubs of the time, they had no official media department to cope with the waves of requests that came their way every day. Many days, requests for interviews and/or information made by us to Ewood Park were transferred through to the club secretary, who, clearly overworked, was often less than patient, and not very forthcoming. On one occasion, I sought info as to whether Ian Pearce had put pen to paper to confirm a move from Chelsea. After my umpteenth call, the receptionist finally said to me 'He's signed!'

'No disrespect,' I replied, 'but I'd like that news confirmed by a source a little higher in the food chain than the phone answerer!' She must have thought me a rude, arrogant prick.

The Rovers manager at the time was Kenny Dalglish, who was famous for his dislike and distrust of the press. Still, for a confident rookie like me, he held no fears – at least, until I foolishly attempted to get one over on him in the early days of that 1993/94 season.

Rovers had been trying to snare Roy Keane, the up-and-coming midfielder from Nottingham Forest, and they thought the deal had been done. But at the last moment, Manchester United had trumped them, and the Irishman headed to Old Trafford instead of Ewood Park. I'd been lucky enough to break the story on Radio Lancs, thanks to a contact of mine who knew a friend of Keane's. The friend had confided to my contact that Keane had let slip his intentions on a brief return to Ireland. We broke the story on a sports bulletin on the Tuesday, and needless to say, Rovers weren't happy, either with Keane, or with us.

Undeterred, I headed to Ewood on the Friday for the usual pre-game press conference, reserved for local journalists only, with Dalglish. Sensing a chance for a good follow-up story, I tried to tease Dalglish (who'd just seen his team lose 3–2 at home to Norwich on the Wednesday) by asking whether he'd seen any weaknesses in his team that might be put right by a foray into the transfer market.

Dalglish's reply was curt. 'Well, perhaps you can tell me what those weaknesses are, and I can point them out to my players?' he said.

Undaunted, I pressed on. On the same night that Rovers had lost to Norwich, Keane had scored twice for United in a 3–0 win versus Sheffield United.

'But you must have had a wry smile at Roy Keane scoring twice for Manchester United Kenny?'

'No son. Just a wry smile at your question,' said Dalglish.

End of interview.

In fairness to Kenny, he was normally very good with me individually. But for some reason, he seemed to take issue with Keith Macklin, a veteran broadcaster from our opposition, Red Rose Radio, an independent station based in Preston. Whatever question Keith asked, Kenny dismissed it. If Keith offered praise, Kenny wasn't having it; if he criticised, Kenny bridled. I felt so sorry for Keith, in the same way I'd felt sorry for Bryon Butler when Alan Shearer had dismissed his question. As I got older, I realised that Keith (who by then was well into his sixties), was probably anxious not to cause ripples with Rovers that could potentially see him removed from his high-profile role; but as a youngster of course, you feel invincible, with your career stretching out before you.

At football clubs, managers (or coaches as they are called in Australia) often set the tone in their relationships with the media, and Dalglish was certainly the dominant figure at Ewood Park. Many of his players (Hendry aside) were often obstructive, or just plain bland in their answers. David May once did an interview with Guy that lasted precisely one minute and 27 seconds – and Guy asked seven questions! For a station that had four hours of live radio to kill every night, it was downright annoying.

Alan Shearer wasn't much better. His reputation for being non-conformist with the media was well founded, and yet having met up with him again at a social occasion in Sydney many years later, when he was splendid company, I understood that this had been a front, put up to deflect interest away from what was fast becoming an incredibly high-profile career. The Rovers players were in on the joke, and they made a habit of walking past and making loud yawning noises whenever we were interviewing him. Either that, or they'd shout 'chicken and beans', a reference to his rather bland pre-match meal. It was painful.

Still, Shearer was a pleasure to watch from the commentary box; and it was certainly a pleasure to call some of his many, spectacular goals. All told that season, Shearer scored 34, and I can remember screaming 'You can't give him an inch, because he'll take a mile!' after he'd impossibly found space to score a typical poacher's goal in a 3–all thriller against Leeds at Elland Road.

Rovers' ascent caused particular angst down the road in Burnley, Rovers' traditional rivals. The two clubs had an enmity that bordered upon pure hatred.

Radio Lancashire had followed the (then) recent trend, by instigating a Saturday night phone-in to supplement our live coverage, and many of the calls were from irate Burnley fans, complaining about our alleged 'bias' towards Rovers, both in our calls and our programmes. It was complete fabrication of course. There wasn't a Rovers fan among the three of us (Guy was an Arsenal fan, Gary Man United). If anything, Rovers made our life so difficult that we'd have been happy to see them fail; but 'bias' is an age-old complaint when it comes to broadcasting. I laugh about it now I'm in Australia, when I'm accused of being 'biased' towards Sydney, or Melbourne. I've been accused of supporting so many clubs down the years, but, as I've already explained, there's only room in my heart for one, and that's Manchester City.

Back to Burnley. The Clarets, like Rovers, were a famous outfit fallen on hard times, but while Rovers had found money, Burnley were still scrapping to get out of the lower divisions. Trips to Turf Moor of a weekend were tremendous because of their passionate, one-eyed fans, but occasionally, it seemed to us that the club had a persecution complex. One of the reasons for this was that Radio Lancashire employed the ex-Burnley winger, Leighton James, as a pundit. Leighton would appear with Gary on the Friday night show looking ahead to the weekend matches and, invariably, he was critical of Burnley, who he still held particularly close to his heart.

One particular Friday, Leighton had slammed Burnley, and their manager Jimmy Mullen especially, for their failure to win away from home. By October, the Clarets had played five matches on the road, and lost the lot. So by the time they visited Bradford City, Leighton had had enough, and made his feelings plain on the show. Specifically, James pointed out Burnley's deficiencies at set pieces, both defensively, and offensively, and opined that, until they sorted it out, they would get nowhere in the old Second Division.

Me? I was gleefully out on the town that Friday, and had heard nothing of Leighton's words (these being the days before Twitter and instant messaging), but I was booked to commentate the Clarets' game at Valley Parade the day after. So, of course Burnley won the game 1–0, courtesy of a set piece. I headed to the post-match press conference blissfully unaware of what was to come, and if I thought I'd get an easy ride from Mullen in the wake of their success, I was mistaken.

As I walked into the packed press room, Mullen had just begun his ruminations to the assembled throng; but out of the corner of his eye, he spotted my arrival, stopped what he was saying mid-sentence, and pointed straight at me.

'And as for you, you Radio Lancashire…!' he frothed, unable, in his fury, to form the epithet he wanted to use. 'I suppose YOU think that win today is all down to Leighton James!'

I went bright red, while the reporters around me giggled nervously. It was only later I learned the truth.

Later that season, Burnley briefly stopped talking to us at all, in protest at James's opinions, and I also had the rather unpleasant experience of being jostled by the players at their training ground as they bristled at yet another James missive. It was all good, character-building stuff – although it didn't feel like it at the time. I once said to John Kosmina, after a spiteful exchange on air in Australia, that I'd had far worse in England – if he's reading this, then he'll now know what I meant! Kossie would also be aware that managers in England experience far worse abuse than they get in Australia. Mullen for example, eventually quit Burnley in 1996 (long after I had left the area), after a gang of yobs tried to set fire to his wife's dress, as she went to pick up a Chinese meal from a local restaurant. Whatever disagreements I had with Jimmy, he didn't deserve that. Unbelievable.

Preparing for commentaries in those days was also a little different to how it is today. In the modern era, the commentator has everything at his disposal via the internet. Player facts, club histories, YouTube replays of matches, they all are at your fingertips. Back in 1993/94 no such things existed, in fact, we were only just beginning to work on computers in the office. In my early days at Red Dragon, each journalist was equipped only with a typewriter and a landline telephone. The latest stories came via a teleprinter in the corner of the newsroom, noisily chugging out hourly updates from a central feed in London; while the best 'live' service came via teletext, then a relatively modern script-based system, available via a red button on your television remote control.

In preparation for my commentaries in those days, I would often phone the clubs involved, and ask for them to fax pen pictures through of the players. Imagine that! Statistical records were cross-checked via the football reporter's bible, the *Rothmans Football Yearbook*. I also used to keep yearly football diaries to have a statistical database to hand, writing longhand the line-ups, scorers etcetera each weekend, just like I'd done all those years ago as a kid at home. How times have changed.

Technology wasn't much better at the grounds either. As a radio reporter, crosses were done via an ordinary telephone. We at Radio Lancs had our own line at every one of our local grounds, plus one for the opposition BBC reporter. The other local BBC stations around the country had the same set up so we'd borrow their line when we went to, say, Fratton Park, and vice versa.

For commentaries, you couldn't spend 90 minutes holding a phone to your ear, particularly when you needed to get the thoughts of a summariser as well, so something different was needed, and that meant the 'reporter-phone'. This was a rather odd-looking device; in essence, a square box with a traditional telephone dialling pad on the top. At the side was a socket for the microphones and headsets to make things a little more comfortable for the commentator and his offsider. But it wasn't until 1995 that the quality of the actual broadcast was improved, with the advent of 'ISDN' (Integrated Services Digital Network), a system which gave studio quality audio, as technology advanced towards the next century. The reporter phone then became obsolete, as the 'Glensound' ISDN box took its place – a much more user-friendly piece of equipment, which is still in existence today.

I was on the reporter-phone when I delivered what I consider to be the best commentary of my time at Radio Lancashire, a thrilling 4–all draw between Swansea City and Blackpool at the old Vetch Field, back in South Wales.

Blackpool were 4–2 down when they sent on sub Neil Mitchell, who proceeded to score twice in the closing minutes. I got completely lost in the drama of the game and was screaming away with excitement, when I suddenly remembered that the gantry on which we were perched was directly above the Swansea fans, who duly began throwing plastic bottles at me and my co-commentator! We stayed up there for some time after the final whistle, to ensure they couldn't get at us.

Blackpool were by far the most welcoming club of the four Lancashire outfits. Their manager was the genial Billy Ayre, a quietly-spoken Geordie who was well aware that his struggling club ('Pool were in the third tier at the time, and only just avoided relegation that season) needed all the publicity they could get. But his grizzled central defender, Gary Briggs, was a rather different beast.

Briggs was coming towards the end of a long career, played mainly at Oxford United, where he won the League Cup in 1985. He'd joined Blackpool in 1989, and had such a fearsome reputation, he was nicknamed 'Rambo' by the supporters. Long-standing injuries meant he often trained away from the main group, which further added to the legend. Even his own teammates didn't really seem to know what made Briggs tick. So when I criticised his performance live on air one Saturday afternoon, it probably wasn't my wisest move. Blackpool lost at Bradford (there was clearly something about that ground), and Briggs was to blame in my opinion, having let his striker get away from him twice.

By Monday, Gary Hickson arrived in the office white as a sheet. As he lived in Blackpool, Gary was detailed to get the thoughts of Billy Ayre on a Monday after training. While he was chatting to Billy, Briggs had sauntered over and, seeing a Radio Lancashire sticker on Gary's tape recorder, asked a question.

'Are you Simon Hill?'

'No – Gary Hickson,' replied Gary.

'Tell him I want to see him,' growled Briggs, holding Hickson's gaze for several seconds before taking his leave.

Gary recounted this to me still trembling; and it didn't do much for my disposition either. For the next few months, I made sure I stayed well out of Briggs's way at matches.

Preston North End was the fourth member of the local quartet. Like Burnley and

Blackpool, they were trying to recapture glory that, for them, existed only in sepia-tinged photographs.

North End had the ubiquitous John Beck in charge – he of the crazy dressing room antics, such as throwing buckets of cold water over his players pre-game in order to 'psych' them up. He was also infamous for his love of the long ball game. He once dropped goalkeeper Kelham O'Hanlon for not being able to kick the ball far enough to get onto the head of giant striker, Mark Sale. Yet for all his madness, I liked Beck. He was the only local manager who would call us personally in the office and feed us stories. He also liked to play practical jokes. He once called me to announce he'd signed Ian Bryson from Barnsley, and I excitedly patched him through to the studio to conduct an interview regarding his latest acquisition. Problem was, John couldn't hear me. Time and again after pushing various buttons, I queried whether he was getting my audio feed. Time and again, all I could hear was 'Hello…hello?'

Finally, in exasperation I cut his link to the studio and called him back on a landline, at which point I could hear him and assistant Gary Peters collapsing in a fit of giggles. 'I could hear you all the time you stupid cunt!' he said. No, I didn't quite get it either.

On a more serious note, Preston provided me with the most challenging moment in my young broadcast career, and one in which, I have to say, I didn't really cover myself in glory.

North End were away to Mansfield one wintry afternoon, and my dad (proud as punch at his son's profession) had accompanied me to Field Mill. I got him a press ticket, sat him next to me in the press box, and asked him to keep quiet while I got on with the business of providing full match commentary back to the studio.

Halfway through the first period, North End took the lead through their prolific marksman, Tony Ellis but as I described the action, I suddenly became aware that there was something of a commotion going on underneath me in the director's box. It soon became apparent that someone had been taken seriously ill and my dad, in his eagerness to help me make sense of what was going on, started furiously writing down all the information he could gather from those journalists alongside him who weren't (as I was) engaged in play-by-play commentary.

The scenes below us were getting ever more chaotic. The poor man had clearly had a heart attack, and paramedics were quickly on the scene, complete with a defibrillator, as they frantically tried to restart his heart. As all this unfolded, I was desperately trying to focus on the game but Dad then pushed a note onto the table in front of me which read 'Preston North End director seriously ill.'

Commentary can do weird things with your brain. Such is the intense concentration required to keep talking coherently for 90 minutes as you try to explain live action that is constantly unfolding in ever-changing ways, you sometimes fail to think clearly. It's as if the 'logic' button is temporarily disconnected. I had one of those moments.

Call it inexperience, call it rank unprofessionalism, but I blurted out, almost verbatim what was written in front of me. Within seconds, I knew I had made an almighty mistake. Running through my head now were visions of panicking families listening to the radio back in Preston, desperately trying to reach people at the ground, trying to ascertain whether it was their beloved relative in mortal danger, or not.

The whole episode was an utter nightmare, and to make matters worse, other journalists (who'd heard my words) now felt like they had no option but to report it too. I'd created a monster. The rest of the game was a blur – probably the worst call of a game I ever put to air. When, in the second half, news filtered through that the poor guy had died en route to hospital, my dad furnished me with another note saying 'Preston director dead – official.'

Thankfully, this time I ignored it, but I felt sick all weekend. I didn't even know the deceased, but the thought ran through my head that I should attempt to ring the family to apologise. But I couldn't be certain they'd even heard my faux pas, and I could potentially be making matters worse. In any case, they were dealing with their grief, and they probably didn't want some reporter adding to it. I was in turmoil.

BBC Radio Lancashire dealt with the matter very professionally. On the Monday, I was called into the office to speak to the MD, Steve Taylor. I half expected to be sacked, and I'd have had no complaints if they'd taken that decision. But Steve told me that, as luck would have it, they hadn't received any complaints. He told me to chalk it down to experience, and to learn from it. I did. I would never, ever, make such a mistake again.

All of these experiences were, incredibly, packed into just nine months in Blackburn. As it turned out, I wouldn't even see out the end of the 1993/94 season in Lancashire, thus missing Rovers' triumphant march to the Premier League title just 12 months later…with a certain Robbie Slater in tow.

4

CHAPTER FOUR

HITCHIN, HITCHED & HITCHES

I never thought much could conquer my love of football, but in 1994, I left Blackburn for love of a different kind. With my relationship growing ever more intense, my busy schedule was causing problems. My girlfriend was having to travel up north every week to stay at my flat in Darwen, so we could actually spend some time together. Far too quickly, I grew tired of being so far apart, and Guy and I began to argue over which rest days we took. Now with the benefit of hindsight, I can see how silly and impatient I was. Guy was working just as hard (indeed, it affected his own relationship with his partner, Shelley, for a time too), but I could only focus on the damage I felt it was doing to my own love life.

My girlfriend had her own career, and genuinely didn't mind the constant toing and froing, but by March 1994, I'd had enough, and decided to do something about my perceived 'situation'. I asked her to move in with me. But being an old-fashioned sort of girl, she was adamant the only way we would live together would be as man and wife. In haste, I proposed during a wonderful, if brief, holiday in Gran Canaria.

Blackburn was not really a place I wanted to set up home. As exciting as my professional career was, I wasn't overly fond of being back in the north after spending so many years further south. My flat, on the A666, linking the old mill towns of Blackburn and Darwen, was cold and unwelcoming, and the slate grey skies of Lancashire weren't exactly manna from heaven for a 26-year-old looking to start married life.

I started to sniff around. There was a little bit of interest from BBC GMR in Manchester. Andy Buckley, their sports editor, was looking for a new commentator. I was interested, but there were two problems. Firstly, the job was still in the north; secondly, the job was commentating on Manchester United. Sacrilege. A quick conversation with my dad settled things. The look of sheer disappointment on his face when I told him I might apply told me all I needed to know. I didn't, or rather just couldn't, pursue it.

So, I started looking for a move further south. Three jobs appeared in quick succession in the BBC press – one in Bristol (fantastic), one in Nottingham (second choice) and then, unbelievably, a head of department job, in Worcester…the city where my girlfriend lived.

I applied for all three. Bristol declined, which was a disappointment. But BBC Radio Nottingham was interested. After an interview with sports editor, Martin Fisher, I was offered the job as the Nottingham Forest commentator, and was all set to accept, until a late phone call from James Coghill, Assistant Editor of BBC Hereford & Worcester. James explained that he wanted to call me for an interview, and while there could be no guarantees, he thought I stood an excellent chance of becoming their new sports editor. I had a decision to make, and after careful consideration, I opted to turn down the role in Nottingham. A mistake.

After my initial delight at being offered the job in Worcester (a week after I'd said 'no thanks' to Nottingham), I started making plans to move to the midlands. But the warning signs were there already. Guy was aghast that I'd leave Radio Lancs, a station that had transformed its sports coverage to reflect a vibrant football culture, to go to a sleepy backwater like Worcester, where the only major sporting team was Worcestershire County Cricket Club. At the very least, Guy reasoned, I should have opted for Nottingham, where Forest were still a major (if declining) club with a strong support base, and where I'd be commentating on a good level of football every week.

But I was having none of it. I was going to Worcester to set up home with my wife to be, and stay there for good. I was wrong – on both counts.

In Blackburn, Guy and I had been a swashbuckling new team; a breath of fresh air that swept away the rather staid way that Radio Lancashire had presented its sport. We were young, we were new, and we felt we could take on the world. The listening Lancashire public were very encouraging, quickly embracing our fast-moving, hard-working style of radio presentation and commentary – accusations of 'bias' aside. It was a style that reflected the gritty northern towns we were representing. But Worcester was a very different sort of place.

Set in the foothills of Birmingham to the north, the rolling countryside of Herefordshire to the south, and the mountains of Wales to the west, Worcester was a pleasant enough city with a beautiful cathedral, wonderfully manicured lawns and a lovely river which, I later learned, flooded every year. The 49-year-old me would probably love living there – the 26-year-old me quickly reasoned it was as boring as bat shit. Within weeks I knew I had made the wrong move.

My last game for Radio Lancs had been at Sheffield Wednesday, where Blackburn Rovers had won 2–1 in front of 25,000. My first game for BBC Hereford & Worcester was in the Endsleigh League Division Three – a midweek clash, involving Hereford United and Scunthorpe United. Less than 2000 were there to see the Bulls win 1–0 in a dour game; the contrast was startling.

A few weeks later, I had to cover a Bob Lord Trophy game (Conference League Cup) between Stafford Rangers and Bromsgrove Rovers. On the same night, Aston Villa were at home to Inter Milan in the UEFA Cup, and as 40,000 people headed up the motorway to Villa Park, I bypassed them en route to Marston Road, where precisely 356 people (I counted them) watched Rovers win 4–1. Afterwards, as I was interviewing Rovers hat-trick hero, Recky Carter, the lights were switched off at the stadium. It felt like an ominous sign.

Still, I set about my new job with relish, seeking to recreate the success we'd had at Lancs by giving the sports department a thorough shake-up. One positive about my new job was that I was now the boss of my own department, although in truth, that meant being only boss of myself and Dave Bradley on a full-time basis. 'Bradders' as he was universally known, was a local who'd applied for the head job too. He'd been around the station for years, and he was very popular. But if he held any grudges against the blow-in for stealing the gig he probably had every right to think was his, he didn't show it, and he tried to back me to the hilt.

But others were less keen. The freelance staff were a happy, close-knit team, who'd probably wanted Bradders to get the gig to ensure continuity – not some brash northerner, hell-bent on making his mark in their rural idyll.

My first targets were two reporters who I felt were below the standard required for broadcasting on the BBC. After explaining what it was I wanted from them, I gave them a chance until the end of the 93/94 season to prove their worth. Neither, in my opinion, were up to the task, so I thanked them for their efforts and told them they wouldn't be required for the following campaign. They weren't best pleased, and I sensed the other freelancers were nervous around me from that moment on; understandably so.

Next, I set about revitalising the Saturday sports show, changing the format from a sport and music mix to a faster moving, all speech, four-hour extravaganza. I made new opening titles, with more modern music as backing tracks, and introduced a Friday night preview show, looking ahead to all the weekend's football action. The problem was, neither Hereford nor Worcester was particularly football-mad. Hereford United only occasionally roused the local passions when they had a good Cup run (think Ronnie Radford's goal versus Newcastle in the seventies), while Worcester City were a fair to middling non-league outfit, playing out of the dilapidated St George's Lane to no more than a few hundred diehards.

The other two clubs in the region, however, had potential. Kidderminster Harriers actually won the Conference title that season (1993/94) but were cruelly denied promotion to the football league because their Aggborough home didn't meet the required standards. Down the road were Bromsgrove Rovers, who were also in the Conference, and had finished second the year before Harriers' success. The two had a budding rivalry that I thought we could make good use of.

I recruited ex-Everton striker Peter Eastoe as my main pundit, and promoted local personality Colin Shepherd (who'd taken village team Pershore Town to the final round of FA Cup qualifying, leading to them being featured on BBC television) to be the senior summariser.

Colin was a great character, but he had a slightly parochial view of the world, which came to the fore the day he and I set out to cover Hereford United's FA Cup tie with non-league Hitchin Town in late 1994. Worcestershire to Bedfordshire was only a hundred miles, if that, so after I picked him up, I headed for the M5, which would take us north to the M6 for the cross over to the M1. The entire journey would take no more than 90 minutes. But Colin had planned a cross-country route, that would take us through Evesham, Chipping Norton and Buckingham – a route that would have taken hours. He wasn't much used to driving on the major roads, and wasn't impressed when I told him which way we were heading.

'I don't like them motorways,' he said in his rich Worcestershire dialect. I giggled and inquired as to whether he'd like to go by tractor.

Colin's approach to life was pretty typical of the area, and while on occasion it could be funny, mainly it just frustrated me. I was a 'townie' – used to the hustle and bustle of city life, while they were country folk, who liked to take their time. Even the radio station's official catchphrase 'from the black country, to the black mountains' I felt was clunky, and indicative of a region that really didn't know what it was, or wanted to be. The Black Country is the industrial heartlands on the fringes of Birmingham, while the Black Mountains represent the rural farmland in Herefordshire, backing onto South Wales. There was very little identity; the local towns themselves, I felt, existed only as a reference to somewhere else.

This apathy became evident when Hereford United, our senior club, let go of their manager, John Layton, towards the end of 1994. The story broke on the Friday of our preview show, and I excitedly prepared the programme to be a live phone-in to discuss his dismissal. Despite heavily promoting the phone-in during the day's sports bulletins, and leading the show off with a discussion as to the merits of the decision with Peter Eastoe, a quick glance at my 'call' pad five minutes into the show showed not a single person had phoned in to offer their opinion.

In Lancashire, the departure of a manager would have been met with either howls of protest, or a plethora of 'good riddance' messages from passionate supporters, but sleepy Hereford either didn't have a point of view, or (more likely) just didn't care.

Eventually, one line flashed red and I put a caller to air, asking him breathlessly what his view on the Layton story was. His answer summed up the whole area. 'Well, if it ain't broke, don't mend it,' said the caller. There may even have been a lamb bleating in the background, but I can't be sure.

And that was it. One paltry call. I was fuming, but more at my own stupidity in having taken a job without having thought things through properly.

Hereford United did provide me with one unique experience however, and it was all down to the aforementioned FA Cup tie with Hitchin. Hitchin Town had never been further than the first round of the famous old competition so when, after being 3–2 up against the Bulls, they scored a fourth in the closing minutes to put their progress into round two beyond doubt, their fans went ballistic, and invaded the pitch.

The referee panicked, and blew his whistle for full-time, despite there still being several minutes left on the watch. Hereford were livid and their CEO, Robin Fry, got himself into hot water by making his feelings plain to the match officials. We'd mentioned the discrepancy during our commentary, but, as the game was clearly beyond Hereford's reach anyway, we thought no more about it. That was, until Fry called me a day or two later, saying he had been summoned to appear before the FA disciplinary panel in London to explain his conduct. Fry wanted to know if I would speak on his behalf at the hearing, and produce taped evidence of our commentary, proving his point. I agreed.

So a couple of weeks later, I headed for the hallowed halls of the FA at Lancaster Gate in London. It was a surreal experience. Just sitting in reception at FA HQ was enough to put anyone ill at ease. The place reeked of history. On the walls were pictures of Bobby Moore lifting the World Cup, Paul Gascoigne crying at Italia '90, and long-forgotten internationals, captured for all-time in black and white. Every nook and cranny was filled with a cup here, and a plaque there. I felt like I'd wandered into a stately home full of national treasures – football's crown jewels if you like.

So by the time I was called into the hearing, I was as nervous as a kitten. I wasn't helped by the fact that the Chairman began by giving me a solemn lecture on how these briefings were conducted in the utmost secrecy, and that if any of the details were broadcast to the public, he'd see to it that I never set foot inside the FA again. I was petrified!

Anyway, I proceeded to give my evidence, but it didn't do Robin much good, as he was fined and cautioned as to his future conduct. On the way out, the referee involved (who'd escaped with just a warning), breezed by, laughing and joking, and said something to me about 'remembering my name in the future'.

Little did I know then, that Graham Poll, me – and Australia – would meet again in very different circumstances, a decade or so later. He wouldn't be so sure of himself that night.

Away from the radio station, my girlfriend and I were preparing to get married. We'd bought a house in a pretty area of the city called St Peters, and I'd moved in, ahead of our wedding in September 1994.

However, my gut instinct that we were singing from the same hymn sheet was starting to evaporate. She was only 23 and I, 26, and with the benefit of hindsight, I can see now that we were just both too young, and had spent too little time together (we dated for just over a year before we were married). Most crucially, we hadn't discussed the really serious issues all marriages have to deal with. Specifically, I wasn't interested in having children, but when we talked briefly about this fairly fundamental issue during our courtship, we glossed over it. I thought that, as I matured, I'd probably change my mind. My girlfriend perhaps thought she could change it for me. But as the wedding grew closer, her family started to make noises in that direction, with her sisters joking about the house being a lovely 'family' home.

So, on 10 September 1994, we were joined in holy matrimony at a little church in Kempsey, Worcestershire. It rained.

Things didn't improve in 1995 either. After several years of trying to build my broadcasting career, I'd rediscovered the joy of playing football again, which I did for a side called FC Milton in the Worcestershire Sunday League. I loved it so much that when a charity game was organised involving media 'celebrities' and numerous ex-pros, I readily agreed to participate. Everything was going well until a freak accident occurred during the match. I was involved in a heavy tackle with former Coventry City star, Greg Downs, but got straight back up and went to sprint forward as my team was on the attack. But with my first step, my leg unexpectedly gave way and I crashed to the turf in an instant. Whether I had weakened the tendon in my knee in the tackle, I can't be certain, but my kneecap had dislocated, and my left leg was sticking out at an unnatural angle. The game was played on an artificial surface, in other words, hard ground, so, not expecting my leg to give way, I'd not broken my fall by putting my arms out, and had crashed down on my elbow, which was giving me grief as well.

I howled out in pain as people gathered around me to see what the problem was and then quickly recoiled in horror, as they saw the distorted angle of my mangled knee. Within minutes, an ambulance was on the scene and I was receiving oxygen. After gently lifting me onto a stretcher, I was off to hospital, with every bump in the road pure agony.

It's fair to say that the medics at the hospital didn't give me the best care either. Not only did they give me a shot of pethidine to numb the pain in the wrong leg, but after putting my knee back in place, they merely strapped it up and told me to come back the following morning.

After an uncomfortable night, I returned to the hospital the next day and my left leg was encased in plaster from thigh to ankle. I was told it would remain that way for six weeks. Years later, I was informed that such a procedure was one commonly practised in the 1970s, but not in the 1990s. The knee has never been the same since, and I have dislocated it twice more – both times playing football. Eventually, I will need a knee replacement.

Twenty-four hours after that, the pain in my arm was diagnosed as a fracture. So that too was put in plaster, and off I hobbled, looking like a car crash victim, not someone who'd fallen over playing a game of football.

The recuperation process was slow, and I was incapacitated for weeks. Mundane tasks such as going to the toilet required Houdini-like manoeuvring. I couldn't even put my left shoe on, so my wife would put it on and leave me in bed before going off to do her daily chores.

I did, however, manage to go to London for an interview for a temporary job at Radio Wimbledon, the in-house service that operates for those attending the two weeks of 'The Championships' in SW19. My wife put me on the train in Worcester, and I somehow navigated the tube system; I think the journey took me about four hours, door to door.

Despite my rather weird appearance (or perhaps because of it), I got the job, which the BBC had given me permission to do during the English summer. Before long, I would be in London for good.

Finally, the casts were removed from my arm and leg (leading to severe muscle wastage in both areas) and I was free to resume my able-bodied life. But the sequence of events in Worcester had made me unhappy to such an extent that I wanted out – of the city, if not yet my marriage. So when an opportunity presented itself in the BBC internal press, I decided I'd have a stab at it. The job was a six-month attachment (BBC-speak for an extended trial) to the World Service, at Bush House in London.

Despite my relatively comprehensive CV in local radio, I was still young, and I wasn't sure I'd get it, and my wife wasn't keen, to put it mildly – particularly as I, unwisely, only informed her of my application after the event. I tried to assuage her fears by saying I didn't think I stood much chance of getting it anyway.

I thought my suspicions had been confirmed after a less than spectacular board (BBC jargon – a board is an interview). The managing editor, Linda Spurr, seemed happy enough with my performance but one of the other members of the three-person panel seemed to have taken an instant dislike to me.

Sports Editor Harry Peart was a BBC veteran. A regular drinker, chain smoker and with a face that had more wrinkles than a discarded serviette, Peart was old school, and I didn't think he was impressed with me in the slightest. Every response was greeted with either a grimace, or a slightly raised eyebrow. I thought I was toast, especially when he only half-heartedly shook my hand on my way out. Little did I know then that Harry was to become, in many ways, my mentor, and someone who I not only had a huge amount of respect for, but liked immensely.

So, it was a huge surprise to learn a week or so later, that I had got the job. I was elated. Not only was it another step up the ladder, but a chance to move to London, one of the most exciting cities in the world. Most importantly, it was my ticket out of the nightmare in Worcester. I felt that I could get both my career, and my marriage, back on track in a new, and very different environment. This time, I was only half-wrong.

Things weren't all bad in Worcester however. In a professional sense, I reacquainted myself with cricket, and got to commentate on a one-day final at Lord's between Worcestershire and Warwickshire. Despite my childhood disappointments, I still enjoyed the game very much, and the one upside of living in Worcester was that the local team was, in those days, one of the best in the country.

Along with Bradders and freelancer Chris Williams, I would commentate on the many Sunday League matches at the picturesque New Road ground, and elsewhere. It was a different challenge to football, with so many 'down' moments during play that had to be filled. The county also had excellent players, like Zimbabwean-born batsman, Graeme Hick, then *the* up-and-coming star of the English game, wicketkeeper Steve Rhodes, captain Tim Curtis, and big Tom Moody, the Australian import.

In May 1994, just a few months after I'd arrived, Worcestershire won through to the final of the senior one-day competition, the NatWest Trophy. Adding further spice to the occasion was that they were facing their biggest local rivals, Warwickshire, all at the traditional home of cricket.

BBC Hereford & Worcester arranged for full ball-by-ball commentary on the day of the final, 3 September 1994. But as per usual during my time in the county, things didn't exactly go according to plan.

After the morning session, during which Brian Lara set Warwickshire up for a big total – en route to a magnificent 81 – the rain came tumbling down. We thought it would only be a short shower, but the grey skies just wouldn't lift, and by midafternoon, the umpires decided to abandon play for the day, and come back on the Sunday to finish things off.

That, however, presented us with a problem. We'd booked out the entire day's schedule, so that meant filling hours and hours of airtime. The afternoon's football got us out of a hole; we offered full match commentary from Worcester City's home game at St George's Lane (for the benefit of at least several people, no doubt), but that still left us with big gaps.

In the end, I think we interviewed every single Worcestershire player, the groundsman, the umpires – probably even the tea lady. By 7 pm (the scheduled close of our broadcast), we were the last people in the ground, and the cleaning staff were sweeping up around us with the main stadium lights long since turned off. The joys of live cricket on radio during a wet English summer!

A day later, we returned and saw Worcestershire lift the trophy, a majestic 93 not out by Graeme Hick enough to overhaul Warwickshire's total. It had been a hell of a long weekend in London, but a good test of our broadcasting capabilities nevertheless.

But such days were too few and far between, and so, by April 1995, I was eagerly preparing for my next challenge with the World Service. My wife, however, was digging her heels in.

I pushed on regardless, more determined than ever to pursue what I saw as a brilliant opportunity. In April, the BBC helped find me an apartment in Pinner, Middlesex, and as part of the relocation package, they said they would pay my mortgage in Worcester for the duration of my attachment, while I sorted out the rent in London. That, in the short-term, was the perfect solution. My wife was free to remain in Worcester, and we bought some time – six months for us to think things through, and six months for me to prove my worth to the World Service. After all that had happened, I was determined that there was no way that I would return to Worcester.

When I look back on my first marriage, I find it astonishing how rushed everything seemed to be, and how little we knew about each other before making such a big decision. As a husband, I wasn't honest enough with my feelings regarding children, and was overly-obsessed with (what I thought was) my faltering career. Crucially of course, I didn't consult her before applying for the job in London. That was wrong.

At the time, I couldn't grasp why the move was such a big deal. For me, it was a promotion, with more money, and only two hours down the road. For her, moving away from her family was a huge wrench; but of course, I'd done all that years ago. I was insensitive to it, no doubt.

Having come so close to failure as a teenager, I was too single-minded in my pursuit of professional success. I was the product of a small-town northern environment, more accustomed to a rather mundane existence. But now, having had a glimpse of a different life, I was scared to death of seeing it disappear. Jointly, we were guilty of nothing more than wanting different things out of life at that time. She was happy in her environment, keen to settle down and start a family.

Me? I wanted more. Much more…and nothing was going to get in my way.

CHAPTER FIVE

5

BUSH, BIERHOFF AND BURKINA

If there is such a thing as love at first sight when it comes to your career, then that was me and the BBC World Service.

From the very first day I walked into Bush House on the Strand, I felt right at home. I already had a good vibe about London itself after my stint at Radio Wimbledon the year before, where I had made good friends with people such as Rupert Bell (a racing journalist by day) and one of my new BBC colleagues in the capital, Mary Rhodes. It was a little taste of being back in the big time after my experiences in Worcester, and I interviewed stars such as the bubbly Arantxa Sànchez Vicario, Gabriela Sabatini, and the gorgeous (yet moody) Anna Kournikova.

Even going on the tube to work every day made me feel important, part of a thriving, happening city. It couldn't have been more different to the almost comatose pace of life in Worcester.

Bush House was a fantastic melting pot of cultures. In total, there were 44 different language services, and going for a beer in the basement in-house bar was like taking a round-the-world trip without leaving the building. I made myself at home immediately at the beautiful old ornate building, and met interesting people such as Orin Gordon, born in Guyana, whose bulletins for the BBC Caribbean Service contained fascinating yarns on things I'd never heard of – such as the lesser spotted mealybug, a pest which kills off crops in the region! Shafi Naqi, whose encyclopaedia-like knowledge of cricket in Pakistan was combined with a background in law and current affairs work for the

BBC Urdu Service, and Rob Minshull (World News), who'd seen service in the Israeli army, and whose political and sporting interests dovetailed perfectly with mine – he being a Manc, a City fan, and left of centre politically.

Within my own department, senior journalist David Coles and I became inseparable, and along with Harry Peart, we proceeded to drink London dry for months on end, while Harry in particular, gently, but firmly, set about polishing my craft as both a presenter and a journalist.

Harry would pull my writing apart after every bulletin. He was a stickler for the definite article, and also for introducing stories by naming the sport at the very top. He hated the modern trend of presenters leading into a story by merely saying (for example), 'John Terry has been appointed England captain.'

Harry's view – and it's something I've stuck by ever since – was that not everyone in the audience knew who John Terry was, nor which sport he played. Therefore, the World Service introduction would read thus, 'In football, the Chelsea defender, John Terry, has been appointed as the England national team captain.' So simple, but he was spot on.

Harry fiercely protected the values of the World Service, which had an attention to detail that is rarely replicated today, and I think journalism (and broadcasting in particular), is the poorer for it.

After a few months of doing shifts preparing and presenting the 'Sports Round-Up' bulletins – which, incidentally, had an audience of millions – I began to receive fan mail from all corners of the globe, like many of the other presenters did. It was my first experience of this, but it hit home to me just how respected the BBC's international coverage was, especially in areas of political instability, or oppressive regimes, where press neutrality couldn't be guaranteed.

We, of course, were only covering sport, a pastime of little importance in the great scheme of things, and yet people were so passionate about it, and our football coverage in particular. As the late Pope John Paul II once said, 'Of all the unimportant things in life, football is the most important.'

I once received a letter from a girl in Pristina, Kosovo. The writer told me, in broken English, that she was a Manchester United fan (we all have our issues), and that she listened religiously to our broadcasts every day of the week. She told me she loved my voice, and hoped I'd write back to her. I did, but never heard from her again. With the Bosnian War still raging in her part of the world, I often wondered whether she received my letter – indeed, whether she even survived.

Others, particularly in Africa for some reason, simply liked to list their favourite presenters, and it became obvious over time, that the longer you were there, the more you became part of their consciousness. When I first started at the World Service, my name barely appeared on such lists in letters shown to me by other presenters. Then, after I'd been there a while, I moved up the pecking order, and by the time I left three years later, I was near the top. It was a lesson that, in broadcasting, longevity is just as important as ability in the eyes of the public because they simply become used to you being in their living rooms. An invited, familiar, and welcome guest, rather than a stranger.

Towards the end of 1995, our managing editor, Linda Spurr, held a meeting, in which she told her staff that she wanted our coverage to become more dynamic, and that she was looking for ideas both to revamp the programmes, and for 'special' projects.

She told us that the world was our oyster, and that for the best ideas, there was a travel budget. This was one of the great joys about the World Service. We weren't limited to what happened in England, nor even Europe. If there was a story happening in Somalia, it was our story as much as anyone else's. We had complete free reign to let our journalistic minds run wild. I loved it.

I helped put together an idea for a new short programme entitled *Football Extra* which was much pacier than the usual World Service output. On a whim, I also decided to put a programme idea together for the midweek magazine show called *Sports International.* Every week, different members of the team were assigned to work on the half-hour programme, which pulled together stories from around the globe. Occasionally, they'd do in-depth feature programmes on a specific topic. My idea was simple, and it had an ulterior motive. I'd never been to Asia, and for some reason, Japan really appealed to me. So, how about a half-hour special on Japanese sport?

I spent a couple of weeks preparing my proposal along with costings for flights, accommodation, internal travel etcetera, and eventually came up with a six-strand programme idea.

Japan was preparing to host the 1998 Winter Olympics in Nagano, and had also recently won the rights to co-host the 2002 World Cup with South Korea. Preparations for the two events would give me two features, but not enough for a half-hour show. So, I expanded the football theme, reasoning that the annual Intercontinental Cup match in Tokyo every December was the perfect time to go. If I could get accredited, I could grab some interviews in the mixed zone afterwards. Japan was also in the process of building a new Asian football academy in Fukushima – I would travel there too.

That left just two slots to fill. I opted for a two-part interview with an American-born journalist, who'd been based in Tokyo for years covering both baseball and Sumo wrestling, Japan's other two big sporting passions.

I didn't hold out much hope of my proposal succeeding, but I was desperate to take advantage of the World Service's global scope. To my amazement, Linda Spurr loved the idea, and told me that if I could sort out flights, accommodation and organise the interviews and accreditation, the BBC would fund a week-long trip.

Before heading to Japan however, there were other things that needed attention. With my job going as well as I'd hoped, the World Service had quickly agreed to make my role permanent, even before my attachment had finished. I couldn't sign quickly enough. I'd even dipped my toe into cricket waters again, covering a one-day international between England and India at Old Trafford, which meant sharing a commentary box with the legendary Henry Blofeld – something of an education.

'Blowers' spent the whole day checking out the various pretty young girls wandering around the stands via his binoculars, and sipping Pimm's in the members stand. He didn't seem to be watching the game at all. But whenever he was scheduled to report on a wicket for BBC Radio 5 Live, he was flawless, merely asking his fellow commentators whether the unfortunate batsman had played forward or back. He then delivered a word perfect 30-second summary, before returning to his binoculars. I thought he was utterly brilliant.

Professionally I was making rapid strides. But what about my wife? She was not enjoying life alone back in Worcester, so, a little reluctantly, she agreed to join me in London, and move in to the flat in Pinner. We put the house in Worcester on the market, and she set about finding work in the capital. After a while, she started to enjoy being in a different environment, but for me, the horse had already bolted. After four months without her, I had been having the time of my life, both professionally and personally. With mates old and new (a lot of my student friends from my days in Portsmouth were now London-based too), I was out on the town three or four nights a week, and had no intention of slowing down to accommodate her arrival.

Things came to a head during Euro 96 – the first football tournament England had hosted in 30 years. I was accredited for the tournament, and reported on several games in the group stage, including the famous England/Scotland game in which Paul Gascoigne scored one of the great international goals.

England's final group game was against the Netherlands, but I wasn't working for that one, so my wife and I went to the local pub in Pinner to watch it. England put in one of their best displays in years to thrash the Dutch 4–1, and we had a great time in a packed pub, singing, cheering and drinking with some friends we'd met there. It was a rare night when we'd clicked again and had enjoyed each other's company, and so, we both agreed we'd go back there for the quarter-final against Spain on the Saturday.

But, a trip to see my parents at a holiday campsite just outside London on the morning of the game (we'd planned to leave early to return to the capital in time for the game) went awry when her parents unexpectedly turned up too. My wife wanted to spend more time with her family, and I ended up driving back – in a fit of pique – on my own. We were approaching the end of our marriage.

The final of Euro 96 was at Wembley, between Germany and the Czech Republic. I was delighted to learn that World Service were going to offer full commentary, and that David Coles and myself had been chosen to call the game. This was to be my second major final in the space of a few months, after we'd relayed coverage of the FA Cup Final between Manchester United and Liverpool to the world – another lifetime ambition achieved.

For the Euro final, we were perched high on the second tier of the old Wembley (before its redevelopment in the early 2000s), and the atmosphere was tremendous. The game went to extra time, when Oliver Bierhoff netted the 'golden goal' winner for the Germans. I had the pleasure of calling it, and felt my career was once again heading in the right direction.

London had quickly become home from home, but earlier in 1996, I had been reminded of the perils of living in the big smoke, when I had a rather lucky escape. The Good Friday peace agreement was still two years away from being signed, and the major cities of the UK were still a target for the IRA as they waged their war of terror, aimed at securing a united Ireland.

On 18 February of that year, I was walking from Holborn tube station to my shift at Bush House. I had just reached the office and sat down at my desk when there was an almighty bang, and the huge windows of our office, facing onto the Aldwych, started to shake so violently, I was sure they would shatter at any moment. I sat open-mouthed, several colleagues likewise – had it been an earthquake, or some sort of gas or electrical explosion?

The truth was more sinister. Twenty-two year old Edward O'Brien, an IRA volunteer, had accidentally detonated the 2-kilogram Semtex bomb he was carrying on the number 171 bus, just 200 metres or so away from us on the Aldwych. Two passengers and the bus driver were all injured in the explosion, and I'd been fortunate I had arrived some minutes earlier into work. Had I been later, I may have been even closer to the bus.

In December 1995, I jetted off to Japan for my half-hour documentary special for *Sports International.* I attended the World Club Cup game between Juventus and River Plate (in which a young Alessandro del Piero netted the winner), travelled to the ski fields of Nagano, and headed north to Fukushima on the bullet train. Many years later, the facility would play a vital role as the recovery base, following the devastating tsunami that struck the region in 2011.

I actually experienced an earthquake on that trip, though thankfully a much smaller one than caused the tsunami. In my Tokyo hotel one night, I was starting to nod off when I became vaguely aware of a distant rumble. I woke with a start, as my bed started to inch across the floor, as though someone was giving it an almighty shove every few seconds. Then, it stopped. I thought I might have been dreaming, but a further check confirmed the bed was at least a foot nearer to the door than when I'd got into it. I phoned the hotel reception, and the girl giggled, saying she had answered quite a few calls in the last few minutes, that it was 'only an earthquake' and not to worry!

Back in London, my wife and I tried to put down some roots, buying a three-bed semi in North Harrow. But even there, things refused to go smoothly. Within a few weeks of moving in, we were burgled, with the thief only making good his escape as my wife put her key in the door as she returned from her day's work. I got a tearful phone call at work and made my way home immediately, to find our home had been ransacked – jewellery, items of clothing, video recorder all gone, with the upstairs drawers overturned and emptied in the search for valuables.

My wife was understandably nervous about being in the house on her own from then on, and even though we made the house more secure by installing high fencing at the back (which is where the robbers had made their entrance), it only added to the strain we were under.

By mid-1997, we'd reached the end. My wife had thrown a party for her birthday, and we'd spent the entire night in separate parts of the house. She moved out a month later, and our divorce was finalised in 1998.

Fortunately, work was a great distraction from my personal problems.

By the end of 1997, I got word that I was in the frame to cover the African Cup of Nations, to be held in January 1998. The tournament was a mainstay of the World Service's coverage, and they needed a commentator to call the latter stages of the Cup, to be held in the west African nation of Burkina Faso.

I had no idea where Burkina Faso even was, but some research taught me that it was a land-locked nation, wedged in between six countries – Mali, Niger, Ivory Coast, Ghana, Togo and Benin. It was also the fifth poorest nation on earth. After confirmation I had got the gig, we flew via Paris to the Burkina capital, Ouagadougou, a few days before the tournament started. It was to be one of the best experiences of my life.

We arrived in the middle of the 'dry' season, when the hot Saharan wind blows in straight from the desert, meaning temperatures can rise as high as 45 degrees. Not much fun for a lad from northern England, although if I'd known then what I know now, I would have said it was good preparation for an Australian summer! Every day felt like someone had wrapped me up in a blanket and put me in the oven. It was a searing heat quite unlike any other I had experienced.

On the first day, we also got an insight as to how the Cup of Nations (known locally as the CAN) was going to operate. We took a taxi down to the main stadium to check out whether our broadcast facilities had been put in place for the opening ceremony and opening game.

Normally with major tournaments, you have to pass through a phalanx of security, but not at the August the 4th stadium in Ouagadougou – so named after the date when the Marxist revolutionary, Thomas Sankara, had overthrown erstwhile President, Jean-Baptiste Ouédraogo in 1983. Sankara was, in turn, murdered by supporters of the (then) current President, the football-loving Blaise Compaoré, who'd taken power in 1987, and had personally guaranteed the success of the tournament by building two new stadiums. Compaoré was standing for re-election in 1998, and no doubt the two events were related.

Anyhow, no-one batted an eyelid at our arrival, so we simply wandered through the gates, the stands, and then onto the pitch itself!

The following day we acquired our media accreditation at Ouaga da Mil, a specially constructed 'IBC' (International Broadcast Centre), which every major tournament must have for the traveling media. We also had a special guest in tow – more of which shortly.

The night before, we'd been relaxing at our hotel having a quiet drink. 'We' in this case being a team of BBC journalists sent over specially to cover the tournament via the various language services.

For the English-speaking section, there was myself, African service veteran Martin Davies, engineer David Haye, and producer Marcus Prior. For the Swahili service there was Saed Ali Muse from Somalia, Durosimi Thomas, who'd escaped the civil war in Sierra Leone by fleeing over the border to Ghana, and from South Africa, there was the devout Muslim, Mohammed Allie, and the giant (at least 6 feet 8 inches) Afrikaaner, Mark Gleeson.

To service Portuguese speakers, there was Eleuterio Fenita from Mozambique, who walked with a pronounced limp after having contracted polio as a child (not that it stopped him from acquiring a bevy of female admirers throughout the tournament) and, for good measure, a local helper from Ouagadougou with rheumy eyes that suggested a serious alcohol problem. The BBC Africa (French) Service also had Pierre Kazoni and Charles Bambara in tow. It was quite an eclectic mix.

All were detailed to provide the best coverage for the BBC, whose daily African news bulletins began with the delightful tradition of the African proverb. These are an integral part of the culture on the continent, and I used to love listening to them before we'd start our daily broadcasts. Here's just two examples:

'When the leopard has a toothache, then the goat can go and collect a debt!'

'Better to stumble with the foot, than the tongue!'

One man who rarely stumbled with his tongue however, was late. We were awaiting – with bated breath – the arrival of a broadcasting legend, Mr Dennis Liwewe. Dennis was known as the 'voice of Zambian football' and, as we waited, my colleagues recounted various stories of his exploits – telling me he was quite a character. When he finally arrived late into the evening, I wasn't to be disappointed.

Liwewe had been delayed on a connecting flight from Switzerland. Why was he in Switzerland? In his own words, and with a heavy African accent, 'I have to go to Zurich, because last time I in Europe, I buy watch for my wife, and she no like. I say whaaaat? She want change. So I have to fly to Switzer-laaaand and get new one!'

We were staying at the Hotel Yibi in downtown Ouagadougou, a pretty basic hostelry, where hot water was never guaranteed, and where locking your room meant wedging your chair underneath the door handle. But the Yibi had an even more famous guest than Dennis Liwewe staying and, as we continued to drink our fill in the bar, we were about to meet him.

Above the hubbub of our general conversation, we became aware of a shouting match taking place in reception. The gentleman concerned was clearly unhappy that his luggage had been lost en route from the airport to the hotel, and was letting the poor concierge know about it, all in a broad Geordie accent.

We stuck our heads around the dividing wall to see what all the commotion was about and there, in front of us, stood Bobby Robson. Robson was then General Manager of Barcelona after Louis Van Gaal had succeeded him as manager at Camp Nou, and he was in Africa to scout potential new talent for the Catalan giants.

The next morning, Bobby was riled again – complaining to the receptionist that no-one had come to pick him up as arranged, he claimed, to take him to Ouaga da Mil to get his accreditation.

At which point, I stepped in, and offered Bobby a ride to the IBC (where we were heading too), in order to get his precious badge. Robson readily agreed, and I could hardly believe my luck, as I sat next to him on the 20-minute cab ride, listening to his stories about Italia '90, Ipswich Town and his experiences at Barca.

On arrival at Ouaga da Mil, Robson hopped out and headed off for his badge – but I wasn't going to let him get away that easily. I reasoned that, as we'd helped him out, he owed me an interview at the very least. I asked whether he'd spare us a few minutes, but Robson turned tail, and said something along the lines of 'You journalists twist my words around.'

'If it wasn't for us journalists Mr Robson, you wouldn't even be here!' I countered.

At which point, he admitted I had a case, and gave me a three-minute interview as to why he was in Burkina Faso. Exclusive number one, signed, sealed, and delivered.

Robson wasn't the only football personality we encountered on that trip. We spent a raucous night in a restaurant with Basile Boli, the former French defender famous for headbutting Stuart Pearce during a game against England ('I was…er…how you say…angry!'), and I had a fascinating conversation with ex-Cameroon goalkeeper, Joseph Antoine-Bell, about the social problems affecting his native country.

Really, the football was just the backdrop to a hugely educational month and a half. The Burkinabe were truly the most hospitable people I had ever come across. They had nothing and yet, as a rare overseas visitor to their impoverished country, they wanted to share everything with you. An example of which was a Lebanese expat, who, upon hearing of our visit via the World Service, drove 80 kilometres from his dusty outback home to our hotel, and demanded to see us. We nervously appeared, wondering who on earth was waiting for us. After explaining he was a lifelong fan of the World Service, he insisted we go with him to his restaurant on the edge of town, where he proceeded to give us free dinner and beer, before driving us back late into the night. The power of the BBC.

When the tournament started, we didn't know what to expect. We'd spent two days attempting to acquire mobile phones (then in their infancy) but every meeting with the local company took hours, and ended in nothing but frustration, as they demanded more and more money for their fairly rudimentary services.

Engineer David Haye then attempted to rig up a 'sat-phone' in order to feed pieces back to London. This, in pre-digital days, meant shinning up the side of the hotel onto its roof, in order to position a rather bulky piece of equipment, which in turn, gazed up into the sky, pointing optimistically at an ever-moving satellite, in the vain hope of getting a signal back to the UK.

I accompanied him on this little voyage of discovery, the type which would have health and safety up in arms these days. But after an hour of rigging, pointing and sweating in the intense heat (and all to the roar of planes taking off from the nearby airport), we were getting nowhere. Time after time, David tried to dial in to London; time after time, he failed, prompting him to reposition the hardware at a slightly different angle, in order to try again.

Eventually, after the umpteenth failure, I threw my hands up in the air and exclaimed, 'What the hell are we doing here?!' To which, David (experienced at these types of delays) calmly replied, 'Collecting stories for our old age.' He was dead right!

Come opening night however, all our ducks were in a row. Mobile phones? Check. Sat-phone? Roger. But nothing had prepared us for the opening ceremony, or the crazy African fans.

The 4th of August Stadium was packed for the match between hosts, Burkina Faso, and regional giants, Cameroon. But first was the ceremony. Now, even as long ago as 1998, opening ceremonies were pretty lavish affairs, full of whiz-bang technology, laser beams, fireworks and dancing girls. Not in Burkina Faso though.

We were treated to half an hour of the most chaotic yet brilliant fun only Africa could muster. First, four parachutists dropped onto the pitch from the four corners of the stadium, or at least, that was the plan. Three made it safely enough, but the fourth missed his target by quite some distance, colliding with one of the floodlights and clinging on for dear life until he managed to disentangle himself from his canopy, in order to be able to climb down. Thankfully, he wasn't the one delivering the Cup itself, otherwise he may have had to have thrown it to the fans below, who were already at fever pitch – we might not have seen it again!

Then, musicians appeared on the apron of the pitch. Their rhythms were fabulous, but the acts that followed them made their continuing procession around the circuit rather precarious. For some reason, the organisers thought a demonstration of the local wildlife was a great showcase for the country, so in behind the musicians traipsed an assortment of pigs, goats, chickens and guinea fowls. However, faced with 30,000 roaring football fans, they understandably got a little nervous. So, while the more nimble footed of the beasts bolted to try and find cover, those that were more firmly tethered simply shat themselves, all the way around the track. As you can imagine, this made walking (while concentrating on playing the right notes or beats) extremely treacherous for the musicians. It was farcical. By the end of the ceremony, you couldn't work out who was officially part of the entourage, and who was there merely trying to round up – or clean up after – the assorted animals.

But for all that, it was something completely different, and quintessentially African. The organisation of the entire tournament was chaotic, but as Marcus Prior remarked (and this wasn't his first CAN), 'The bureaucracy is not there to help you...but it's not there to hinder you either!'

When the football started, Burkina, playing in just their second CAN since 1978, were clearly nervous too, in front of such an expectant crowd. They had to change their colours which perhaps didn't help, as their normal green strip clashed with Cameroon. In fact, most of the African nations played in a combination of green, red and yellow. I was told that the reasoning was simple in most cases – the green represented the land, the yellow the sun, and the red was the blood that had been spilled! Anyhow, in a change strip of white, Burkina Faso lost 1–0 to an Alphonse Tchami goal, and their fans weren't slow in making their feelings known at their substandard performance.

That presented us with a problem too. We had to attend the post-game mixed zone, which was located across on the far side of the field, to conduct interviews. The 4th of August Stadium was built in the traditional 'communist' bowl style, with the area for spectators only slightly raised above ground level, in one continuous loop.

As we walked around the track area, it became clear that we were sitting ducks for any projectiles launched from the still-packed stands, and so it proved. Thankfully, the missiles launched at us weren't dangerous – but they were disgusting. The Burkina Faso fans' weapon of choice was a deflated balloon, filled with piss.

After negotiating the obstacle course outside, we were, at last, safely in the inner sanctum, and I made a beeline for the Burkina coach, Philippe Troussier, a Frenchman who was later to be linked with the Australian coaching job. Troussier was well versed with African football, having led Ivorian side, ASEC Abidjan, to three consecutive domestic league titles and he wasn't overly concerned by his team's opening-day defeat, spelling out why his own particular brand of magic would take them deep into this tournament.

'Are you concerned by this loss?' was my opening question.

'Non, non. You see, I am zee White Witch Doctor, and my power will take us to the last four at least. Zis, I promise to you and all fans of Les Etalons [which translates to 'the Stallions' – the nickname of the Burkina team]' said Troussier. Troussier had picked up the label of the 'White Witch Doctor' in Nigeria, and clearly enjoyed the moniker, believing it was a good publicity tool, in a continent still keenly in thrall to the concept of voodoo, or 'muti'. Events would also prove him to be a fairly decent judge of his own capabilities.

Outside, we made our way through the thousands of disappointed (but mainly good-natured) Burkina fans, and came across the tiny cluster of traveling Cameroon supporters. I decided to get their views on their team's success, from a dude inhaling deeply on some sort of pipe, which clearly didn't just contain tobacco.

'Football,' he said into the microphone, before taking another deep breath of the noxious smelling substance, 'is our bizz-ness.' The 'bizz-ness' part of his statement took a good three seconds as he exhaled a huge plume of smoke. It was broadcasting gold.

Talking of gold, the BBC had issued each of us with a gold American Express credit card to settle our hotel bills but we soon learned they were utterly useless in west Africa. Not only did Hotel Yibi not accept plastic, but they demanded payment for our room and board on a weekly basis, and we were staying for the best part of six weeks.

So, every Friday, I had to go and line up at the local bank to withdraw (using travellers cheques, issued as a safety net for this very scenario) huge bundles of the local currency, the CFA.

Being the only white man in a queue of 30 Africans certainly raised eyebrows among the locals – and the bank tellers were just as unnerved. Every Friday was the same ritual, with the teller refusing to part with such a large sum, before leading me to an upstairs room where I had to give chapter and verse to the branch manager as to why I needed the money.

From the bank, it was a quick scurry back to Hotel Yibi. Burkina was a peaceful place (by African standards), but I had stacks of notes hidden in my socks, my underpants and even under my baseball cap, so I didn't want to take chances. It is a credit to an impoverished people that no-one ever tried to mug any of us. Sadly, things were to take a turn for the worse for the country many years later, when Compaore was overthrown in yet another coup. In 2017, he is due to stand trial for his part in the violent crackdown of the 2014 uprising, which saw him removed, and the 1987 killing of his former comrade, Thomas Sankara.

The social side of things in Ouagadougou were another highlight. After a few days, we'd quickly hooked up with other touring journalists on the same beat as us. Piers Edwards was a freelancer working for the Hayters agency, and he was to make his mark at this tournament by breaking the exclusive story of Algerian Moussa Saib's impending move to Spurs. Adam Docker and Guy Oliver were shooting stories for the excellent *Futbol Mundial* while Alan Duncan was writing for the now-defunct *African Soccer* magazine. His editor, Emmanuel Maradas (later to work for FIFA, and a close ally of Sepp Blatter), was also on the trip.

Rogan Taylor, the Liverpudlian lecturer who'd become something of a celebrity in the UK for his work campaigning on behalf of the families of the victims of the Hillsborough disaster, was also in Ouagadougou. Rogan was great company – a brilliant raconteur, and his sharp Scouse wit had us in stitches, as did his peculiar peccadilloes when it came to travel in the Third World. Rogan couldn't go without his daily fix of Weetabix, so he simply wrapped the breakfast biscuits individually into his supply of socks prior to every trip!

We had some brilliant evenings out at Jimmy's, the nightclub adjoining our hotel, which was full to the brim every night with some of the most beautiful women I had ever seen.

Being newly single, I found it hard to resist their charms, but Eric Mnene, an ample-framed BBC journalist who'd recently arrived at the tournament from the BBC Swahili bureau in Kenya, wasn't much impressed. Eric wore the traditional white African robes, along with a colourful fez on his head. He looked like a priest, and for a long time one night, he sounded like one too.

I was trying to tease Eric into admitting that he found some of the girls in the club attractive but he was having none of it. Every girl I pointed out, he simply shook his head or tutted. That was, until an extremely large, older lady arrived. Eric's face lit up. And with that, he sprang into life on the dance floor, gyrating purposefully next to the apple of his eye for the next few tracks.

But with all of us young bucks working, and playing hard, it was perhaps inevitable that some couldn't last the pace. The food in Burkina was delicious, with grilled meat being a particular speciality. But as with any environmental change, foreigners have to be careful with what they eat on tour so I erred on the side of safety, and kept to a very basic diet, for which I was mercilessly teased. One of my colleagues wasn't so lucky however.

Martin Davies loved his seafood, and being in deepest, darkest Africa wasn't going to stop him eating his favourite dish. When he asked for fish one evening in a Ouagadougou restaurant, we asked him whether he was sure he wanted to go through with it.

'Don't be soft' he said, and insisted he'd be fine. However, the smell of the fish was, shall we say, a little bit different, and between mouthfuls, Martin became a bit unsure if what he was consuming was actually fresh. He called the waiter over.

'Is this fish fresh?' he said. 'Oh yes sir,' replied the waiter. 'It was caught fresh in Lome [Togo] four days ago, and was brought here on the truck straightaway.' Martin spat a big mouthful out, and didn't touch another morsel. Too late. For the rest of the trip, Martin suffered horrendous diarrhoea. He probably lost about 5 kilograms in weight, and lived off Imodium to such an extent, we thought that the local chemist was going to run out of supplies. By contrast, the worst I suffered was a touch of athlete's foot, due to the constant sweating inside my trainers because of the heat, thus making my feet smell rather badly. For the remainder of the tournament, Martin and I had pet-names for each other.

'Morning arse,' I'd say to Martin.

'How's it going feet?' he'd reply.

Meanwhile, the tournament was progressing well. I was enjoying the unique flavour of a tournament filled with teams and players I had barely heard of. Ghana in particular impressed me in their opening game. They defeated Tunisia 2–0, with a display so brilliant, I thought they were odds-on to win the tournament, particularly as they had a large contingent of support from just across the border. Their team was packed full of talent: the tricky Peter Ofori-Quaye, the majestic Samuel Kuffour and the veteran Abedi Pele, playing in his last major tournament at the age of 35. But the Black Stars then fell victim to that oldest of African problems – they fell out with each other over money. The coach was unable to mollify either them, or the Ghanaian FA, who were refusing to pay them their agreed bonuses, and they lost their next two games, bowing out at the group stage. It was a travesty.

Burkina Faso had recovered well from their opening day loss to Cameroon, defeating Algeria 2–1. But they got their opening goal due to a rather dubious penalty, and when, in the third and deciding game, the official opted to send off Guinean Pablo Thiam when he was at least a metre away from his alleged 'foul' I smelt a rat.

The day after Burkina Faso's 1–0 win (which guaranteed them a place in the knockout phase), I recorded a package for *Sports International* saying that the standards of refereeing had been rather questionable, hinting that the officials were 'leaning' towards the home team a little too much. I did, however, stop short of calling them cheats.

A day later, the head of referees at the Confederation of African Football, Farah Addo, called a press conference, and in front of a throng of journalists, proceeded to berate my story, which, he, 'couldn't believe had appeared on a network normally as reliable as the BBC.'

Whether there was collusion or not, I couldn't be sure. But my gut feel told me I was right, and my package contained 'grabs' of powerful figures such as Joseph-Antoine Bell, who also believed it to be true. Burkina Faso needed to have a long run in the competition – they were the only nation which filled the stadiums – and President Compaore had invested a lot of money in staging the event.

Big Mark Gleeson stood up for me at the presser, admonishing Addo for his rebuttal, saying, 'If an organisation so respected as you say the BBC is, is saying these things, then perhaps you should take it seriously, and investigate Mr Addo!'

The ref in question, Omer Yengo of Congo, didn't referee another game at the tournament, perhaps as if to underline the point.

Although unrelated to this particular incident, Farah Addo was later found guilty of embezzlement by FIFA and banned for 10 years. Sadly, such is the distrust in the way the world governing body does its business these days, that is not necessarily an indication of his guilt. Addo died in 2008.

Interestingly, the FIFA Presidency was also hotting up in Ouagadougou, after long-time supremo João Havelange had announced his retirement. The two candidates were Lennart Johansson (the overwhelming favourite), and Havelange's then General Secretary, Sepp Blatter. I interviewed both, as well as Havelange, and remember just how shattered the normally jovial Johansson looked, as he was beginning to realise he was losing the political games that FIFA would (later) become so infamous for.

Blatter ultimately won the vote in Paris in June of that year.

Lennart Johansson looked pale and drawn after the CAF Congress at Ouaga da Mil, and so too did our producer, Marcus Prior, after falling victim to the dreaded stomach bug, just a few days before the end of the tournament.

On the morning of the semifinal between Burkina Faso and Egypt, Prior appeared in the lobby of the Hotel Yibi, not looking his usual chipper self.

'Everything okay Marcus?' I enquired.

'Dunno really,' he replied. 'I went to the toilet with a bit of a funny tummy late last night, and woke up this morning face down in the shower with shit all around me!'

After we'd got the giggles out of our systems, we realised that this could pose a major problem. Later that morning, we'd hired a taxi to take us for the six-hour trek south to Burkina Faso's second city, Bobo-Dioulasso, which is where the semi was being played.

The reason we'd hired the services of a cab? Well, the train lines between the two cities took up to 10 hours, and were highly unreliable, and with only two flights per week between Ouaga and Bobo, the only other option was to fly via military aircraft. Martin Davies had chosen the military option for an earlier game in Bobo, deciding he couldn't expose his rather delicate stomach to the long car ride.

Martin told us later that the plane had just two seats, for the pilot and his deputy. He, the only passenger, was deposited in the hold, where there were no windows. The plane then took off at a ferocious rate of knots, due to a short runway at the military airfield. Martin, caught by surprise at the rapid elevation, didn't have a firm enough grip on the side of the plane. He slid some five metres in a matter of two seconds, banging his head on the back of the fuselage for good measure! I don't think Martin would go back to Burkina Faso on his holidays…

Meantime, we were preparing to set out on our marathon journey, but in addition to Marcus's problematic bowels, we had another issue. Alan Duncan, who was accompanying us on the trip, was the only fluent French speaker among us. So when the taxi driver quietly had a word in his ear, Alan turned to us and breathed a heavy sigh. It turned out that our driver had not only never been to Bobo-Dioulasso before but he had also never driven in the dark. This was particularly prescient, given that this was a night game, and he would be driving us back in the wee small hours. Despite our misgivings at learning this information, the driver assured us he knew the way, and so we set out on what was to be, by far our craziest day in Africa so far – and we'd had a few already.

Perhaps, because he'd never been to Bobo before, our driver seemed to want to get the journey out of the way as quickly as possible. That's the only reason I can give for the way he drove for the first two hours, which was, like a madman. After numerous requests for him to slow down, we nicknamed him 'Schumacher' after the F1 speedster, and, perhaps being one of the few words of English he understood, he eventually he got the message.

After three hours, we had our first pit stop – enforced due to Marcus's dicky tummy – although to be fair, he'd done well to last that long. He disappeared behind a mud hut with the roll of toilet paper he'd sensibly brought along, and reappeared 10 minutes later looking suitably becalmed.

Schumacher had slowed down, but the over-laden trucks that zipped past us with their precarious cargo, certainly hadn't, and, as dusk approached, we realised just how hair-raising this trip could potentially be. Maybe Schumacher had been right after all. The problem with the roads in rural Burkina Faso is simple – there aren't any. Once you get an hour outside Ouagadougou, the tarmac disappears into mud tracks so keeping your distance from cars (and more pertinently, trucks) heading the other way on your patch of dirt becomes a question of judgement.

The way they do this in Burkina is to use indicators. When you see a car coming the other way, you put on your right indicator, and the other guy does likewise so you can judge the distance between the edges of your two vehicles. Good in theory, but in practice those distances can feel very small indeed when you are on a bumpy dirt track doing 70 kilometres per hour, and there is no sunlight or street light, to help you. When it's a ten-tonne truck coming the other way, it's downright frightening. This then, was our six-hour journey to Bobo-Dioulasso.

Having arrived – somehow – in one piece, we found the place was buzzing, a riot of colour and noise. In fact, riot was a very apt word for what was to happen later. I made my way to the commentary box along with Marcus, who was to help me out with some summarising – and his toilet roll. Alan and Piers, the fourth member of our travelling quartet, went off to the press gallery.

Burkina Faso had never been this deep into a tournament before, and the packed stands fully expected them to complete the job. Philippe Troussier's squad had made great virtue in the build-up of their togetherness, forged in the wake of their early disappointment against Cameroon. But Egypt were far too strong for the rookies, and ran out easy 2–0 winners, with Hossam Hassan scoring both goals, en route to winning the golden boot with seven.

But there was more fun to be had as the final whistle sounded. Desperately disappointed, the local fans gave vent to their frustrations by invading the pitch. The military wasted no time in wading in, and amidst a flurry of batons, the unmistakable waft of tear gas began to fill the air around us.

Tear gas stings like the devil, and we had no way of avoiding it. By the time we got out of the stadium, we were stumbling around like drunken fools. Eventually, we led each other, hand in hand, back to the safety of Schumacher's taxi. Literally, the blind leading the blind. He was already revving the engine, anxious to leave.

After rinsing our eyes with water, we were starting to calm down after our exciting day – and so was our driver. It was nearly 1 am, and Schumi, having (he informed us) not slept, in fear of being mugged in his taxi, was starting to tire. We had to take it in turns to keep watch on him, screaming 'Attention!' (the French version) every time his eyes started to close, and a truck hove into view around the corner of the next mud bank.

To keep him conscious, Alan dug into his rucksack and found an old-fashioned cassette of The Verve and their new album (hey, this WAS 1998!). This seemed to do the trick, and for half an hour, we happily sung along to 'Bitter Sweet Symphony' and 'The Drugs Won't Work'. Even Schumi hummed a few bars.

Then, at around 2.30 am, Schumi pulled over to the side of the road and stopped the car. He mumbled something to Alan in French and got out of the vehicle.

'What's he up to Alan?' I said.

'You won't believe it. He says he has to go and buy some onions for his mother!' was the ridiculous reply.

What?! Here we were, in the middle of the Burkina Faso hinterland in the dead of night, and our driver had gone walkabout to try and find onions! For 20 minutes we waited, staring up at the jet black African night sky, all to the strains of Richard Ashcroft, wondering whether Schumi would return. It was a surreal moment.

To his credit, he did eventually reappear, and lo and behold, in his hand, he had a bag of onions! Where he acquired them, I have absolutely no idea.

That wasn't quite the end of our escapades with Schumi. Finally, we saw the lights of Ouagadougou appear on the horizon, and we felt we were going to survive our ordeal with civilisation so close. But another exchange with Alan in French had our colleague hitting his head on the dashboard in disbelief.

'For Christ's sake Alan. What is it NOW?'

'He says he forgot to get petrol in Bobo, and he doesn't know if we have enough to make it home,' said Alan, wearily.

It's a good job Schumi didn't speak any English, because I remember promising to 'wring his neck!' if he didn't get us home. But of course, he did. We eventually limped back into the capital at 4.30 am, frazzled but grateful to be at our hotel. We drank until the sun came up.

That memorable tournament came to a close on 28 February 1998, with Egypt claiming their fourth title, defeating South Africa 2–0 in the final. A day later, I ticked another box in my broadcasting career, filing a piece for the BBC's famed *From Our Own Correspondent* programme, about our experiences in west Africa.

I have never been back to Ouagadougou – but I'd like to. I wonder if Schumi is still driving his taxi?

Later in 1998, I achieved another one of my lifetime's ambitions, when I was selected to be part of the small World Service team to head to France for the World Cup Finals. The downside was that, this time, there was to be no commentary duties, as the World Service didn't have the rights. Our team consisted of myself, David Coles again, Tim Maitland and Harry Peart, who by now had moved on from his role as assistant editor to become sports news correspondent, filing reports into the highbrow *Newsdesk* and *Newshour* programmes.

In comparison to the shenanigans that went on in Burkina, this was a much more business-like trip, but it did give me the chance to secure the biggest interview of my life, and one which led to my next move, albeit across the newsroom floor.

The disparity between the size of the World Service team (four of us), and the BBC Radio 5 Live crew was enormous. Radio 5 Live, which started in 1994, had quickly gained a big reputation for excellent sports coverage, and they left nothing to chance for the big event, taking nearly a hundred staff over to France. Their budget dwarfed ours, and yet despite their big numbers, we scooped them when it came to getting the biggest interview.

This came when arguably the world's greatest ever footballer, Pele, arrived in Paris doing his usual round of interviews just ahead of the final (featuring his native Brazil), which helped promote his major sponsor, Mastercard.

Radio 5 Live weren't going to bother sending anyone to the press conference, so I suggested I go along, in the vain hope I might just get an exclusive with the great man. David Coles, the head of our small team, agreed.

The media scrum at the hotel where the conference took place was unbelievable. I had never seen so many journalists and cameras. After the main conference finished, the MC said those wishing to conduct 'one-on-ones' with Pele should register at the desk, and they would do their best to get through as many as they could. For two hours, I waited nervously after registering my interest, believing at any moment, he would tire of the endless round of questions and call it a day, but eventually, my number was called. Such was the volume of media wishing to speak to him, that when it got around to radio, we had to go in pairs. I was coupled with a guy from *Voice of America* whose name I can't remember, but I will always remember what he looks like, courtesy of what happened next.

After being ushered in to meet the great man, we began the interview. But in our brief conversation outside, it had been clear to me that my American friend didn't have much of a clue, either about 'soccer', or the football legend we were about to meet. So, I gambled, and let him ask his questions first and my suspicions were proved correct. After two relatively mundane questions, his knowledge gave out, and he looked to me to carry on. I kept Pele talking for a good five minutes, despite his security guard angrily pointing to his watch within my eyeshot. When finally we were through, I thought I'd push my luck even further, and ask for a photograph.

The guard shook his head and said Pele had to leave but, gentleman that he is, the Brazilian great overruled him, and agreed to my request. Quickly producing my camera for the guard to (rather grumpily) take the shot, I took my place next to Pele, smiled, and then watched in disbelief as my American friend threw himself into the shot on the other side of Pele. Click. I couldn't believe he'd ruined my photo of a lifetime! The cheeky sod even asked me to send him the snap in the mail afterwards.

So, on my wall at home I now have – in perpetuity – a shot of me, the best footballer of all-time, and some American dude who didn't even know much about the legend he'd (briefly) interviewed. Prat.

Still, after I'd calmed down, I had a five-minute exclusive with the great man and neither David Coles, nor our colleagues at 5 Live, could believe it.

'Did you want to run it on Five Live?' I asked breezily to their head of programmes, Gordon Turnbull.

'Er, yes please, if that's okay?' he replied. It was a little moment of triumph for the World Service team, because if truth be told, 5 Live had treated us like their little brother on the trip.

I criss-crossed the country at that tournament, going anywhere and everywhere in the hope of getting stories and exclusives with the many stars that are drawn, like moths to a flame, by the World Cup. My final excursion at the Cup was to Marseille, where the Dutch were scheduled to play their quarterfinal with Argentina. I booked my train tickets and hotel early, reasoning they would quickly sell out, and arrived at my accommodation well in time to take in a Netherlands training session. The only issue was, the Dutch had opted to make their training base in Monte Carlo, a good two hours away. I probably would have had no other option but to book further train tickets, but an old mate came to the rescue.

Wandering through the streets of Marseille on my first night, I spotted my former colleague, Guy Havord, there working in his new role with Sky Sports. He was going to the training session too, and he offered me a lift – perfect.

The Dutch training session was intense – too intense for Winston Bogarde, later to become the most famous Premier League misfit of all-time – as he snapped his cruciate ligament in a tackle, his howls of pain bringing back horrible memories of my own knee injury some years previously.

But the Dutch media conference that followed was a wonderful example of why they garner such admiration around the world. I was used to the chaotic media days of English Premier League clubs – of unhelpful managers, moody players and obstructive media officers, that is, if they actually employed one at all. The Dutch though, had everything organised down to a tee. TV crews in one corner of their hotel, radio in another, press in a different area. The coach was available for 'one-on-ones' with everyone, plus three squad players on any given day. Maximum time allowed was five minutes, at which point, a Dutch media officer would quietly arrive to usher them away to their next port of call. It ran like clockwork; everyone got what they wanted, there were no raised voices, no press claims of unfair treatment, no jostling in a scrum to get close to disinterested players. It was all over in an hour, and I remember thinking, why, when it was all so simple, could clubs in England not be run along these lines? After all, even in 1998, the media coverage had been instrumental in the gargantuan leap in player wages. The two of us needed each other – and still do. The Dutch knew what their duty was to their supporters back home, and got on with it, invariably without complaint. Little wonder they got such good coverage.

Mind you, their team helped. It was truly a galaxy of stars. Even now, they trip off the tongue so easily: Van Der Sar, Reiziger, Stam, De Boer (x2), Cocu, Kluivert, Seedorf, Davids, Overmars, and of course, the inimitable Dennis Bergkamp. All coached by the masterful Guus Hiddink, who I was to meet several times over the next few years.

We had observer tickets for the game with Argentina, and arrived early for a drink near the port area of Marseille, ahead of the short stroll to the Stade Velodrome. We revelled in the noisy atmosphere around us, the orange-clad Dutch fans mingling happily with the Argentines, all of whom seemed to carry some sort of musical instrument. It was all so different to watching England games, where the atmosphere was always tense. My compatriots had sadly disgraced the country once again in France, having fought running battles with their Tunisian counterparts in the same city earlier in the tournament. They disgusted me.

Even so, England was still the country of my birth, and, as Argentina had defeated Glenn Hoddle's team on penalties in the Round of 16, I was leaning slightly towards the Dutch.

Actually, that reminds me of a funny story about the England–Argentina game. We'd been working at the IBC in Paris that night, and finished late. The game was about to kick off, so we hurriedly found a restaurant nearby and settled down to watch on a small TV at the venue. At halftime, we finished our meal, paid our bill, and rushed back to the hotel to view the second half, arriving just a few minutes after the second period had kicked off.

Of course, in that time, a certain David Beckham had been sent off by referee Kim Milton Nielsen but we were blissfully unaware. No-one in the mainly French-speaking hotel bothered to tell us, so we watched the rest of the game cursing what we perceived to be, Hoddle's negative tactics. I think David Coles even made the comment that 'Beckham has been anonymous.'

A few months later, I interviewed Glenn Hoddle in the wake of his dismissal as England manager, as he launched his memoirs of the tournament. I recounted this story, and he thought it was hilarious. I still have a copy of his book, which he signed, with the quip 'I hope the meal was worth it!'

Anyway, back to Marseille, where, as we walked to the Velodrome, we were confronted by two impossibly tall Dutchmen, who wanted to know who we were supporting? I said I was neutral really, at which point, he plonked a foot long orange cardboard tube on my head, and said 'You for Holland now!'

We sure were. The Dutch fans created a wonderful atmosphere in the cavernous stadium, and we cheered as loudly as anyone when Dennis Bergkamp scored one of the all-time great World Cup goals to clinch victory in the 89th minute.

That put them through to face another South American team, Brazil, in the last four. I extended my stay, and then received a phone call from Harry Peart, still stuck at the IBC in Paris. You could always tell when Harry was after something, because he'd talk around the issue, and wait for you to suggest what he really wanted. This was one of those phone calls. The conversation went something like this:

'Hey Simon, Harry here. How's Marseille?'

'Good thanks. What's occurring your end Harry?'

'Oh, nothing much, just enjoying watching what's happening down there in Marseille.'

'Yep, it's great.'

'Hmmmm, yes, I'd like to come down, and I think World Service would like me to. Only problem is, all the hotels are booked out.'

'Ah, that's a shame Harry.'

'Yes, yes it is really. I don't really know what I should do.'

'Would you like to come and stay with me Harry? There's a sofa bed in the room.'

'Oh, are you sure? That'd be great. I'll book my train tickets.'

So, down came Harry to drink the minibar dry, and smoke himself senseless in my room! I didn't begrudge him after all the help he'd given me in the previous few years; not even when he stole some of my interview material from a press conference ahead of the Brazil game, and passed it off as his own work in a 'special dispatch' for the news programmes the day after!

My work at those two major tournaments that year had attracted the interest of Radio 5 Live, with whom we were due to have closer ties anyway on our return from Paris. The two sports departments were due to merge, with us World Service types moving into their premises at Broadcasting House in Oxford Circus. I smelt an opportunity.

I held several informal discussions with Gordon Turnbull at the World Cup, and on my return, I made it clear to World Service that, after three years, I fancied doing some work for the domestic-based network. David Coles, who'd taken over from Harry as assistant editor, wasn't hugely impressed. In his view, switching to a network where the focus was more towards Grimsby's game on a Tuesday rather than Gabon's World Cup qualifier on a Wednesday, wasn't a promotion. He had a point.

But I was keen. Within BBC circles, 5 Live had an infinitely higher profile, and, as wonderful as the big football tournaments were, the next one was more than two years away. I wanted to commentate on a more regular basis, and the start of the new BBC News 24 television channel had caught my eye as well. I'd never had any real aspirations to be on television prior to my move to London. Indeed, even radio wasn't on my horizon when I'd started my journalistic journey back in Portsmouth. I had wanted to be a newspaper journalist, a writer. But that had all gone out of the window, as my career had taken a very different path. Several of my colleagues were taking their first steps into the world of television, and the small screen interested me.

So, as the 1998/99 football season drew near, an agreement was made between 5 Live and World Service for me to transfer across the floor. I was to become part of the network's football reporting and commentary team, and I was put on the rota to work one day a week with the fledgling television channel. I would also continue presenting the flagship Saturday show *Sportsworld* on the World Service, when the need arose.

The big time awaited. But for me, my really big break wouldn't happen at the BBC, nor even in England.

CHAPTER SIX

HARRY, HAGMAN & THE HAWTHORNS

Although I may not have hit the heady heights I dreamed of at the BBC, I wasn't far off. My three years at 5 Live were another intense learning curve, not least because they gave me an insight as to just how tough it was to break into that upper echelon of broadcasting.

So far, my career path had been relatively smooth. I'd moved around at my own pace, almost forcing my way through into the positions I wanted. Now was the time for a little more patience, and, as I was a little bit older, and working in a city I liked, I was prepared to bide my time.

My regular working week was still challenging enough, however. On Mondays, I would spend the day on the BBC News 24 channel, learning how to edit packages via the (then) new 'AVID' system. This wasn't as easy as it looked. I was used to dealing with audio packages only, now there were pictures to take into consideration, and I learned all the little tricks of the trade on a training course at Elstree, the famous recording studios in Borehamwood. There, we studied how not to 'cross the line' (a TV term for ensuring continuity of pictures when cutting between locations), and how to 'dissolve' 'wipe' and 'trim'. We learnt about 'OOVs' (out of vision tape pieces) 'SOTs' (sound on tape pieces) and 'UPSOTs' (literally 'upping' the sound on tape to reveal a grab of the person in question) – it was fascinating stuff.

But as useful as all this technical info was, my core business was still at the front of the shop, and I was eager to get in front of the camera for the first time.

Eventually, my big moment came; I was to host the midday sports bulletin, and my first ever piece of live television would be a 15-second 'tease' as to what was coming up.

People think presenting on TV is easy – just look at the camera and talk. Simple! In reality, when you are inexperienced, the camera is hugely daunting and it can trip you up in all sorts of ways. I was about to have my first taste of its evil ways, and the hush that descended upon the newsroom as I prepared to go on air did nothing to calm my nerves.

As I sat in the chair waiting for my debut, I was initially confident I had the skills required to make a success of it. After all, I was an experienced broadcaster by now, well used to talking in front of an audience. But this was different. In radio, I worked mainly with a pair of headphones and a microphone, with my focus shifting between the action, and the desk in front of me, while keeping one eye on my notes or scripts. Here, the words were on the autocue, directly at eye level, and that was it – just me and the camera's eye. The microphone was clipped on to my tie, which presented another new problem – what to do with my hands. I opted to put them on my lap underneath the desk.

Increasingly, as the minutes passed by, my heart started to thump, and my mouth became dry. My only link to the studio wasn't via a big, familiar pair of headphones, but a tiny 'IFB' (interruptible fold-back), a small earpiece that was attached via a 'curly' – a piece of wire that clipped into a radio pack, secured to the belt of your trousers.

The producer spoke to me down the IFB and asked if I was ready – I said I was, in between coughs, splutters and facial contortions, all designed to try and relax me and ensure my voice was going to work, for a 15-second link that was already shaping up as the longest quarter-minute of my life.

Then, I was on. I managed to get the words out without a stumble, and left the set elated, feeling like I'd passed some sort of exam. Easy. That was, until Karen Mullally, the senior producer, beckoned me towards her, saying she had a few pointers for me to take note of, ahead of the main bulletin in half an hour. A few pointers? In 15 seconds?

Karen was right though. Nothing prepared me for the house of horrors that awaited me watching back that short excerpt of television. First of all, there was the physical. Television tends to exaggerate any physical imperfection – and I knew already that my ears tended to stick out. Here, I looked like the FA Cup, a large Toby jug of a presenter. The upshot was, I needed a different, slightly longer, hairstyle than my (then) close-cropped look. Not much I could do about that in the short-term.

Next was my posture. I was slumped in the seat with hunched shoulders – a bad look on television, making me appear disinterested and far too casual. I also hadn't smiled; in fact, I didn't only look nervous, I looked downright miserable, like I didn't want to be there. Karen told me I needed to at least put my mouth into 'neutral' mode, because my mouth had a tendency to slump downwards in my 'normal' mode, thus presenting the visual of a man who'd just realised he'd left the iron on at home.

I was also a bit 'shiny' on the forehead, meaning I didn't have enough make-up on. Again, no surprise; the make-up artist had asked me how much I wanted on ahead of my debut, and being a typical bloke, I'd said 'Not much', being totally unaware of how the hot studio lights (and my tension) would make me sweat.

My wardrobe was also completely unsuitable. These were the days when waistcoats were the height of fashion in London and I had on, what I thought, was a pretty smart piece of cloth but both it, and my rather lurid tie, 'strobed' horribly on screen.

Next, I needed to move a bit. Television is a two-dimensional medium, so if you sit stock still (as I had), you look like a mannequin, and the viewer quickly becomes disinterested. Karen suggested that I work on what was known as the 'cross' theory, which, in essence, meant moving your head at regular intervals from north to south, to east to west, as if you were making the sign of a crucifix with your noggin. Not too fast though, or you looked deranged. Finally, my intonation, while fine for radio, was nowhere near good enough for television, which needed rather more enunciation.

So there it was. Just 15 seconds of television had revealed I was, after all, a complete and utter novice at this new form of broadcasting. I was thoroughly chastened. It took months before I improved.

The next few days of my working week were taken up with working on the 'desk' of 5 Live. This meant preparing and presenting the hourly bulletins – much more familiar work for me, and I was quickly into my stride, occasionally working with my old Polytechnic pal, Ian Kemp, later to be my best man at my second wedding.

Weekends were where I really polished my craft, however, as one of the commentators out on the road covering Premiership, and lower-league football. Working on the Saturday show *Sports Report* gave me particular pleasure, as it had been essential listening for me as a child on the old Radio 2, in the days of Jones and Butler et al.

Now, here I was, the ordinary Joe from the north, rubbing shoulders with the BBC elite, and working alongside such luminaries as Ron Jones, Stuart Hall, Alan Green and James Alexander Gordon. JAG, as James was known, was part of the furniture at the Beeb, coming in every Saturday to read out the football results in his unique, brilliant style.

JAG's intonation has become legendary. You always knew which team had won, even before you heard the score, as the pitch of his voice would rise, or fall depending upon success or failure for the team involved. You also knew exactly when JAG was entering the room, because his arrival was always accompanied by a big smile and cheery 'hello' to everyone. I'd give him an extra G on the end of his nickname. He was Just A Great Guy.

Stuart Hall's match reports were a thing of great beauty, although there was only room for one of his type amongst a team of reporters. Stuart's flowery use of the English language always took precedence over the details of the game he was covering; often, you couldn't even take a stab as to which side had won, until he gave the score line at the end of his report. In the meantime, you'd be treated to some Latin prose, or vivid imagery of far-off lands. Here's an example, when he was covering a game at Manchester City's Maine Road, during one of the regular crisis periods. The following is probably not verbatim, but you'll get the gist:

'And lo, did the faithful gathered, look out toward yonder hills in hope, and wonder whether they would ever see the promised land, the Premiership, a wonder of the world akin to the hanging gardens of Babylon? But no…'twas only the Pennines, and beyond it, Oldham.'

Stuart saw football – indeed, life – as fun, and he refused to take either too seriously. Sadly, as we learned many years later, his idea of fun with young girls, unbeknown to any of us, was to get him into serious trouble with the law.

But if Hall was all about the lighter side of life, then Alan Green was his polar opposite. A bluff Northern Irishman, Green was an excellent play-by-play commentator, but to call him opinionated is like saying the Pope is just a tad Catholic.

Green was incendiary. He fell out with so many people, I wondered whether he had a friend left in the world. The BBC of course, felt that was part of his appeal – he divided opinion like no-one else, and got people talking. A classic case in point came when I was commentating with him at one of the biggest games I ever covered for 5 Live, a Saturday lunchtime game at Old Trafford, between Manchester United and Liverpool.

It was the first time I'd called with Green, who, along with Mike Ingham, was the senior caller at 5 Live. I had a good relationship with most of the commentary team; many of them were up and comers, like me, who had a healthy respect for each other. John Murray, David Oates (who was to die tragically young), Simon Brotherton, Dave Woods and Ian Brown to name but a few, were all excellent practitioners of their craft, and there weren't too many egos amongst them. We all worked happily together, in the days when 5 Live used two commentators per game plus a summariser – these days, they've cut back to one.

Green though, was a little different. In the build-up to games, commentators would normally share notes and a joke in the press room pre-match, building a team spirit that would help you get through a game together. Ahead of this game though, a huge fixture for a relative rookie like me, he ignored me for the most part, and instead chatted at length to summariser Jimmy Armfield, the former England international.

The unwritten protocol for 5 Live commentators was that the 'senior' guy (if there was one) would take the second part of the commentary. So, for this game, I, being the junior, would lead off, doing the first 22 and a half minutes, before handing over to Green. The pattern would be repeated in the second half. The problem was the other part of the unwritten protocol – that a handover would only take place during a natural break. In other words, once the ball went out of play, or if the ref stopped the game. Theoretically, this meant there was a possibility of overrunning your allotted time, and this is what happened to me at Old Trafford.

As I was preparing to hand over at the 22.30 minute mark, the ball just wouldn't go out. As per protocol, I kept calling, only to see Green's outstretched arm come towards me, tapping his watch impatiently. I ignored it, waited until the ball had gone out (no more than a minute or so later), and handed over.

'A bit late son, but better late than never I suppose,' he said condescendingly.

Towards the end of the first half, Gary Neville launched into a tackle on one of the Liverpool players – a mistimed, rather than crude attempt at winning the ball – and Green went ballistic. He spent the next few minutes castigating Neville, demanding sanctions be taken against the England full-back.

When it came to the start of the second half, he still wouldn't let it lie. As the United players came back out and I prepared to take the microphone, Green began grumbling in my ear that Neville was still out there, and that Sir Alex Ferguson should have substituted him. I felt he was trying to influence my reading of the game in favour of his own opinions. What I – still learning my craft – really needed at that moment, was a clear head to call such a big encounter.

It wasn't the last time I called a game with Green, and in fairness, he was more convivial with me after that; but I was wary of him following that experience. He didn't do interviews with managers after games, which meant he was free to be as controversial as he liked during commentary, but it left us 'lesser' mortals having to pick up the pieces, with some managers using the opportunity of a BBC interview to let us know exactly what they thought of our colleague.

Many years later, I was to meet him again at the World Cup in Germany, when I agreed to do an interview for the BBC in Munich, during my time at SBS. Green said he didn't remember ever having met me, but that didn't stop him from trying to pick my brains as to the likely Australian line-up against Brazil!

But the other football staff were magnificently supportive. Senior producer Charlotte Nichol was always encouraging, as was her number two, Roy Calley, and it was Calley who gave me my one of my most prized career moments.

Most weeks, I would report on a game on a Saturday, then commentate on a Sunday, but this particular week, I had a rare Saturday afternoon off. I was preparing to put my feet up, until Calley called me with news that one of the regular commentators on *Match of the Day* was sick, and wasn't fit for work. *Match of the Day* was, and probably still is, the most famous football show in Britain, and I'd grown up watching it religiously on Saturday evenings, with its various hosts, from David Coleman, to Jimmy Hill, Desmond Lynham, and now, Gary Lineker.

The programme normally featured two 'main' games, with commentary done at the ground. The third game was the pick of the other matches, and had commentary 'dubbed' onto it in the studio, late on Saturday afternoon. Roy wanted to know if I'd be interested in filling in? There wasn't much of a decision to be made there. So, that Saturday night, I made my debut on *Match of the Day* calling a five-minute edit of Coventry City's match with Everton. I had to pinch myself as Lineker read out my name in his introduction to the game that night, with my name also appearing in the credits at the end.

I also had a good working relationship with the many summarisers utilised by the Beeb, in particular, Steve Claridge, then only just retired from a long and fascinating career. Claridge was great fun to work with, and every inch the working class lad, despite his huge profile. Many times he arrived late to games because he'd missed his train connection, or the tube was busy – no limousines or private chauffeur for Claridge.

I was commentating games at famous venues up and down the country. The Stadium of Light was a favourite, particularly as I had the good fortune to be given a Tyne–Wear derby between Sunderland and Newcastle to cover. I called games at Anfield, Highbury, Villa Park, Goodison Park, White Hart Lane, and even on occasion, Maine Road.

White Hart Lane actually gave me one of my more interesting days in the commentary box. The game was Spurs against Coventry, which Tottenham won 3–2. Calling games at the Lane were always a challenge because of the low-slung commentary booth, which was situated just behind the dugouts, but also because Spurs were rather a difficult club to deal with at the time. I'd already had problems getting interviews at Spurs' training ground in Cheshunt, but when they put up the barriers this particular day, they actually did me a favour.

In the wake of their success against Coventry, I was asked, naturally enough, to try and grab a Spurs player for his reaction. Rights holders would make the short journey to the players' tunnel, and make the requests via the club media officers. But this particular day, they appeared to have gone AWOL, so I was reduced to shouting out to the players as they came out of their dressing room. Despite having won the game, not one was willing to stop, and the Spurs stewards seemed to take great delight in the fact their players were giving the media such a hard time. In my desperation, I spotted Coventry's Mohammed Konjic coming out of the opposite dressing room, and asked him if he'd be gracious enough to talk. To my surprise, he said 'Sure. No problem.'

Thinking on my feet, I reasoned that an interview with a losing player (and not a particularly high-profile one), wasn't exactly going to make for great radio. So, after asking a couple of perfunctory questions about the game, I moved on to ask him how he – a Bosnian – had arrived in the Premier League.

Konjic was brilliant. He went into great detail about how his family had suffered during the Balkan War, and how he'd grabbed at the chance of a career in England, in order to be able to send money back to his family. He got quite emotional about it – perhaps no-one had asked him these questions before? Whatever the truth, the interview went down well, and I even got a text message later from fellow broadcaster, Simon Brotherton, congratulating me on one of the 'most interesting interviews ever heard on Five Live.'

Spurs weren't the only club that caused us grief. Chelsea were especially hard work. Although their media liaison guy at the time, Gwyn Williams, tried his best, there was always the feeling at Stamford Bridge that they couldn't be bothered with all this stuff. Jimmy Floyd Hasselbaink was particularly rude to me one day after he'd scored a bagful in a routine FA Cup win over Gillingham – breezing past me, and then getting annoyed when I pointed out that Gwyn had okayed an interview. 'I'm going to speak to my ladies!' he growled as he sashayed across to a couple of glamours from Chelsea TV. Funny how these things stick with you.

Other clubs could not have been more helpful. West Ham were always welcoming (more on them soon), and Ipswich Town almost laid out the red carpet every time you happened to visit Portman Road, or their picturesque training ground in Suffolk. The north-east clubs were great too, and always seemed grateful the 'London media' had bothered to travel to take an interest in their club. But a few were suspicious, defensive, obstructive even; a symptom I suppose, of football's ever-growing profile in England, and the constant demands on players and coaches. It wasn't as if we didn't understand, but sometimes I felt they forgot we were just doing our jobs. Some treated us like we were fans trying to get autographs. Maybe some were?

My burgeoning profile also led to other opportunities.

In my second year at 5 Live, I swapped my Monday TV shifts to a different day in order to host the 'Monday Match' (that night's live Premiership game) on the radio network, and then, when West Ham United were on the verge of qualifying for Europe via the Intertoto Cup, I was given my first taste of commentating on the continent.

The Hammers were everyone's second-favourite club, and I enjoyed going to Upton Park immensely. The staff were friendly, the players amenable, and their manager, Harry Redknapp, was one of the great characters of the English game.

So, in August 1999, I was delighted to be chosen as the Hammers' commentator, for however long their European campaign was to last. The first trip was to France, for the final of the Intertoto Cup against Metz. The game itself was unremarkable, except for the local gendarmerie, who used water cannons to quell a minor disturbance among the West Ham fans on the terraces. I interviewed a young Frank Lampard afterwards – he'd scored one of the goals in a 3–1 win to put the club through to the first-round proper – and, in faltering English, Paolo di Canio, who was already a cult hero in East London.

The second-round draw paired the Hammers with Osijek, a small club from the east of Croatia, and this was a more interesting trip, coming as it did, only shortly after the end of the Balkan war. We flew into Zagreb and spent the night in the capital, a beautiful city, reminiscent of Paris. The connecting flight to take us to Osijek was a day later and we landed in a city still clearly scarred by earlier battles.

Osijek reportedly received in excess of 50,000 shells during the conflict, and every building was a testament to that, being pock-marked, partially destroyed or burnt out. The locals were still suffering – economically, if no longer physically. I'd never seen such a collection of poorly-dressed people. It looked like we were on the set of a Dickensian play.

But that was nothing in comparison to West Ham's next excursion, to Romania to play Steaua Bucharest. For this game, we actually flew on the team plane, and upon arrival in Bucharest, we were bundled into a tatty-looking coach for the short trip to the hotel. Bucharest was the only city where I saw women begging in the streets topless, in the hope of getting a few more 'lei' for their families. It was pitiful, especially as temperatures outside were barely above freezing.

The entire trip was, in fact, an eye-opener into the disparity in wealth between Romania's elite and its ordinary citizens. We were staying in the lap of luxury at the Hilton, but the local newspaper's main headline was about how people were struggling to stay alive in their icy-cold flats in the middle of the harsh Romanian winter. Dominating the entire skyline was the obscenely large palace, built by Nicolae Ceausescu during the communist era.

Meantime, West Ham were setting about their preparations for Steaua, and I managed to secure an interview with the likeable Harry Redknapp. Harry had told me to come up to his room for a bit of peace and quiet, so I arrived, and switched my tape recorder on.

One of the questions I wanted to ask Harry was about one of the (many) players he'd signed recently, but who wasn't on this trip. Here's a rough transcript of what happened:

SH: 'Harry, what's the story with your new signing? He's not on this trip. Why?

Harry: 'Well, that's a good question Simon, and I'm pleased you've asked me that one. [He's] currently having talks with Hibernian with a view to a loan. Unfortunately, they haven't yet been able to agree on the financial side of things (whispering aside) I think the little c*** thinks he's going to Real Madrid!'

Clearly, I edited that part of his answer out of my final piece, but Harry was hilarious – always ready with a quip, a one-liner. No wonder the press loved him. Once, when he signed the aesthetically pleasing Portuguese attacker, Dani, he'd famously said to the assembled journalists, 'He's so good-looking, I don't know whether to play him, or fuck him!'

Yet for all his 'second-hand car salesman' persona, Harry was a very good manager, and seemed to have the respect of all his players. His team were very competitive too. A young Rio Ferdinand marshalled the backline alongside the abrasive Neil Ruddock, while in midfield, Trevor Sinclair, Joe Cole, Frank Lampard and Marc-Vivien Foe (later to die tragically on the field of play) supplied the exciting frontline of Paolo Wanchope and Di Canio. But Bucharest was to be where their journey would end in that year's UEFA Cup. The Hammers were beaten 2–0 that night, and could only draw the return leg 0–0 at Upton Park.

Those up-and-coming Hammers weren't the only stars we glimpsed that night at the Ghencea Stadium however. Pre-game, the genial John Murray, producer Caj Sohal and I, were going through our usual rituals, checking our notes and making sure our pronunciations of the Romanians matched, when a huge kerfuffle erupted in the press room. We looked around, thinking that perhaps a Romanian football legend such as Gheorghe Hagi had walked in, or some political or royal figure. But the truth was stranger than that. John turned to me and said, 'I don't believe it!' as we glimpsed a wide-brimmed Stetson, unmistakably plonked on the head of Larry Hagman, aka, JR Ewing, from the American hit soap, *Dallas*!

What the hell was he doing there? Good question. Apparently, re-runs of old episodes of Dallas were huge in that country, and Prince Paul of Romania had not only invited Hagman over, but paid for his flights and accommodation. In return, he was asked to come to the game we were about to cover, and be introduced to players from both teams.

Hagman took a seat, not caring in the slightest about the rumpus going on around him; he was probably used to it, in fairness. I thought I'd chance my arm, so I fought my way through the scrum, approached him and asked him would he mind giving me an autograph.

'I've been told not to,' he said in his broad Texan drawl. 'It might start kind of a rush.'

There were other European trips to come too. I went back to Bucharest with Liverpool, who played Rapid in the UEFA Cup, enjoying the fabulous company of summariser, Bobby Gould, who'd won the FA Cup as manager of Wimbledon in 1988. In the bar following the game in Romania, Gould beckoned over Gerard Houllier (then the Liverpool manager), and I sat in thrall as the two exchanged wonderful (and often hilarious) stories. I'll recount just one.

Gould recalled that during his brief spell as manager at West Bromwich Albion, his team had performed particularly badly one day in a local derby against Birmingham City. As the team trudged off at full time having been well beaten, he and his players were subject to some pretty forceful abuse from the Albion fans. Gould, who was apparently at the end of his tether by this stage, got halfway down the tunnel before turning on his heels and making his way back to the terrace, where he proceeded to invite two fans into the dressing rooms with the players.

'You explain it to them!' he allegedly said to his players, leaving the fans inside the dressing room, as Gould slammed the door behind him!

Another trip took me to Germany with Tottenham, for another UEFA Cup tie, this time with Kaiserslautern. I didn't know it at the time, but the Fritz-Walter Stadion was to become a very special place for me (and Australia) in years to come, but that night, on a freezing evening at the Betzenberg, Spurs lost 2–0 to a Youri Djorkaeff inspired 'Lautern, to crash out of the competition.

Still, another professional companion made the trip worthwhile. Chris Kamara was in his early days in the media then, but he had me in stitches telling me the tale of the day he opted to resign as manager of Stoke City. Kamara told me he'd tried to sign a player to improve the club's perilous situation near the foot of England's second tier but for whatever reason, the move had fallen through. Kamara was at his wit's end, and decided he was going to quit.

He drafted a letter of resignation, and faxed it over to Jez Moxey, then Stoke's CEO, but had a change of heart. He then had to get to Moxey's office to retrieve the fax before Moxey received it. It involved a good deal of subterfuge, but as I remember, he made it in the end – only to be sacked shortly after! He has since become one of the most recognisable faces on Sky Sports' football coverage, and on that trip, he was superb company.

Away from the slightly ethereal trips abroad, life descended into a familiar routine for me at the BBC over the next two years. I had bought a flat in West London (which I own to this day) with my share of the profits from the sale of the house in North Harrow, and the regular pattern of News 24 shifts, Monday night matches and weekend games and commentaries continued. Except that I was, by now, becoming a real social animal.

As you might have gathered, I'd always enjoyed a drink, but between the ages of 30 and 33 I was rarely sober, even during the working week. Having escaped the clutches of a difficult marriage, I was determined not to waste a moment and embrace the last vestiges of my youth. As a result, I entered that rarest of states for me in a professional sense – being comfortable. In fact, to describe it as being almost disinterested in my career was probably closer to the truth.

With work ticking along nicely, and with no prospect of imminent promotion, I turned into a hardened socialite. London was a brilliant playground, and my venue of choice (along with my regular partner in crime, Alan Duncan, he of Burkina Faso fame), was the 'Roadhouse' in Covent Garden, the perfect place for late night drinking bouts and meeting pretty girls.

Already a heavy smoker, London's late-nineties obsession with drugs was starting to take me in under its radar too. One particularly boisterous evening with a BBC producer and various narcotics led to me vomiting all night long, and convinced I was on the verge of a heart attack as I hallucinated.

But all of this was starting to affect my work, and, for the first time in my career, I had very much taken my eye off the ball, so to speak. I knew I'd been sailing close to the wind when I turned up to call an England under-21 international against Finland, one Friday night in Barnsley. The evening before, I'd been out on the town and got so blind drunk I probably shouldn't have driven up north the day after.

By the time I arrived at 6 pm, I was a mess. I was tired, unshaven (not unusual for me in fairness, even today), and stinking of alcohol. My co-commentator that night was one Trevor Brooking, Mr Clean Cut himself. He asked me whether I had been out on the tiles the night before, to which I replied, 'I might have had a couple!' That was the understatement of the year.

The same night, I drove back to London and went straight back on the pop, meeting friends at a nightclub in the centre of town – a night that ended up with me getting a cigarette burn on my face, courtesy of a 'mate' with whom I'd got into an alcohol-induced argument. He decided to stab me in the eye with a fag to make his point…thankfully, he was also drunk, and missed, narrowly. I was on screen the following Monday for BBC News 24; I certainly had plenty of make-up on that day.

Just prior to that, I had completely failed to identify the scorer of a goal during a game involving Arsenal at their old Highbury ground. The reason? I was still hung over from another night's debauchery. I was having too good a time to even notice the damage it was doing.

Many people may think that commentary is merely a perfunctory process, a matter of saying names and describing what is the bleeding obvious in front of you, but believe me, when you start playing with the factors that affect your concentration levels, the end results are quick to show themselves. It is a precise art, which requires the utmost care and attention to detail.

Perhaps then, it should have been no surprise when I got the shock of my life in early 2001. If my commentary standards had been slipping, I certainly hadn't noticed (or cared), but the BBC had.

Joanne Watson was one of the senior producers on the BBC's sports coverage. She had clearly heard my declining powers of reportage, and decided to act. One Monday, I got a call from Roy Calley, asking me to come into the office the next day. I asked what it was all about. He replied (being a loyal sort of a bloke), that it was 'not his doing'. I knew there was trouble ahead.

I sat down with Roy on the Tuesday, and he explained, rather uncomfortably, that he had received word from Joanne, that she was concerned about my drop-off in standards. Her 'solution' was for me to spend time with Ron Jones, one of the senior commentators, and try to learn from him as a sort of 'mentor'. Now I had huge respect for Ron, but I was young(ish) and headstrong. I had no intention of serving penance. If Joanne had a problem with me, I wanted to hear it from her outright.

Building up a head of angry steam, I barged into Gordon Turnbull's office, and demanded to know why Joanne hadn't got the guts to have it out with me face to face. His first words told me all I needed to know.

'Look Simon, there's no suggestion that you are going to be withdrawn from the football team yet…' said Gordon.

What? No-one had even mentioned the possibility that I could be demoted, so I knew instinctively that such a conversation had already taken place. I was fuming. Although I saw the season out at 5 Live (2000/01), I felt the writing was on the wall, especially as Joanne never did confront me. In fact, she avoided me for the rest of the campaign. In hindsight, I can see she was merely doing her job, although another reporter had been pushing his case with her for some time, and it did rankle with me, when he was appointed as my replacement when I eventually left. I felt it had been a *fait accompli.*

Fate was on my side however. As I stewed, two offers came in from elsewhere, totally unexpectedly. First, an old colleague of mine at Red Dragon (Dez Corkhill), got in touch to say his new employers, ESPN Star Sports in Singapore, were looking for a presenter/commentator. I expressed an interest, and within weeks, their senior producer, George Greene, was heading to London with a contract offer. I was handed a one-year deal that could be renewed annually. ESPN would sort out my visa, and the low tax rate in South-East Asia would make my stay highly lucrative. I said I was keen, and would return the contract to him within the week.

In the meantime though, there was another player in the market.

In 2001, two independent television networks decided they were going to challenge Sky as the pre-eminent broadcaster of sport on pay TV in the UK. Carlton & Granada, two regional giants, had joined forces to create OnDigital, a channel that promised to bring top-class sports coverage to the British masses, and give Rupert Murdoch a run for his money.

Two of my old bosses at the BBC, Nick Atkins and Shane Stitt, had been charged with setting up the programming side of things. I liked both of them, so when Shane called me, he was always going to get a sympathetic hearing.

'How's your career going at the BBC?' he said, in his broad Belfast brogue.

'Ah, it's not too bad,' I replied, trying not to let on that I wasn't in a good place.

'Really? I think you could be doing a lot better. Why don't you come and work for me?' said Shane.

The truth was, I had already virtually agreed to move to Singapore. But Shane talked me round, and when he offered me a package worth almost double what ESPN were offering, I'm afraid I let the financial side of things cloud my judgement. Particularly as my role would consist of presenting and reporting, but not commentating.

Singapore was something new, but I wasn't quite ready to give up my dream of hitting the top in the UK just yet. There was also the added bonus of being able to stick two fingers up to the BBC, by switching over to one of their broadcasting rivals.

So, in May 2001, I left the BBC after eight years' service (and Gordon Turnbull was good enough to try to persuade me to stay), and put pen to paper with OnDigital. Within weeks, ITV, the long-standing national independent broadcaster that acts as the 'umbrella' for regional networks such as Carlton & Granada, had given it their backing, and taken over the new venture. With a new deal agreed with the Football League to show lower division football for the next three years, the League Cup rights secured, and some Champions League titbits too, all seemed in place for a long and happy career at my new home.

7
CHAPTER SEVEN

P45s & 457s

Except of course, it wasn't.

The early days at ITV were exciting. Our new network, to be called the ITV Sport Channel, didn't go live until the new football season kicked off in August 2001. That meant a lot of preparation time, and we put it to good use.

One of the other new recruits was my old pal from Radio Lancashire, Guy Havord, who'd taken a gig as a commentator. As I was to be the main 'touchline reporter' for the channel's coverage of the Championship, he and I would be working closely together again; and so, it was decided we'd traverse the country, introducing ourselves to each of the managers at the 24 second-tier clubs.

It was a gesture that was appreciated by most. They were as keen to make it work as we were; after all, ITV were paying a whopping £315 million for the rights. It was a deal, we learned very quickly, that was massively overpriced. In the meantime though, we went from club to club, attempting to put in the groundwork for positive relations.

Two of the more challenging managers to deal with were Crystal Palace's Trevor Francis, and Coventry City's Gordon Strachan. Francis, who strangely later became a co-commentator in the media, was quite open in his dislike for this particular part of his job. He complained that the cameras were becoming too intrusive, and asked what the network's response would be if he were to ban them from training sessions. I replied, without total conviction, that ITV would probably withhold some of the next month's cheque. At the very least, it seemed to put enough doubt in his head for him to dismiss that notion. Job done.

When we called on Strachan, he kept us waiting for quite some time before we were finally ushered into his office at Coventry's training ground. Our brief was to outline what we would need from clubs in the coming season, and to try and develop some sort of professional relationship for us to work together in the coming months. Strachan however, was having none of it.

Guy asked him whether he'd mind giving him his phone number, in order that he could (on occasion) check on how he planned his team to play, what formation etcetera, ahead of a live commentary game.

'I'll tell you how I'm going to play now,' said Strachan, interrupting Guy mid-sentence. 'Four-four-two, it won't change all season. Next question.'

I ventured one of my own; did he have any issues with talking to us immediately after a game had finished?

'I know why you want that – so you can try to catch me out. It's a game between you and me. You're trying to get me to say something I shouldn't, and I'm not going to,' said Strachan.

Strachan would give me trouble after my first live game, a midlands derby between Coventry and Wolves, which Wanderers won with a late goal. Interviewing Strachan afterwards, he was true to his word when I challenged him about a refereeing decision that had led to Wolves' winner. 'Ha ha, yes. Well I know you are trying to get me to say something I don't want to, but I'm not going to…whoever you are from Sky.'

And with that, off he went. The bosses at ITV were livid he'd mentioned the name of our major competitor live on air on just our second weekend, and thus began a rather fractious relationship with Coventry, one which only improved after Strachan was replaced mid-season, to be replaced by the rather more placid Roland Nilsson.

But it was my beloved Manchester City that gave us the most trouble that particular season. Like Coventry, City had been relegated at the end of the 2000/01 campaign, and were expected to challenge for promotion the year after. Kevin Keegan had been appointed as manager in succession to Joe Royle, and he was anxious to prove himself again following his failures with England.

That's where the ITV Sport Channel got off on the wrong foot with Keegan. Our reporter Chris Terry, an amiable cigar-smoking product of middle-class England, didn't have a nasty bone in his body, but he didn't mind asking a tough question. So when he asked Keegan if he was a 'quitter' when things got tough, he set the tone for a campaign of rancour and discontent between City and ourselves.

I bore the brunt of it. Being touchline reporter, it was my job to get pre- and post-game interviews, as well as keep an ear across any news on the sidelines. It needed a decent relationship with the clubs involved, but we were barely on speaking terms with City. I regularly had bust-ups on the phone with City's then media officer, Chris Bird, as yet another request for an interview with Keegan or one of his players was refused, or ignored.

Chris knew I was a City fan, but they were sorely trying our patience, and matters came to a head one day at Watford's Vicarage Road ground. We'd requested – as usual – a pre-match interview with Keegan, and as per usual, he had turned us down. City were furious at having to play on a Sunday with a 6.15 pm kick-off (chosen by ITV to maximise audiences on the back of the afternoon's Premiership game on Sky), feeling it was unfair to their supporters. I sympathised, but I was only trying to do my job.

I attempted to approach Keegan personally to have a chat, and try to resolve matters amicably. He ignored me totally, brushing past me as if I wasn't there. That day, I almost wanted City – the club I had supported since I was six years old – to lose. But they didn't, winning a scruffy game late on thanks to yet another Shaun Goater tap-in.

Man of the Match that day was Australian Danny Tiatto, and part of my job was to interview the best on ground, and then offer him his magnum of champagne, courtesy of league sponsors, Nationwide. When City refused to let Tiatto come out and speak, I was left with a large jeroboam of the fizzy stuff – the Nationwide representative, ex–World Cup Final referee, Jack Taylor, having long since left. So, spotting a City-supporting mate in the stands (who had known I was going to be there, and had hung around for a catch up), I handed him the 'Man of the Match' award. He tells me he still has the bottle at home – but the champagne itself was drunk 10 years later to celebrate City's title success in 2011/12!

Even when I wasn't working on City games, they caused me trouble that year. When City went to Edgeley Park to face Stockport in a local derby in late March 2002, I travelled up to watch as a fan, standing on the open terrace behind the goal with the rest of the City support. County were destined to finish bottom, and won only six games all season – one of which, just happened to be that night. Two late goals from youngster, John Hardiker, secured a 2–1 win; he would score only once more in over 100 games for the club! The result was so unexpected, it had taken ITV by surprise. They had no official reporter at the midweek game, but the senior producer knew I was there, and so he gave me a call on the full-time whistle to ask a favour.

'Can you do a quick interview with Carlton Palmer for the show?' he asked.

'But I'm wearing a City shirt!' I protested.

No matter, I couldn't exactly turn him down, so I fastened my jacket as tight as a I could around me, attempting to cover up my allegiances as I trooped off to find Palmer. My first question to the former England international was a straightforward one. 'Was that win a surprise for you?' I queried.

'Well, no not really…hang on, is that a City shirt you're wearing underneath there? You must be WELL gutted!' laughed Palmer, as he clocked the unmistakable sight of City's old fluorescent away kit under my coat.

I actually wasn't too keen on covering City at all professionally, and not just because of Keegan. During my days at the BBC, I'd commentated on a City game once, an FA Cup tie with Leeds at Maine Road, won by Leeds 5–2, with a certain Harry Kewell among the scorers. But it was an odd experience. City was how it had all started for me but they were from a different part of my football life, if that makes sense. Working at Maine Road that day had been strange; I didn't feel like I belonged in the press box at City. My place there was in the stands. I still feel that way now, and when I go back to the new Etihad, I always sit with the fans when I can, only accepting press tickets when absolutely necessary.

Also, when I'd called one of the goals that day, my colleague Dave Woods felt I'd gone a bit over the top in my commentary, saying at halftime, 'I thought you were going to go into orbit when City scored!'

Personally, I didn't feel I'd commentated Ian Bishop's goal that day with any more, or any less intensity than the many others I had called for 5 Live but, never having hidden my loyalties, I accepted that would always be open to question.

Which brings us to an interesting debate. Should commentators and journalists be open about which team they support? Many feel we should hide our colours, but I take the opposite view. I've always been happy to discuss my allegiances. Why? Firstly, I feel it should dispel any rumours of 'bias' with regards to other teams. People know exactly which team I support, so it should stop all that speculation; and with City, if anything, I am even more critical, because they are so close to my heart.

But second, and most importantly, is this: some journalists today say they actually have no team at all. Really? I find this an odd statement to make. If you don't, or have never, felt a powerful connection to a team, then how on earth can you empathise with the fans, for whom ultimately, you provide your media service?

Some, in Australia in particular, say they just 'love good football'. Okay to a point, but they clearly lack the passion of the committed football fan, who spends their hard-earned every week to watch their team. In addition, if you only 'love good football' then you surely preach disloyalty to supporters – supporters who are needed to be the backbone of any football club. What happens if the club which plays good football suddenly changes to a different style? Does the fan then go elsewhere? Football isn't like that, it's based on tribalism.

Back at ITV, things – Keegan and City apart – were going quite well. I was co-hosting the Saturday night show called *Football First*, a sort of *Match of the Day* for the Championship, along with Matt Smith (who went on to have a long career with ITV). Ex-pros Robbie Earle, Garry Nelson, Jim Beglin, Russell Osman, John Hendrie, David Fairclough, Paul Walsh, Clive Allen, Tony Dorigo and Graham Taylor were all regular pundits, and to a man, they were great guys to work with and get along with.

Robbie and Graham in particular, were a huge help in explaining the tactical side of things, and Graham, the former England manager who'd been lampooned and reviled in equal measure during his time with the national team, still had a keen eye for a player. That season, he constantly made special reference to Portsmouth's gangly striker, Peter Crouch, and Grimsby Town's nippy frontman, Michael Boulding. It was no surprise then the following season, after Taylor had been reappointed Aston Villa manager, that he signed both players. Crouch in particular, would go on to bigger and better things.

The Saturday show finished at 11.30 pm, screened live from our South Bank studios right on the Thames. From there, we'd quickly take off our make-up, get changed, and a car would be waiting to take Matt and myself up to wherever we needed to be on the Sunday for the live Championship game. Often, we'd sleep in the car and arrive at Grimsby, or Sheffield, or wherever, at about 3 am.

The Sunday game coverage was rather typical of ITV's patchwork approach towards its new channel. With Sky covering a Premier League game on the same day, there was a need to 'bookend' their coverage to grab ratings, which meant a rather weird shift for us.

We did a live 'pre-game' show at 1 pm – half an hour before Sky went to air with their own pre-game for the 4 pm Premier League match. Then, we had to sit around all afternoon – often in freezing conditions – to wait for our own game, normally scheduled to kick off at 6.15 pm. By the time the game had been played, post-match commitments taken care of, and the drive back to London negotiated, you were often climbing into bed not much before 3 am on a Monday morning – meaning a 24-hour shift, door to door. Still, shifts like that meant I had to calm down my social activities.

My stint at ITV gave me some real insight into the pressures managers are under at that level. I'd already had to deal with the combustible Kevin Keegan, the fiery Gordon Strachan and the uncooperative Trevor Francis, but a game at my old student stomping ground of Fratton Park took things to a whole different level. In this case, the manager wasn't the one at fault.

The game was Portsmouth against Wolves, who were then managed by David Jones, a Scouser who'd earned his stripes with Stockport County before moving onto Pompey's great rivals, Southampton. Those links were enough to guarantee him a hot reception in any case but this particular fixture came just a year or so after Jones had stood trial on 21 charges of alleged child abuse – charges relating to his former job as a care worker.

Jones had been acquitted of all the charges, yet it had cost him his job with Southampton, and, he claimed, contributed to the death of his father. His post at Wolves was his first since the court case had cleared his name. Yet that was of no concern to the Portsmouth fans, who gave the Wolves manager the most torrid 90 minutes I ever had the misfortune to bear witness to. It wasn't just the verbal abuse around his Southampton links, it was the constant insinuation that Jones was guilty of those charges he had been found innocent of every time he ventured out of his seat in the dugout. Some hilarious people had even brought bags of sweets, and threw them at him – it was horrific.

Through it all, Jones remained impassive, focusing his energies on the game in front of him, and ignoring the uproar that was going on, in some cases, only yards from where he was sitting. It was an extraordinary show of restraint and professionalism.

Perhaps he could do nothing else? I'm not sure but I do know I'd have struggled if presented with a similar situation. I interviewed Jones afterwards, and once the chat had finished, I shook his hand, and told him I was full of admiration for how he'd conducted himself that night – and I meant it. Jones simply shrugged; he probably knew it was coming, but that didn't make it right.

Sometimes, football fans forget how to behave like human beings. It's as if all normal rules of society cease to apply once they get inside the stadium. Now, I've whistled and booed at players, refs and managers in my time on the terraces and in the stands, just like anyone else. But to take a bag of sweets, purposely to throw at an opposition manager when the man had been found innocent, was a return to the days of the mob, and was not only unfair, it was unsettling.

I found other managers to be equally fascinating personalities, at a level of football which is arguably the most cut-throat of the lot. The Championship of today is the gateway to the unfathomable riches of the Premier League, and even in 2001/02, it was a huge prize.

One of my favourites was Gianluca Vialli, a huge star as a player, then managing Watford. Vialli's English was good, but not perfect, and he occasionally struggled with idioms. One time, during a poor run of form, I asked Vialli whether a game at Burnley was make or break for his team's play-off prospects. His response? (In an Italian accent…) 'Yes, yes…I think if we no win this game, then we will have…how you say…we will have had our fish.' Huh? It took me a couple of seconds to realise he meant 'We will have had our chips!' I corrected him, and he giggled.

Vialli was such a friendly guy I wondered whether he was a bit too nice to be a manager. My professional relationship with him was helped by the fact that both he, and his assistant, Graham Rix, were smokers. They'd seen me light up at grounds up and down the country when our paths had crossed – sometimes, Vialli would even cadge a ciggie off me, and we'd puff away furtively down some windy tunnel, me shooting the breeze with one of the greats of the game, before he headed off to his dressing room to begin his team talk!

Similarly, although I'd had a bad experience with Jimmy Floyd Hasselbaink when we covered a game involving Chelsea, his manager, Claudio Ranieri, couldn't have been any more accommodating. Particularly when, after three questions, the word came from my director that there was a problem with the recording, and we'd have to start again. Most managers would have said 'tough' and walked away. Not Claudio. He smiled and said 'No problem, take your time.'

Sheffield United's Neil Warnock came with a reputation of being all fire and brimstone. Yet away from the touchline, I found him to be hugely engaging – a northerner with a very warm and open personality. When I presented a pre-game show in Stoke one night (a League Cup tie as I recall), Warnock was part of our panel, and within two minutes of saying hello, he was bringing out photos of his family to show me. I found him really pleasant company.

By contrast, David Moyes at Preston was very serious, very businesslike, with steely blue eyes that meant you chose your questions very carefully indeed. Gary Megson (then at West Brom), appeared a little nervous and defensive; someone who seemed almost wounded if you asked him a tough question. Peter Shreeves at Sheffield Wednesday was a perfect gentleman, while Nottingham Forest's David Platt was aloof, a trait perhaps picked up from a high-profile playing career.

All were 'living on the volcano' as the title of Michael Calvin's recent book so aptly summarises the job of the manager. It was, and remains, an insanely pressurised environment, and on game day, you could almost literally feel the adrenaline and the testosterone, being so close to the players and managers.

Some of the other characters in and around the broadcasts often made our life difficult, interesting, or even fun too. Take for example, the Gillingham Chairman, Paul Scally, who was one of those who had spent the club's (anticipated) ITV millions on an immediate refurbishment of Priestfield Stadium. Scally, who wore jam-jar glasses so thick, his eyes looked like a panda's through them, could be volatile with the media (he once banned reporters from the *Kent Messenger* group for several years), but he could also be jovial and funny.

He also didn't mind the odd prank and he nearly caught me out with one, ahead of a game involving the Gills that particular season. Scally rushed up to me excitedly in the tunnel, announcing his great friend, Elton John, had decided to grace us with his presence for the match. Would we like to interview him? 'Sure!' I said.

However, when 'Elton' appeared, I had my doubts as to whether he was who Scally had said he was. He was indeed a dead ringer for the singer, but something wasn't quite right. The truck in the TV compound had the same thoughts but the director invited me to press on anyway with the interview. Thank goodness we prerecorded it, and didn't go live.

'So…er…Elton,' I began rather tentatively. 'What brings you here to Gillingham today?'

'Cos I fackin' love football don't I, you caant!' was his reply in broad cockney. End of interview, to the backdrop of howls of laughter from Scally.

Scally by name, scally by nature.

Former referee, Phil Dowd, gave me a very different problem that same season. Before a game at Bradford, ITV had set up the usual monitor in front of my position, placed squarely between the two benches. This was normal, and few had batted an eyelid at the various grounds up and down the country. But as Dowd prepared to blow his whistle to start the game, he caught sight of the monitor, and jogged over to speak to me in front of 14,000 people.

'You have to remove that monitor now. I'm not having the two managers checking over my every decision. If you don't move it, I won't start the game,' he said calmly.

I relayed his words back to the director in the truck, and two minutes of panic ensued, while the crowd (and the players) became agitated at the delayed start. I felt the eyes of the entire ground on me, as time and again, Dowd repeated his instructions. Eventually, Dowd was mollified, and the monitor remained after our floor manager, the kindly Stan, found a solution. Dowd agreed to start the game only on condition that the monitor had a wide-brimmed cover placed over it (in effect, blinkers) to make it impossible for the two benches to view without literally taking my seat!

Stan, who by then was well into his sixties, was a master at soothing egos but another floor manager, the rather younger Chuck Taylor, was the master of keeping us entertained.

A former ice hockey player in his native Canada, Taylor was a big guy who was never going to be intimidated by footballers, and he had an excellent line in humour to deal with anyone who tried.

When Coventry's groundsman tried to give us grief for encroaching onto their pitch for a pre-game show ahead of a game at Highfield Road, Taylor cut him off at the knees with a few well-chosen lines (which sadly, I cannot remember) – and he wasn't averse to telling someone to fuck off either.

He saved his best humour for those of us in front of camera, trying to make us laugh by giving us silly nicknames just as we were about to go on air. His two favourites for me were 'Scoop Amorphic' and 'Zeke Bindertwine' – two fictitious TV anchors he'd invented from back in his native North America.

Often as I was about to take the cue from Matt Smith at a windswept ground somewhere in the north of England, Chuck would grin inanely behind the camera and say in his transatlantic drawl, 'They're about to cue to you Scoop!' or 'This is Zeke Bindertwine reporting!' Perhaps you had to be there, but he never failed to make me laugh and a cameraman was once in such hysterics his lens bobbed up and down throughout my entire cross, as his shoulders bounced up and down in helpless laughter.

But the good times at ITV were not to last.

From the opening weeks of the new channel, there had been much press talk of the low ratings our live coverage was attracting. One game involving Grimsby and Rotherham was watched by so few people, the papers claimed it would have been cheaper to buy all those watching a free ticket and transport them to the games, rather than the money we were shelling out for staff, facilities and equipment, to beam the match back to them in their homes.

The English football bubble – growing inexorably since Paul Gascoigne's tears at the 1990 World Cup – was about to pop, and it would take with it quite a few casualties.

In those early days, I was unconcerned about the negative coverage. We'd been warned by our bosses that it might happen, especially as much of the written press was owned by Rupert Murdoch, the head of our big competitors, Sky. But when a report appeared in the press one week, speculating that the channel was about to fold, we began to get rather alarmed. So much so, that the new head of the ITV Sport Channel, Brian Barwick, saw fit to come down to our offices on the South Bank and give us a 'pep' talk. Barwick told us he was our 'champion', that no jobs would be lost, that the channel was on a sound financial footing, and that these were mere teething troubles, which would be resolved within months.

He was right about a resolution being found within months – it just wasn't the one he'd promised.

By early March 2002, the writing was on the wall for the ITV Sport Channel. The repayments to the clubs on the £315 million deal were starting to cripple the parent companies, Carlton & Granada, who now held out very little hope of a realistic and sizeable return on their investment. The reason? Sky, our competitors, played a smart game.

When ITV launched the sport channel, they did so with their own 'set-top box' technology. To receive the new channel (and others), you had to buy this new contraption. But most people who were interested in watching football on satellite or cable already had a set-top box via Sky, and didn't see the need for another, especially to watch the second tier of the game. That was the first mistake.

The second mistake was that the technology was poor. As an employee, I was given a free box, but the picture quality was rubbish. It constantly froze, and the other channels available were few in number, and poor in content anyway. Then, the black marketeers found a way for the public to access the boxes without having to pay. ITV quickly abandoned the thought that the boxes could make them money, and gave them away for free. When that still didn't work, they attempted to get the ITV Sport Channel available on the more established Sky platform instead.

Except, Sky weren't exactly going to lay out the welcome mat for us. After all, this was a network (ITV) that had been bullish in its intent to challenge the Isleworth-based Sky for supremacy in the British pay-TV market.

Initially, the two parties had talks that apparently went well, and ITV put out a statement saying they expected the channel to be on the Sky platform within weeks. But Sky played a canny game, delaying and delaying. Until, by January, the money had almost run out for Carlton & Granada.

In the face of dreadful ratings and sky-high expenditure, Carlton & Granada attempted to renegotiate their deal with the Football League. It was a final attempt to stem the bleeding and it failed, as the clubs refused to accept a whopping cut from £315 million to £130 million. Many of the clubs meantime had, unwisely, already spent their inheritance.

That would cause many of them to go into administration over the next few years, but we at the ITV Sport Channel, preceded them. On 27 March 2002, less than a year into trading, the parent company, ITV Digital, was placed into administration, and there was no guarantee our jobs would be saved either.

When it became clear that the whole venture was going to be wound up, ITV said they would try to absorb some of our jobs into their main free-to-air network, but in practice, only a few were re-employed elsewhere. Brian Barwick would resurface as Chief Executive of the FA.

In the end, the ITV Sport Channel died due to the lack of a good business plan. It had overestimated the appeal of lower league football, paid way over the odds for it, attempted to broadcast it with substandard technology, and then failed to have a proper Plan B when it all went tits up. In short, it was a catastrophe.

In the middle of all this were people such as me, who now saw their careers flashing before their eyes. The downturn in ITV's business saw other media concerns slash their budgets too, as they saw which way the wind was blowing. Sports budgets were cut at Sky, BBC and elsewhere; all of a sudden, the outlook for someone like me was very bleak indeed. I wished I had gone to Singapore.

Eventually, we were issued with our P45 notices – redundancies in other words – and I was among 60 to be told that my services would no longer be required after 31 May. The journalists union, led by the brave Robin Bailey, managed to get each of us three months' severance pay, but for so many of those I worked with, it was to be the end of their broadcasting careers.

Knowing that the end was nigh didn't make our final months with ITV easy either. We still had to broadcast the games and do our jobs but the intense publicity meant we were easy targets for disgruntled fans and officials, people who now knew that their clubs were potentially in jeopardy too, due to ITV's largesse and poorly thought out plans. Typically, few held their clubs to account for their lavish spending, but as I said before, football is tribal.

In late April, we travelled to the midlands to cover West Bromwich Albion versus Crystal Palace at the Hawthorns. Albion needed to win to earn promotion to the top flight for the first time since 1986, so passions were already high, even before kick-off.

ITV's trucks had branded logos all over them, so there was no mistaking where we were from. As the fans started arriving, one or two began shouting abuse our way, and then a couple started throwing stones at the trucks. None of what had happened was our fault, in fact, we were as much the victims as the clubs themselves, but of course, they weren't aware of that. We took cover, but this was going to be a long day. It could be about the joy of promotion for the Baggies fans or, if they failed, it could be about retribution against us if they stayed down, and had to face the consequences of a severe cut in revenue.

In the end, a 2–0 win for Gary Megson's side confirmed their promotion. As I stood on the pitch at the end, interviewing full-back Neil Clement, the fans began to move towards the front of the stands, in preparation for a celebratory invasion.

As I began my third question, the nearby security guard, whose eyes by this stage were darting everywhere, came and whispered in my ear, 'You've got to go pal,' but I ignored him. Seconds later the security cordon broke, and thousands started to pour onto the field. This time, our guard wasn't so reticent and screamed at me 'Fucking run!!'

I sprinted for the safety of the tunnel, arriving just in time, ahead of the jubilant Baggies fans. But if that had been somewhat fun, what followed next, wasn't.

Because of the chaos in the tunnel, there was no way I could continue conducting interviews in that area – it was too noisy, and there were too many people milling around. So, we tore down the 'sponsor's board' that is used on every TV broadcast as a backdrop to interviews, and started to move it to another area. At which point, a tunnel steward decided to make a joke.

'I dunno why you're bothering to move that mate,' he said 'You won't be needing it as of Monday when you're all out of work! Ha ha!'

Ha ha indeed. I snapped. Turning back towards him, I informed him quite firmly that yes, he was correct, I and 59 others WERE actually losing our jobs, and if he thought that was cause for humour, then I would happily tell him otherwise. In fairness, he quickly realised what he'd said was in bad taste, and apologised.

That was unpleasant, but it wasn't the nastiest experience I had at ITV. Not by a long way.

A week or so later, I was at the New Den for the play-off semifinal second-leg tie between Millwall and Birmingham City – two clubs with a reputation for having violent fans. The first leg at St Andrews had ended in a 1–all draw, so Millwall felt that, with home advantage, they would win through to the final at the Millennium Stadium, and a shot at the Premier League.

But things didn't go according to the script, and with just minutes to go, Birmingham scored to give them a 2–1 advantage in the tie. The mood grew ugly as the final whistle approached, so much so that the referee actually went around the players, whispering that time was nearly up, and to make their way to the tunnel side of the ground as quickly as they could. He knew what was going to happen next – and so did I.

I was again in my role of touchline reporter, and with seconds to go, my director got in my ear to tell me to get ready to go on the pitch to conduct interviews as usual.

'You've got to be joking?' I said. 'Do you know what the atmosphere is like down here?'

'Well, we've got to at least give it a go,' was his reply.

I steeled myself, and as the whistle blew I went to take a step towards the field but it was utterly pointless. The players flew by me at a rate of knots, and then the coins and bottles began to rain down on the turf. I bolted for cover.

For the second time in the space of a few weeks, I heard a security guard say to me 'Fucking run!' but this time, I was almost literally running for my life. I managed to get into the tunnel in one piece before the big iron doors slammed shut behind me, and the stewards put a huge block of 4 x 4 across it to hold it in place. Within moments, the Millwall fans were hammering on the door, then trying to charge it to break it open. It was truly terrifying, but the door, thankfully, held firm.

That night was the worst football violence I ever saw in my life. Or should I say, witnessed from afar. We made our way back to the apron of the ground, towards the ITV trucks. The whole inner area of the stadium was now in lockdown, as the Millwall fans went mad outside.

After two hours, we were finally released, and the scene that met us was one of utter carnage as we wandered back to find our cars – if they were still there, that is. Many vehicles on the nearby streets had not only been turned over and had their windows smashed, but some had actually been set on fire. Whole streets were strewn with rubble, stones used as weapons as around 900 Millwall fans battled with police and the small number of travelling Birmingham fans. We escaped without injury, but it was truly a night of shame for the game, a night which saw 47 policemen injured. It was like a war zone.

Seven days later, the ITV Sport Channel closed its doors for good, after the Division 2 play-off final between Brentford and Stoke City at Cardiff's Millennium Stadium, for which I was again the pitch-side reporter. In a further kick in the nuts, ITV (terrestrial) screened the high-profile Championship play-off final between Birmingham City and Norwich on their main channel, and used their own pitch-side reporter. A year's work covering the second tier of English football and they used their own staff on the showpiece game, then issued our P45s. Thanks ITV.

So, just a year after voluntarily quitting the BBC and having two television networks clamouring for my services, I was, at 34, out of work for the first time in my broadcasting career.

I decided to get away from it all. My old mate from Burkina Faso, Piers Edwards, had been lucky enough to secure tickets through the ballot system for the 2002 World Cup in Japan and Korea. A friend of his had pulled out at the last minute, so I filled in, and in June of that year, I flew to Korea to meet up with Piers.

It was great fun, watching a major tournament in a very different part of the world, without the pressure of having to work. We followed Senegal and Costa Rica through the group stage (seeing the Senegalese spring a major surprise in the opening game, defeating France 1–0), before Piers headed off to Japan, where he had secured tickets for the knockout phase.

But I wasn't going home just yet. Almost as an afterthought, I had tagged on a few extra days' holiday at the end of my trip, to visit an old colleague from BBC World Service.

Rob Minshull is, as I mentioned, a Mancunian by birth, and a City fan. We'd met up at Bush House, where Rob worked as a BBC producer in the newsroom, and over the course of several years, we had attended a fair few City games together. When he emigrated to Australia we'd kept in touch, and the year before, I'd flown to Bali to meet him for a holiday, staying in Kuta.

Rob lived in Sydney, and he had invited me to come and stay with him for a short while. But, if you'd have told me I would be living there within a year, I'd have said you were mad.

I'd never been to Australia before that trip in 2002, so Rob was keen to show me the sights. We took in the Opera House, the Harbour Bridge, the Blue Mountains, Bondi Beach…all the usual cultural icons for a tourist like me. Towards the end of my stay, Rob told me that the media organisation he now worked for, SBS, were considering appointing a new football commentator. He told me I should apply, or at the very least, send him a show-reel of my work in England. He went on about it so much that eventually I agreed to do just that when I returned home. I had no idea what a significant decision that would prove to be.

In the meantime, I had a future to sort out back in England, and, arriving back fully refreshed following nearly a month overseas, I was raring to go. The obvious place to apply was Sky Sports. Sky was – and still is – the dominant broadcaster of sport in the UK, and quite a few of my ex-ITV colleagues had ended up there following the collapse of the ITV Sport Channel.

I was a little reluctant. I wasn't overly keen on the way Sky presented sport, which seemed to a BBC-trained person like me, to be rather brash, and heavily commercial. But it was too soon to consider a return to the Beeb – that would have been undignified – so I stuck in an application.

I was called for a screen test by Andy Cairns, the Executive Editor of Sky Sports News, but he didn't seem overly impressed by my audition, and was reticent about the prospect of finding me work. No matter. I pressed on, looking to carve little niches in the freelance world, and although it was initially unrewarding, eventually I got a break.

It was thanks to my former Red Dragon colleague Dez Corkhill again, at ESPN Star Sports in Singapore, the very same company I'd turned down only 12 months previously.

With the Commonwealth Games heading to Manchester in 2002, ESPN Star needed a reporter on the ground to file daily reports back to South-East Asia, with a special emphasis on Indian, Singaporean and Malaysian athletes. It was only two weeks' work, but it was a start, and a way of serving some penance for having rejected them a year earlier. So I accepted, and set to work trying to put in a good shift every day, before heading to the Sky regional studio in Macclesfield to feed back to Asia at midnight every night.

Being a freelancer was a new experience, and I have to admit, I rather enjoyed it. Not having to answer to bosses on a daily basis, and being in control of your own destiny was somewhat liberating, and the more work I got, the more seemed to roll in.

After the ESPN Star gig came an offer (perhaps borne out of guilt) from ITV to work on their *Goals on Saturday* programme, a free-to-air version of the hugely popular *Gillette Soccer Saturday* on Sky. Hosted by Angus Scott, the ITV version wasn't nearly as successful, but for half a season, it paid very well, and I was grateful for the money.

One of my old producers at the ITV Sport Channel, Rob Sloman, then recommended me to British Eurosport, as they were looking for a new host for their *Eurogoals* show on a Monday night. That also paid very well, and so now I had two days' work guaranteed per week. It was also great fun, working with producers Richard Copeland and David Tunnicliffe (also now living in Australia), and running the rule over the weekend's European action with my studio pundit, ex–Northern Ireland international, Gerry Armstrong.

Dave Farrar, an ex-BBC colleague, also helped me out. He'd carved a real niche for himself in the overseas commentary department, developing fantastic relationships through his time at Eurosport, with Canal Plus in France, and RAI Television in Italy. He asked me whether I fancied being part of the commentary team covering Serie A from RAI's base in Rome, and I readily agreed.

So, once or twice a month, I would fly out from Heathrow to the Italian capital, and call two games 'off-tube' in a studio at RAI, then fly back on Monday morning. I also travelled to Paris with Dave to call European Championship qualifying games for Canal Plus, all done out of a truck in a car park somewhere in the west of the French capital. My first game was Azerbaijan versus Italy, and I remember it clearly, because for the first 20 minutes, I still didn't have an official team sheet for either side. The Italians weren't too difficult to spot with the likes of Del Piero, Totti and Pirlo in their side, but Azerbaijan? Let's just say that their best player, who I believe went by the name of Gurbanov, saw an awful lot of the ball!

In addition, I got the occasional call-up from another ex-BBC colleague, Andy Kay, by now in charge of programming at Capital Radio in London. Every so often, his regular sports presenter, Marcus Buckland, needed time off to fulfil his other broadcasting commitments, and so I added a two-hour football preview show to my burgeoning portfolio, picking up from BBC broadcasting legend Tony Blackburn at 12 pm on a Saturday.

Then, out of the blue, Sky Sports got back in touch.

Andy Cairns wanted me in for a second screen test, which I thought was strange, given they'd seemed totally disinterested the first time around. I nailed the second audition however, and Sky started calling upon me for occasional reporting shifts, though not, as yet, any presenting gigs.

In the meantime, I had done as Rob Minshull had asked, and sent a tape off to Australia but with no real expectation of it leading to anything. I figured they must have a hundred guys wanting the job, and in any case, I didn't have an Australian work visa, and had no idea if I could even get one. So it was with astonishment that a month later, I received an email from SBS, informing me that they were very interested in my application, and could I get myself a work visa for Down Under?

Wow! I spoke to Rob, who told me to get down to Australia House on the Strand (next door to my old premises at Bush House), and see if I could get the required paperwork. But after a short meeting, my hopes were deflated. I didn't match the criteria – not enough 'points' to secure a 457 temporary migrant visa. Disappointed, I asked my interviewer if there was any other way I could get to Australia. She replied that my only possible avenue was for the company concerned to sponsor me.

I wrote back to SBS, apologising for wasting their time, but I did mention the sponsorship angle. A week later, and to my amazement, they replied and said they would look into it, and get back to me.

While all of this was bubbling along, I was happily earning decent money as a freelancer, and was quite taken with my new lifestyle. But things were about to take another dramatic twist, and lead me into a situation where I had to make another huge decision.

First, Sky completed their remarkable turnaround by offering me a full-time contract. I was flabbergasted. The contract, for a presenting role on the Sky Sports News Channel, was for nearly as much money as I had made at ITV. I verbally accepted Andy Cairns's offer, and waited for the formal contract to come through. In the meantime, SBS were back in touch, saying they were now keen to sponsor me to go to Australia, but that the process (involving the immigration office), would take at least a month.

That put me in a real dilemma. Should I take the concrete offer from Sky, the leading UK broadcaster? Or wait on a promise from SBS, an employer I knew nothing about, in a country I'd visited once for a week's holiday?

In the end, I opted to sign the Sky contract. I had a discussion with Andy Cairns regarding my potential opportunity in Australia and he was understanding of my situation. He told me to sign the deal with Sky, and then if something came up in the meantime from SBS, they would hold discussions about releasing me, if I decided that was what I wanted to do.

But something in my head was nagging away. I didn't like the look of the wording of my contract at Sky, which had no break clause inserted into it. I pointed this out to Andy, who dismissed my concerns, saying every contract at Sky was structured in the same way. Just to be sure though, I took the contract to an agent, Jonathan Marks, based in central London. Jonathan and I didn't have a formal agreement, but I'd spoken to him on several occasions during my time at ITV, having been recommended to him by Brian Barwick.

Jonathan gave it the once over, and firmly told me NOT to put pen to paper with Sky if I had any intentions at all of going to Australia. He was a veteran of doing such deals, and he told me that the contract was watertight. Even if Andy had made verbal assurances, there was nothing I could do, legally, if they reneged on that promise.

Now I was sweating. I needed a job, and moreover, I didn't want to piss Sky off to the extent that I'd ruin my chances of going there in the future. On the other hand, I felt like I'd missed out on a big opportunity to go overseas 12 months previously with ESPN Star and paid the price after ITV's failure. I didn't want to make the same mistake twice.

So, after much agonising, I reluctantly told Andy I couldn't accept his offer. Sky weren't best pleased; they weren't used to being turned down, rightly viewing themselves as THE place to be in UK sports broadcasting.

Now I was totally dependent upon SBS coming good on their part of the deal. My career was in the lap of the Gods, resting in the hands of a network on the other side of the planet, in a country I knew next to nothing about.

CHAPTER 8 EIGHT

AUSTRALIA

In November 2002, I received confirmation from SBS that the sponsorship process was progressing well, and that their deputy head of sport, Ken Shipp, would be flying to London later that month to have a chat, and discuss the details of my contract. I couldn't believe my luck.

Things were set in train quickly, and I did my first bits of real work for SBS while still in Europe. In December, I flew to Madrid to cover the FIFA World Player of the Year Awards, although the real intention of my trip was to report on FIFA's impending announcement of a full World Cup qualifying slot for Oceania.

I managed to snare an exclusive with FIFA President, Sepp Blatter, who expressed his delight in having 'completed the world football family' by admitting Oceania. In true FIFA style though, that decision was quickly proven to be one of expedience only. A few months later, they used New Zealand's poor performance at the 2003 Confederations Cup to pull the rug from under the OFC (under pressure from the other confederations), and revert their slot back to a half place. It was an ominous portent to the difficulties the game of football had in its most far-flung outpost.

Meantime, not everyone was doing cartwheels about my imminent move Down Under. My parents were, perhaps understandably, a little upset that their only son was about to up sticks, and go to live on the other side of the world. Especially in lieu of the fact that both my mum, and sister had concerns over their health.

In 2000, Mum had found a lump on her breast, and after investigation, it had been found to be cancerous. After having the lump removed, she underwent bouts of radiotherapy, but her age, strangely, stood her in good stead. Being older, the cells don't tend to reproduce as quickly, so she not only avoided chemotherapy but was given the all-clear five years later.

But just a year later, my sister had the rank misfortune to be diagnosed with the same condition. She too had the lump removed, but being only 38, she couldn't avoid the chemo, and suffered the indignity of losing all her hair. By 2002 however, she too had recovered to an extent whereby the prognosis was good, so, after everything that had happened with my career in the previous year or two, I saw no reason to let this opportunity pass me by.

I met Ken Shipp for the first time in the Langham Hotel on Oxford Street, right next door to my old home, BBC Broadcasting House. Ken was very enthusiastic, 100 per cent convinced I was the right choice for SBS, and that all the immigration department's requirements would be fulfilled.

We shook hands on the deal – which was worth only around half what I'd been offered by Sky, incidentally – and he flew back to Australia while we awaited the authorisation for a temporary 457 skilled migration visa. It was eventually issued in December, and I made the trip back down to Australia House to get my passport stamped with the ticket to my new life.

I agreed to a start date of the second week of January 2003, but before then I had a lot to sort out. First of all, I had to quit my freelance roles, which caused me some angst. I'd really enjoyed putting together a portfolio of work, especially my gig at British Eurosport, where I'd made good friends. But this was no time for sentiment; I had the chance of a lifetime waiting, and so, one by one, I informed my various employers that, come January, I would no longer be available.

I also needed to decide what to do regarding my flat. I was very fond of my one-bedroom apartment in Ickenham, so I decided that instead of selling up, I would attempt to get the property rented out. After all, I didn't know if Australia would be to my liking (and vice versa), so I reckoned having somewhere to come back to, would be sensible.

Then it was the time for farewells. On Boxing Day 2002, I paid my last ever trip to Maine Road. The ground was due to be torn down at the end of the season anyway, with Manchester City due to move to the new City of Manchester Stadium in 2003. This only added to my sense of an era coming to an end, and although City won

3–1, I lingered a little longer than usual at the full-time whistle, at the place where I'd spent much of my childhood, and identified so strongly with.

With my departure date set for 6 January 2003, I also held a farewell party in London for around 30 of my closest friends. It was all rather surreal. Saying goodbye to the only life you have ever known to go and start over in a place you've only ever visited on holiday, is a rather unnerving experience, and I had no idea what I was letting myself in for.

Saying goodbye to my parents (who were staying down in London to help with the removal process), was an emotional experience too. They'd asked if they could come to Heathrow with me, but I refused; I didn't want teary farewells at the departure gate, so instead, we had them outside my flat in Ickenham. I remember telling my parents I loved them – not something I often come out with. It was that sort of moment.

So, with only a suitcase in my hand, I set off on my own for a new life on the other side of the world. My old Polytechnic friend, Andrew Mussenden, had kindly procured an upgrade to business on my one-way flight to Sydney, via a friend of his, Andy Taylor, who worked for British Airways – so, with the emotional side of my departure from England over, I took my seat in the pointy end of the plane, and looked forward to what the next chapter of my life would bring.

I didn't have to wait too long.

One of the very first Australians I met was an attractive blonde flight attendant. I noticed her even before we took off. During the long flight, we got chatting and she asked me about the nature of my trip to Australia.

As I re-boarded for the second leg of the flight to Sydney, I noticed there was a piece of paper stuck to the seat, simply labelled '18A' (my seat number). She had left me her phone number with a message, saying she'd be happy to show me around Sydney if I needed a guide. The first Aussie girl I met (without even leaving the tarmac at Heathrow), was to become my girlfriend for the first year or so of my new life Down Under.

Arriving in Sydney was like arriving in Ouagadougou all those years ago. I'd left London in the middle of winter – the temperature was minus 5 that frosty January morning – in Sydney, it was well over 30 degrees, and it was a rude shock.

Finding a place to live, I was pointed towards the classifieds in the *Sydney Morning Herald,* so, I'd arranged to lodge with Rob for the first few weeks, at least until I got used to my new surroundings. But he dropped a bombshell on me the moment I arrived. He'd taken a job with the ABC in Brisbane, and was leaving to take up the post the following week. The only person I knew in the entire country was upping sticks in less than seven days!

After absorbing that piece of news, I settled into his ground-floor flat in Mandolong Road, Mosman, but already the clock was ticking, as he had handed his notice in to the landlord. I needed to move quickly; I had two weeks to find a place to live.

Thankfully, I had been given a couple of weeks grace by SBS to sort things out before starting work at their Artarmon studios, and Rob knew there wasn't a moment to lose so, on my very first day in Australia, I spent two hours going around Ikea, shopping for furniture, still jet lagged and not really understanding the value of the dollar, nor knowing where these new purchases would actually find a home.

That first night, I didn't even have a bed, as Rob's furniture (save for a rickety old sofa, which belonged to his landlord, and was propped up with bricks) had been transported north for his new life. I'd ordered myself a new one that first day, spotting a van with the logo 'Dial-a-bed!' emblazoned all over it as we drove to Ikea. I called them on Rob's phone, and they promised to deliver the morning after, so I slept on the floor that first evening.

Moving to a new country is an exhilarating, but exhausting experience. You're like a baby learning to walk and talk. I had done some research, but the practicalities of finding somewhere to live, a car to drive, and even your way around, are all a tricky process. Even though the language was English, everything else was foreign – even ordering a pint in the bar was met with a blank stare. So my vocabulary was hastily updated with the word 'schooner'.

After a week, Rob disappeared up to Brisbane, and I was literally on my own. I had rented a car from a place in Oxford Street for the time being, but the layout of Sydney confused me, and the drivers themselves concerned me. Everyone seemed to drive at 100 kilometres per hour, and living in Mosman, I had to negotiate the notoriously busy Military Road.

At least my flat hunting was going well. I'd narrowed it down to two apartments (both in Mosman), and now that SBS had issued me with a mobile phone, I could actually call people back to make, or break appointments.

I made a second visit to a flat in Clifford Street, and decided it was the one for me, signing a six-month renewable lease. I moved all my furniture into the new joint (*all* is probably a bit of an exaggeration – it barely filled a mini-van, with the rest of my stuff somewhere in the middle of the ocean, on board a freighter bound for Sydney Harbour), and started to feel a bit more at home.

My new colleagues seemed friendly enough. I was sharing an office space with fellow presenter, Andrew Orsatti, who was welcoming, as were the rest of the football team who I would be working with: producer Joe di Meglio, analysts Craig Foster and Francis Awaritefe, and head of sport, Les Murray.

To begin with, I was dropped into the programming gently, hosting individual segments on *The World Game,* the iconic Sunday afternoon show which ran an incredible six hours. During the week, I reported for, and occasionally hosted, *Toyota World Sport.*

Coming from the UK, where even long-standing football shows such as *Match of the Day* ran for only an hour, I couldn't quite believe SBS's commitment to a show of that length. It was admirable, but I felt the quality of the show suffered. The network wasn't hugely resourced, and many of the segments seemed to be little more than a succession of talking heads, gibbering earnestly about their passion.

Of course, I later learned that a long history of the game was, for many football fans, their lifeline to a sport that was largely ignored, and even ridiculed in other areas of the Australian media. Indicative of this was one of the first Socceroo internationals I watched on a rival network. Back in 2003, Channel 7 still held the broadcast rights to both the national team, and the domestic NSL. In mid-2003, Australia played a friendly in Dublin against Ireland, and I sat down to watch it at my flat in Mosman.

The host, Bruce McAvaney, was, and is, a hugely respected sports presenter. I've met Bruce, and I like him as a person, and his easy presenting style. But he clearly wasn't overly-familiar with football. Introducing the game, he talked over pictures from Lansdowne Road, referencing Irish rugby, and historic battles between the Wallabies and the Ireland team. The football – or soccer as they insisted upon calling it – was almost an afterthought.

When the action began, it didn't get much better. Although the match commentators couldn't be faulted, the producer and director seemed to have little idea as to the ebb and flow of a game of football. When Australia won the game's first corner, Seven unbelievably cut to an ad break, before realising their mistake and crashing out of the ad, back to the action literally seconds later. It was appalling. That, I was to learn, was how many in the mainstream media approached 'soccer' – they were either contemptuous of it, or just didn't understand it.

The attitude towards 'soccer' was often mixed seamlessly with casual homophobia too. A few weeks after moving into my apartment, my belongings arrived from the UK, and the company arranged delivery to my flat. Two guys were assigned to unload the van and carry the stuff up to my second-floor apartment, and as they emptied the boxes ready to take back to their depot, they were surprised to find a serious collection of football literature.

'You've got a lot of soccer books mate,' said one.

'Yeah, it's my job. I'm a football commentator.'

'Game for bloody nancy boys, mate.'

My new country – and its culture, more specifically – found other ways to shock me too. Back in England, I was aware that in Australia, we Brits were referred to as 'Poms'. I was expecting it, and to be honest, I didn't think it would bother me one bit. In the UK, there are all sorts of nicknames for people of different nationalities. Americans are 'Yanks', the Irish 'Paddies', the Scots 'Jocks', the Welsh 'Taffs', the South Africans 'Saffas'. As a native of the north-west of England, I'd been called a 'northern monkey' so many times I'd lost count. Whippet-chaser, flat-cap wearer; you name it, I've copped it.

But all of that was pub talk. Banter between mates – if you knew them well enough. Britain's long history of troubled race relations meant almost everyone, with the exception of those of limited intelligence, knew roughly where the boundaries were. That didn't seem to be the case in Australia, where casual racism (and often, homophobia) appeared to exist on every level, and especially in the media, which often sets the tone for a nation's cultural discourse.

Right from my first days in Australia, I realised this was going to be an issue with which I would really struggle – and that remains the case, even today.

In those early days, I happened to tune in to a conversation on a radio station while driving to work. It was in the early stages of the 'bird flu' outbreak which had just taken hold in China. The presenter was interviewing a politician about the prospect of the disease being transported to Australia. The conversation went something like this:

Presenter: 'Minister, is there a chance that bird flu could hit these shores?'

Politician: 'No, I don't think that will happen. We have good safeguards in place, and I think we are protected.'

Presenter: 'Unless the bloody Asians bring it in.'

I nearly crashed my car.

Another day, I heard a shock-jock presenter refer to a person involved in the Sydney Mardi Gras as a 'pillow-biter'. Now, I've heard that a thousand times in a pub – but on a mainstream radio station?

Things were even worse when it came to the English, who, I quickly came to realise, were both loved and loathed in equal measure. The two nations have, of course, a long, close and somewhat troubled history. I understood the sporting rivalry, particularly on the cricket and rugby fields, and expected some stick if England lost – and I anticipated dishing some out if the reverse happened. What I wasn't prepared for was the sheer vitriol of the Australian media whenever these contests came around. I had been in the country only a few weeks when Australia defeated England 3–1 in a friendly at Upton Park. The Aussies thoroughly deserved their win, yet for a nation which showed precious little interest in 'soccer' the victory was celebrated with incredible hubris. These were eye-opening experiences for a new immigrant, and worse was to come later in the year.

The Rugby World Cup was played in Australia in late 2003. I am not much of a rugby fan, but the way the Aussie media covered the tournament incensed me. It wasn't so much the digs at the England team, its coach Clive Woodward, nor its star, Jonny Wilkinson. That much I expected, especially as England were the clear favourites to win the tournament. But to me, the one-eyed patriotism went way too far. One article, in which a current Wallaby was quoted, called England an 'arrogant nation, because they wore red coats to go to war'. There were regular pops at the Queen, references to generals at Gallipoli, disrespecting of the national anthem, and various other minor things that, for me, went way beyond sport, and crossed the line into something approaching racism.

I'd been offered tickets to the final (inevitably between England and Australia), but I turned them down. I couldn't guarantee that I wouldn't lose my patience should Australia win and some of the (by now, regular) insults started flying. Instead, I went with my girlfriend to a World Cup party thrown by several (Australian) friends of hers, and whom, she assured me, were not prone to the sort of overt nationalism I'd heard all too often in the previous weeks. The final was probably the first, and only game of rugby union I've ever been emotionally invested in due to the circumstances, and when Wilkinson slotted home the winning points, I couldn't help myself. The house in which the party was being held was festooned with green and gold balloons. I went into the kitchen, grabbed a knife and popped every single one of them.

With hindsight, perhaps Australia's media was just ahead of the game. When I return to the UK these days, I see the same sort of parochialism displayed in the media, even on the BBC, where reporters have virtually become cheerleaders. The Beeb, though, does draw the line at calling the Aussies 'convicts' live on national television. Australia, a nation which prides itself on successful multicultural assimilation, still regularly uses 'Poms' to refer to England or Englishmen. Racism, or xenophobia may be difficult to get rid of in the pub but the media can set an example. To my mind, a nation's media not only has a duty to inform and entertain, but also to set some sort of standard. That's not some highbrow BBC condescension, it is accepted journalistic, or broadcasting fact – good media coverage requires some level of detachment, or impartiality. Too often, the newspapers I read in Australia, or the television I watch, sink to the level of pub talk. Perhaps that is the true nature of an egalitarian society? I'm not convinced.

Another argument I hear all the time in Australia is that 'Pom' is a term of endearment. Really? Then why do I hear about 'Pommy bastards' or see adverts inviting me to 'tonk a Pom' during the cricket? The accent is always – always – towards the negative. Imagine, using the same construct, if Australia were playing Italy, and the Italians were referred to as 'wog bastards' – how would that be received?

I have never, ever, heard a television bulletin introduce Theresa May as 'the Pom Prime Minister' or announce that the 'Pom pound' has risen several points in the financial markets. Why? Because it doesn't work in anything but a negative context, and deep down, people know that only too well. The term is an insult, and anyone who says differently, clearly hasn't been on the receiving end of it, so how on earth would they know?

The oddest thing is, no-one in Australia seems to know what a 'Pom' actually is. The two main theories centre around the first convicts eating pomegranates on the way to Australia, or that it's a short form of 'Prisoner Of Mother England'. Whatever the truth, it is clear it relates in some way, to the first wave of convicts transported down under over 200 years ago. So, here's the question, particularly for those Aussies with Anglo surnames. Who are the descendants of those 'Poms' – you, or me?

Still on the same subject, and back at work, it was becoming crystal clear that my Englishness was going to define me in my new country. On one of the first shows I presented, I made some comment regarding a certain team being a 'rabble' after a poor performance. That led to my first piece of viewer correspondence, a letter from a lady who was outraged at my use of the term, as apparently the word had been used by an English official at the 1956 Olympics to describe the Australian team. She thought it instructive that I was of the same breed. A fairly long bow I thought.

Similarly, Les Murray had no problems in regaling me with a story of his trip to Upton Park for the aforementioned friendly between England and Australia, when he'd felt insulted at being mistaken for being English.

On the other hand, there were those who couldn't praise me enough when I first appeared on screen at SBS. At first, I was flattered. After a while, I realised it was because of my accent, not necessarily the quality of my work. For British expats (and there are plenty of them in Australia), it was perhaps a welcome reminder of home, and my BBC connections helped too. For some Australians, having a British voice was all they'd ever known when it came to football; perhaps they found it comforting?

Either way, all of the above added to my growing sense of insecurity. Here in this strange new land, I didn't really know where, or even if, I fitted in.

Aside of the Rugby World Cup, my first year in Australia passed relatively uneventfully. With the old National Soccer League struggling along in its dying years, and the broadcast contracts being held by other networks, there wasn't really much football to sink my teeth into.

The Champions League provided a welcome injection of 'live' action, with SBS holding the rights, and I called many matches off tube from the Artarmon studios, sometimes with Craig Foster as my co-commentator.

'Fozzie' and I hit it off right from the start. I remembered him vaguely from his time as a player in England with Portsmouth, and along with Orsatti and Awaritefe, the four of us started to hang out at some of the nightspots in Sydney – Establishment on George Street being a particular favourite, and Ravesis in Bondi becoming another regular haunt.

Foster had an excellent, deprecating line in humour and on set he was articulate and clearly knowledgeable about the game. Orsatti was funny too, in a different way. A little more sensitive than Foster, and his Italian temper occasionally flared. Awaritefe was often the butt of the jokes, but a genuine bloke.

Relations between SBS and the newly reconstituted FFA were tense. Although SBS had been a supporter of reform of the struggling domestic game (as outlined in the Crawford Report), many felt the broadcaster held too much sway, both in the court of public opinion, and within the game itself. As the only media network remotely interested in the game, perhaps that was understandable, yet I didn't quite realise how deep these connections ran.

As a newcomer to Australia, I didn't pretend to understand all the politics. I read Johnny Warren's book *Sheilas, Wogs and Poofters* along with Ross Solly's excellent *Shoot Out* to try and gain some sort of grasp of the inner workings of the game Down Under, but prior to the establishment of the A-League, it all seemed (to my foreign eyes), to be a little petty, with different factions squabbling over what seemed, in all honesty, a relatively tiny pie.

I began to dip my toe into the water of the local game, attending a Northern Spirit game at the picturesque, but wholly unsuitable (for football anyway), North Sydney Oval, along with some friends. I travelled over to Marconi with Francis Awaritefe (where he was, unbelievably, refused entry into the media suite due to his lack of a pass – this was a guy who'd played over 100 games for the club), and took in a match at Parramatta Stadium, watching the Power versus Sydney United, where the crowd numbered barely 3000, and where the Sydney United fans threw a flare, like they were in some seething European hotbed. It was an odd landscape.

Covering the penultimate season of the NSL was left to Orsatti, Awaritefe, and on occasion, Foster on *The World Game.* They seemed to spend more time talking politics than actual football.

Today, I can see that while this state of affairs was (and no doubt still is), bewildering for newly-arrived foreigners, it's the legacy of a game which has historically struggled for mainstream traction. Until you've been in the country for a few years, you don't quite understand how hard people have to work, just to keep the game alive.

Now I've been in Australia for many years, foreigners' attitudes towards the game of football here can come across as condescending, and irritate me too – I'm sure I was no different. When you come from Europe (or elsewhere), where the game is king, you have no idea of the gargantuan efforts needed here, given all the obstacles the game has in front of it. I appreciate it, and value it now, but then, new to the country, I probably didn't.

Two men who fought harder than most on behalf of the sport they loved, were Les (Murray) and Johnny (Warren), considered to be the guardians of the game in Australia. So much so that they were dubbed 'Mr and Mrs Football'; and it was easy to understand why. In a country where the game was marginalised, they had (through their work at SBS primarily) kept the flame alive for fans, giving the sport a coverage that, in such a hostile environment, was second to none in Australia.

Les was not only one of my new colleagues he was also my new boss and was still hosting most of the sports programmes himself. However, most accepted this anomaly at face value; being football fans as well as journalists, it was taken as read that Les was 'one of us' and he was trusted not to abuse his dual role. Les was gregarious, and excellent company away from the office.

Johnny I found rather different; and quieter, especially towards newcomers.

In my early days at SBS, I heard rumours from those outside the organisation that the football department tried to 'run the game' from the television studio. I dismissed these notions as the paranoid rants of those slighted on air by the *World Game* team. This wasn't a new accusation; I'd heard similar complaints regarding the BBC and Sky (in particular) during my time in England.

I felt the Australian national team were particularly distrusting of SBS. I learned several players simply refused to talk to the network, while the coach, Frank Farina, had a challenging relationship at times with Les and Johnny.

I took all this on board with a healthy pinch of salt, especially as my colleagues assured me it was all rubbish. But a request to have the respected (and kindly) Ron Smith come on *The World Game* gave me a little clue that this was not just the usual player-coach/journalist type of distrust. Smith took my call, and politely, but firmly, declined my invitation to appear on the show.

Still, I was having a good time in my early months at my new network, and in my new country. I particularly enjoyed living in Mosman, with the beautiful walk down the hill to the picturesque Balmoral Beach and its little waterfront cafes.

SBS seemed pleased with my progress too. I'd fitted in nicely to the on-air presentation team, while commentary duties with Fozzie on Champions League mornings gave us a welcome respite from the lack of domestic football on offer.

The NSL rights were still held (at that time) by Channel 7, who were so disinterested in the local product, they buried the weekly highlights in the wee small hours of a weekday morning, when precious few were watching. I remember the start of the final NSL season being greeted by a solitary paragraph in the *Daily Telegraph* – the local product was virtually invisible.

Later, of course, it transpired that the shabby treatment of football had an ulterior motive. Seven's Steven Wise admitted (via an email in 2000, later made public) that the network had bought the rights for the NSL (and Socceroos) expressly to

Above: Mum and Dad (George and Audrey).

Left: With my sister, Fiona, as kids – I don't know where the blond hair went!

Above: School photo circa 1978, with goofy teeth and bowl haircut, nice.

Above: The football-crazy kid with Man City socks on, and City patches sewn onto the tracksuit for good measure.

Above: The not-as-crazy-about-cricket kid, wearing my county cap at the age of 13. I don't know why I'm in my pads – I couldn't bat to save my life!

Above: My first band, Molotov Cocktail. Me on the drums with schoolmates Rhys Enfield (bass), Russell Reason (guitar, back to picture), Michael Bearpark (partly obscured), and Jason Arber (vocalist).

Above: Reporting for SBS in Frankfurt at the 2005 FIFA Confederations Cup.

Above: Meeting one of my boyhood heroes, Franz Beckenbauer.

Above: Doing a piece to camera ahead of the vital qualifier in 2005 between Uruguay and Australia. This was in Buenos Aires, Argentina, where the 'Roos had their training camp.

Above: The 2006 SBS World Cup team. Back row, left to right, Mike Tomalaris, me, Tracey Holmes, Emma Simkin, Les Murray. Seated, Craig Foster, Stephanie Brantz, Andrew Orsatti.

Above: Orsatti, Foster, me and Les in happier times.

Above: With Rob Minshull on holiday in Bali, 2001, holding the beloved sky blue jersey. Rob was the catalyst in finding a new life for me in Australia – I owe him plenty.

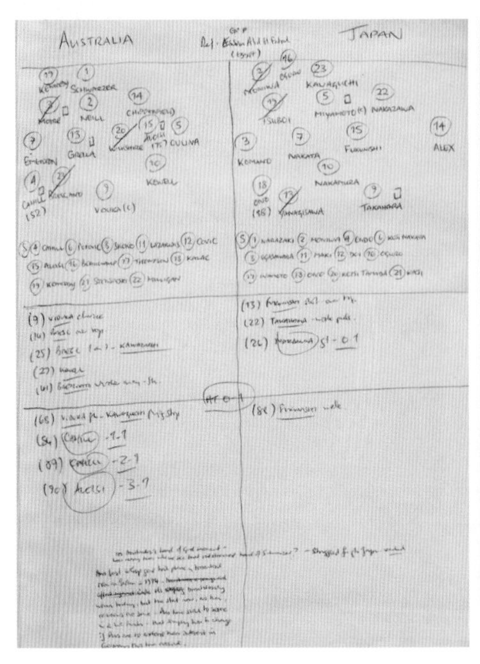

Above: My match notes from Australia's first-ever World Cup win over Japan in 2006.

This page and next: Various accreditation passes, publicity shots, haircuts and uncomfortable expressions – I hate having my photo taken!

Simon Hill
SBS Sport
sbs.com.au/sport

ATHENS 2004
SOUTHBANK
PRODUCTION
Simon Hill
1-30 August 2004

TELEVISION
SIMON
HILL
SBS
LIBRE CIRCULACION-CAMPO DE JUEGO

NATIONAL
ORGANISATION SBS TELEVISION
NAME SIMON HILL
PASS No. 0149
ACCESS ZONES
MEDIA
2003/2004

FIFA CONFEDERATIONS CUP
GERMANY 2005
FIFA
HILL
SIMON
United Kingdom
SBS Australia (AUS)
RTV2
1
3
6
7
8

2006
FIFA WORLD CUP
GERMANY™
FIFA
HILL
Simon
United Kingdom
SBS Australia (AUS)
RTV2
BahnCard
1
3
6
7
8

Above: With Tim Cahill at the 2005 FIFA Confederations Cup. He's given me some of my best moments in commentary down the years.

'suffocate' the game, in order to promote Australian Rules Football, an astonishing business – little wonder the game struggled to make headway.

SBS, despite having no domestic club football to show, was still clearly the 'home' of the game. As well as Champions League rights, the network was contracted to show one live English Premier League game every Saturday night, and with the rights secured to the 2006 World Cup in Germany, it was plain that for a football broadcaster in Australia, SBS was the only place to be. But not for long.

Things began to change early in my second year Down Under. First, in September of the previous year (2003), Channel Seven confirmed its intention to give up their broadcast rights to the game, in response to pressure from the new Chairman of the Australian Soccer Association, Frank Lowy. Lowy had been appointed (headhunted would be a better word) on the back of the publication of the Crawford Report, a government enquiry into how the game had been run. One of its recommendations was that the previous board resign en masse, which they did, albeit hugely reluctantly. Lowy was seen as the messiah who could revive the games fortunes as both a figurehead, and a driver of change.

These events had, in turn, been prompted by the extraordinary ratings success of the 2002 World Cup in Japan/Korea, bringing in audiences of millions to SBS, who took full advantage of the (Australian) time-friendly kick-offs by picking up secondary broadcast rights from Channel 9. The then Prime Minister, John Howard, took notice, and wondered why on earth Australia wasn't competing at the World Cup. The Crawford Report was commissioned and told him, and everyone else, exactly why.

Australian 'soccer' was a mess and one of the main reasons was a television deal with a network that was, unbelievably, hostile to the game it had paid good money to supposedly broadcast. Lowy recognised that was one of the first things that needed to change, and thus, the deal was ripped up. It was to be the first of many such wins for the astute Lowy.

From an SBS point of view, this represented a major opportunity. As the 'home' of the game, the network was in the frame to pick up the rights to any domestic football going. This it did, and late in the 2003/04 season, I commentated my first-ever game of Australian domestic club football – an Elimination Final between Marconi Stallions and South Melbourne.

The game wasn't up to much. It was a blindingly hot day in Sydney's west, and the part-time players struggled with the heat. It ended goalless. Two weeks later, and I was back in the commentary box for the Major Semi between Parramatta Power and NSL powerhouse, Perth Glory. The game was entertaining enough, but I found myself bewildered by the crowd, which only numbered about 6000. Some of them seemed rather confused by the spectacle unfolding in front of them. I heard applause for rather ordinary passages of play, and overheard terminology such as 'penalty' for a free kick, and criticism of the 'umpire'. It was like watching football on the moon.

Parramatta won 4–2, and thus won through to the Grand Final; another rather odd addition to my vocabulary, having been brought up in a country where the team that finished first were proclaimed champions. Perth won through in the Preliminary Final, and so the same two teams would meet again in the final, scheduled for 4 April 2004.

By then, it had already been decreed that this would be the last ever NSL season. The league, Australia's first truly national sporting competition, was moribund. Clubs were financially in peril (due in part, it must be said to the ridiculous broadcast deal, which effectively killed off any potential advertising or sponsorship revenues), the in-fighting and ever-present factionalism. In addition, the ethnic identities of many of the teams left the rest of Australia cold.

So keen was the new Australian Soccer Association (which, under Lowy, had changed its name from Soccer Australia) to distance itself from the NSL, the last Grand Final was a very low-key affair. Few of the major ASA administrators showed up, and the inclement weather rather reflected the state of the game.

Parramatta Stadium was grey, but dry, at kick-off that April day. Soon after kick-off however, the heavens opened with almost apocalyptic force. The surface quickly resembled a quagmire, and it seemed only a matter of time before the game was called off. A crowd of just under 10,000 headed to the back of the stands for shelter, as the last, desperate moments of a once-proud competition were played out.

Power had been the pre-game favourites but the conditions killed their natural passing game. It turned into a scrap, which went all the way into extra time before substitute Nik Mrdja put everyone out of their misery by turning home the winner for Perth, on the mud heap that was once the pitch.

And so, with Mrdja's kick, the NSL faded into history. Few seemed to mourn very much but the question was, what next? Club football in Australia had a history, however chequered, but did it have a future? The answer was to be the A-League – but not yet.

Before that, I had duties to perform at the Olympics – or the Olympics in Melbourne, to be more precise. SBS had secured secondary rights to the Athens Games in partnership with Channel 7 and their output was to be produced from their Melbourne studios. I was to host studio updates, and provide commentary on the two Australian football teams taking part, the Olyroos, and the Matildas.

Spending time in Melbourne was another part of my Australian education. This was (and is) a city which has Aussie Rules in its blood, and despite a heavy migrant presence – it is home to the biggest Greek community in the world outside Greece – 'soccer' has faced hostility there on a scale that even other Australian cities fail to match.

That much became clear during our stay in Melbourne that winter of 2004. Some of the Seven staff were openly dismissive of anything to do with the broadcasting of 'soccer', even though the Australian games (men and women) were to be relayed live on their main channel, rather than SBS. More than once I heard the term 'wogballers' used to describe their own countrymen representing the nation of their birth at the Olympics. It was extraordinary prejudice, the likes of which wasn't attributed to any other sport.

Still, the games themselves were enjoyable enough, although neither the men, nor the women made it past the quarterfinals. I enjoyed hosting the regular daily shows too, and our stint ended in a magnificent piss-up in a Greek taverna, with Les dancing on the tables. None of the Seven team were with us needless to say; it was almost like broadcasting apartheid, with SBS stuck in its 'ethnic' ghetto. Being Anglo, yet a football fan and an SBS employee with no axe to grind with any community, yet again I felt unsure as to where, or even if, I belonged.

Culturally, it seemed to me that people were compelled to make a choice. If you wanted to belong to Australia, you had to follow Aussie Rules, or Rugby League. Either would do. The only thing most seemed to agree on was that 'soccer' was a foreign sport, and most definitely didn't belong. It was (and is), ridiculous of course ; it's just a game, and one that has been played Down Under for just as long as the other codes, being no more 'foreign' than cricket, Rugby League or Union, all of which have their modern roots in England, just like football. Even Aussie Rules, the so called 'indigenous' game, has its roots in the early games of 'folk' football played in England, where Tom Wills and other pioneers of that code, were educated, or even born. Many people enjoyed watching all the different sports, in defiance of the unwritten rules. Yet such attitudes ran so deep, it seemed to me they were almost a part of the national identity.

When I first arrived in Sydney, I was open to all sports. Football had always been my number one, but I had no particular problem with League (given where I'd grown up), and was curious about Aussie Rules. I even paid for a ticket to go and watch State of Origin in that first year Down Under, although I found the atmosphere to be rather muted. I seemed to spend most of the game getting out of my seat, to allow people past, en route to either the bar, or the toilet. Few appeared to be interested in the game itself – it just felt like an event.

The only thing people of a non-football persuasion seemed to agree on, was that they hated 'soccer'. In fact, such was the hostility I encountered with anything to do with the game, I quickly resolved that if this was the way it was going to be, then I knew where my allegiances lay. I reasoned it might also be one way in which I could satisfy the immigration criteria, which had stated that I had to 'offer something significantly different' from a local. Oh, I was going to be different alright. I was going to fight against these silly ingrained prejudices and myths to my last breath.

That same month as the Olympics, SBS lost the rights to broadcast the English Premier League – acquired exclusively by Fox Sports, a relatively new player in the game, but whose power was starting to grow. We at SBS were a little shocked at losing one of the network's 'crown jewels', even though we had only been broadcasting one Saturday night match. It was to be the start of an avalanche.

Not just yet, however. SBS had taken over the rights to the national team games, and I'd already made my debut calling the Socceroos in January of that year, when the team drew 1–1 in a friendly in Venezuela. The call was 'off-tube' in the Sydney studio, and there was anxiety when the pictures from South America still hadn't come through with only 10 minutes to go before kick-off.

Yet even at SBS, the prejudice towards football was evident. As Jenny Hiscocks, our unit manager, scurried around in master control (the hub of every TV network where pictures come in via satellite from overseas), desperately trying to ascertain whether it was all going to work, a voice cried out from the assembled crew, 'Relax! It's only bloody soccer, nobody cares.'

My call of the game itself was pretty average, with the grainy pictures from South America hardly helping my cause. The nicest part of the day was a text message from Paul Williams, the man I'd been brought in to replace. Paul wished me the best of luck, and told me that calling the Socceroos was an honour and a privilege, and that I should treat it as such. I've tried to remember that advice ever since. Tragically,

Paul took his own life a few years later, after suffering depression for many years – a sad waste of life for a lovely, sensitive man, and a very gifted commentator. May he find peace in death that he couldn't find in life.

I was beginning to realise why the SBS football crew were so wrapped up in the game on every level. To an extent, very few people *did* seem to care about the game, at least on the surface. A feeling that only grew when I called my first 'home' international in May of that year.

New ASA Chief Executive, John O'Neill, had been a mover and a shaker at the Australian Rugby Union prior to his switch to football. His success with the oval ball game had come largely on the back of the national team, the Wallabies, and he reasoned he needed to do the same thing with football.

Incredibly, before O'Neill's arrival, the Socceroos hadn't played a home international in almost three years, as the game stumbled from one crisis to another. Famously, in 2002, defender Scott Chipperfield had paid for his own flights to New Zealand, in order to represent the country at the Oceania Nations Cup. An understrength Australian team (shorn of its other major European stars, who weren't quite as accommodating as Chipperfield), lost to the Kiwis in the final, and thus missed out on a vital payday, via qualification to the Confederations Cup.

O'Neill knew he needed to get the national team front and centre again, as part of Frank Lowy's plan to restore the game to health. So in 2004, the ASA organised a two-game friendly series against Turkey, with one game to be played in Melbourne, and one in Sydney. SBS had the rights to broadcast both, but the scene that greeted us at Sydney's Aussie Stadium as I took my seat ahead of kick-off dismayed me. There were around 25,000 gathered at the venue – not a bad turnout – but most of them were wearing the red and white of Turkey!

I looked quizzically at Craig Foster, and asked him for an explanation. He didn't have one. 'This is football in Australia,' he said, almost apologetically. I scratched my head. How on earth was the game supposed to grow if the locals wouldn't even cheer their own national team?

In those days, the national team players were barely known in Australia. With the exception of Harry Kewell, Mark Viduka, and perhaps the likes of Mark Schwarzer and Lucas Neill at a push, they were unrecognisable to most Aussies.

The Socceroos lost both of the friendly encounters, but calling the national team at home had been a thrill, and I felt that the team, at least, had potential. Frank Farina's side contained a smattering of good, European-based pros, and when the

World Cup qualifying series started in Adelaide soon after, a certain Tim Cahill had been added to the mix.

I'd interviewed Cahill back in England in 2002; another reporting assignment for SBS after I'd agreed to join them, but before I'd actually emigrated. He was desperately trying to gain clearance from FIFA to represent his country, after he'd played in a junior tournament for Samoa a few years earlier. I knew him to be a handy player at Championship level for Millwall, but I doubt many of us envisaged just what sort of an impact he would have for Australia – and he would go on to provide me with some of my most memorable commentary moments too.

Before all that could eventuate however, we had a year without any domestic football in Australia, as the NSL was dissolved, and plans were put in place for a new competition.

While Frank Lowy and co were getting on with that particular job, my personal life was changing. My girlfriend and I had been an item for well over a year, but fate intervened when SBS advertised for a new sports newsreader in 2004. The post had previously been held by Mieke Buchan, who was heading off to pastures new in America. SBS wanted a female to replace her, probably to try and balance out the testosterone in the football department.

Senior producer, Joe di Meglio, had the task of sifting through the potential candidates, all tasked with reading an autocue for a mock *Toyota World Sport* bulletin. Although we'd teased Joe about his 'casting couch' it wasn't an easy job. Most of the girls hadn't been in front of a camera before, so although they looked the part, very few actually had the skills required. After two days, an exasperated Joe walked into the office, threw a few VHS tapes my way, and said 'You choose one. I'm done with it!'

Only one, in my opinion, had anywhere near the talent required to appear on TV. Her name was Stephanie Brantz. Steph had already done some work for SBS back in 1999–2000.

From Steph's first appearance on *The World Game* it was clear there was a bit of chemistry between us; the others even joked about me 'flirting' with her on air, which wasn't strictly true, but I liked her easy manner, her eagerness to learn, and of course, I couldn't deny that I found her attractive.

In the early days, our relationship was purely platonic. We had coffee at SBS's studios, we played the occasional game of tennis, and we caught up at other social functions where SBS personnel were also present. But when Steph told me her marriage was as good as over, things changed, and I had to make a decision. I was smitten, even though the circumstances were problematic, not least because Steph had children. But you don't choose who you fall in love with, and we've been together as a couple ever since. I'm not 'Dad' to Steph's children – they have their own father, who is very much involved in their lives – but I hope I'm their friend.

Back at SBS, things were ticking along workwise, though the issue of how to modernise *The World Game* programme was causing headaches for plenty of people – including me.

Ken Shipp, keen to revamp the show, had suggested I take on an additional role, that of associate producer, working alongside the executive producer, Joe di Meglio. But while I initially agreed, the title proved to be more trouble than it was worth. The problem with the four-hour programme, one that Joe and I in particular were wrestling with, was that it just wasn't snappy enough. Sure, it had all the football content the purists wanted, but there just weren't enough of them tuning in, and ratings remained average at best.

The action footage was supplemented by several lengthy panel 'chats', which more often than not, took on the air of a governmental cabinet meeting. Old men in suits, sagely discussing policy matters. It may have been important stuff (and for sure, no-one else was debating these issues), but as live television, it was as dry as a camel's armpit.

By this time, one of the panel regulars, Johnny Warren, had fallen ill. We knew Johnny had been diagnosed with cancer, but, initially we were told the prognosis was good. It wasn't until we happened to be in the Oaks pub in Neutral Bay one day, along with Johnny, that his vastly reduced physical state became apparent. He looked very frail. He also became much warmer towards me, gently chiding me for my smoking habits (with good reason – he'd been a lifelong smoker), and indulging in the sort of basic human conversation we should probably have had at the outset of my SBS career. Maybe his illness (which he'd kept quiet in its early stages) had been the reason for that.

Being from a different background of course, I was largely unaware of Johnny's contribution to football in Australia prior to my arrival Down Under. I'd read his book once I knew Australia was my destination, which gave me some idea, but I had little clue as to the reverence in which he was held by many fans. As if to underline that status, when Johnny passed away in November 2004, he was given a state funeral. We were to broadcast it live on SBS, and Craig Foster and I would be providing the audio feed. Commentary on a funeral? Another career first. Foster and I tried to 'call' the day with as much dignity as we could muster from our position in a side pew, but I suddenly had new-found respect for those TV people who have to talk their way through such sombre events on a more regular basis.

Foster's brand of knowledge, humour and (relative) youth, made him the obvious replacement for Johnny at SBS, but those weren't the only changes in the offing. Joe and I also thought that Andrew Orsatti needed a more challenging role, and so the plan was for him and me to front a new-style show, aimed at connecting with the younger generation. That, however, presented a problem as Les had been the staple of SBS football broadcasting since the 1980s. Perhaps he could be persuaded to relinquish some of his *World Game* commitments and do a pre-recorded segment for the new show, where he'd interview a top personality of the day? That was the plan. But the SBS management structure got us into all sorts of problems with this, and ended my working relationship with Joe di Meglio for good.

Easing Les aside from *The World Game* was no easy task. The programme was his baby, he'd even coined the term 'The World Game', and people worshipped him for keeping the game alive for all those years in such a hostile environment. So, we knew it had to be a gentle process of suggestion. Especially as he was also our boss.

Joe, however, agreed that with Johnny no longer around, Les needed to be moved into a different role. I left it to Joe (as the more senior producer) to put his theories to management and was therefore surprised to be called into the boss's office one day to discuss 'a few things'.

When I was asked what we had decided needed to be done to revamp *The World Game*, I presumed the same conversation had already taken place with Joe, so I disclosed exactly what Joe and I had discussed, and left 15 minutes later. Within five minutes, Joe appeared in my office, and said something along the lines of my having had 'clandestine meetings with the bosses'. Huh?

I had no idea what Joe meant, but sensed something was amiss. Within a week, I found out. Joe's contract wasn't being renewed. I had been made to look like the bad guy, with Joe believing – not unreasonably – that I'd gone into the boss's office to say Joe himself was the problem. It was untrue, but I could do little to assuage Joe's belief.

Whether that was the only reason for his departure, I couldn't say, but it all left a very sour taste in the mouth, and so I told Ken I no longer wanted the title of associate producer. I should never have accepted it in the first place anyway. Les remained a fixture on *The World Game.*

With all this bubbling away in the background, FFA was setting about trying to instigate a new domestic competition. With the announcement of the A-League, due to commence in late 2005, things appeared to be looking up for the game in Australia, and as if to demonstrate SBS's willingness to lead the way, the network decided it was going to send commentary teams to all the Socceroos away matches, starting that year.

For me, that meant a trip to South Africa in January 2005, as the Socceroos started their preparations for the World Cup campaign in earnest. But my spot on the plane to Durban was in doubt, due to an unwanted blast from the past.

CHAPTER NINE

CROCKED KNEE, CRANKY FRANKY & CRICKET

In late 2004, Steph and I were at Balmoral beach on a hot summer day – an ideal spot to take the kids on their school holidays. We brought with us a football – a round-ball type naturally – and for half an hour we ran around in the sand, with the kids laughing and screaming. That was until my dicky knee gave way on the shifting sands. Bang. Down I went, with the knee dislocated again, and me in agony.

Remembering the last time I'd experienced this pain, I knew there was only one way to relieve it – at least in part. I screamed at Steph to put the knee back in place, which is easily done, by simply straightening the leg back out – grabbing the ankle and giving it a gentle tug. But Steph wasn't keen, so there was only one thing for it. I punched my own knee back into its socket. Not recommended, and very painful, but better than the alternative, which (with the ligaments and tendons stretched beyond their normal remit) was absolute torture.

With the kids in shock, Steph helped me hop to solid ground, where she brought her battered old Barina (which had barely enough room for the kids as it was), and manoeuvred me into the back, me nursing my knee, which by now, had started to swell to almost double its size, with the skin drooping to the side, literally a bag of blood from the damage I'd done internally. All because of a kick about on the beach! I tried to reason that this was payback – football had given me so much, so I suppose occasionally it was entitled to give me a kick in the bollocks.

The upshot of the recurrence of my knee problems was that I needed an operation to 'clean out' the joint, and restore it to some sort of health. That wasn't the problem. It was my impending flight to Durban for the Socceroos friendly in January.

My surgeon, David Parker, said he could have me in the operating theatre by the Thursday of that week, leaving me around three weeks recovery time before the flight to South Africa. Even so, that was still a bit of a risk. Because of the swelling that invariably follows knee operations, it is not recommended any patient fly (particularly long distance) for at least a month, due to the risk of blood clots.

Still, there was no chance of putting surgery off. I had chipped a fair portion of bone off the back of my patella, there was considerable scarring, and the cartilage needed a trim too. I wasn't having much luck with my health in Australia, already having had an op in late 2003 for undiagnosed nasal polyps, which left me sneezing blood for months. The Australian medical care however, was thorough, and brilliant – much better than I was used to in the UK.

So, after undergoing surgery (which David kindly filmed for me to watch later), I entered three weeks of intensive physiotherapy and rehab, along with gulping down anti-inflammatories, to try and get me ready for the long flight to Durban.

A couple of days before the trip, David reckoned I was okay to travel, but he advised me to wear compression socks in order to reduce inflammation, and take blood thinning tablets in order to lessen the chance of clotting. It was a bit of a gamble, but I was loath to pass up the opportunity – this was going to be a big year for the Socceroos.

This was my first real, extended look at Frank Farina's team, and although they played well enough to earn a 1–1 draw, there were clouds on the horizon – and not just inside the stadium, where an electrical storm overhead knocked out our signal back to Australia for several minutes, with me continuing radio-style commentary without pictures.

As I've already mentioned, it was clear some in the Socceroos party had a problem with SBS. Although I'd covered a couple of home internationals, this was the first time I'd been on the road with the team, where you tend to see them at close quarters, attending training every day, and the tension was palpable. Some of the senior stars were less than enamoured with our presence. Given the travelling press contingent from Australia was tiny (as it normally is, even today), I felt this was a strange state of affairs, and rather petty.

Stuart Hodge, the then FFA media officer, believed it was the legacy of a long-running feud, between Frank Farina and SBS. A subsequent column from Andrew Orsatti on the fledgling World Game website had hardly helped matters either.

Orsatti's piece, written in mid-2003, entitled 'Let's be Frank!' had criticised Farina after a friendly international loss to Ireland. Orsatti opined that Farina had spent more than four years trying to mould a group of talented individuals into a cohesive unit, before answering his own question, 'Has he succeeded? NO.'

Farina had taken exception to the article, and we were bearing the full brunt of that animosity, especially as Orsatti was on this trip with me as a reporter. Things came to a head at the team hotel, where I'd been designated to conduct pre-game interviews with several players. We'd set up in the lobby area on an upper floor of the hotel, which was just around the corner from the team dining room. After interviewing Danny Tiatto, I asked him whether the next interviewee was ready. Danny said he wasn't sure where the player was, but told me to follow him into the dining room to check as to his whereabouts. This I did with some trepidation. Knowing how teams value their space from my days in England, I didn't particularly want to encroach into a private area, but Danny assured me it was okay, so I followed him. I probably only got two paces inside the dining room when the team manager, Gary Moretti, clocked me and got out of his chair.

Gesturing me back into the lobby area, he tore strips off me for entering the players' area, without pausing to hear any explanation. In a way, I could understand his anger, but I wasn't keen on the way he handled things so publicly.

I apologised and tried to explain, but this didn't seem to be enough. Eventually, after running out of steam, he reiterated his stance that we were to 'respect our private space' and wandered off with the hotel staff looking on agog. We completed our interview commitments, but I wouldn't forget that little contretemps.

Twenty-four hours after our fall-out, we were having dinner at our hotel (nearby, but separate to the Australian team hotel), and as we finished up, I noticed that, lo and behold, eating dinner at one of the tables in our restaurant, was Moretti, and several other members of the backroom staff. I sensed my moment.

Wandering over, I smiled and held out my hand to say hello, ensuring that the rest of the table heard my greeting. I then proceeded to inform him, quite forcefully, so the restaurant staff could hear, that this was a media hotel, and we really didn't appreciate having Federation types in our dining area, and could he please respect our privacy in future? Yes, I know it was childish, but it made me feel a bit better.

Later on in 2005, the hostilities between SBS and the national team developed into all-out war. In March, the Socceroos played a friendly at Sydney's Olympic

Stadium against Iraq. The fixture served two purposes: firstly, to give the team some much-needed experience of playing at home ahead of the vital World Cup qualifiers later in the year; and secondly, to try and earn some money for the still financially-strapped governing body.

To try and generate some interest, the two teams flew into Sydney on the same plane, with me slated to host a press conference at Kingsford Smith airport on a hastily arranged stage in the arrivals lounge. I thought this was a great idea, as most of the Socceroos were still unknown to many Australians, a fact that was confirmed upon my arrival at Sydney airport. Despite there being a crowd of fans waiting to greet the teams, just as it had been with the Turkey friendly the year before, nearly all of them were wearing the colours of Iraq.

Before I moved to Australia I knew it wasn't a traditional football country of course; I was prepared for that apathy, at least to an extent. But what I wasn't ready for, was the outright antipathy towards a sport that was, after all, the most popular on the planet. In those early days of the game's recovery, there was so much hostility towards 'soccer', it became nearly impossible not to react.

One piece, by Richard Hinds in the Fairfax media, summed up the tone of the language being used at the time. His piece in December 2004 described football fans as 'zealots' and 'soccerholic pedants' for daring to use the term 'football'. The proposed A-League was described as being 'full of bravado' and the author summed his own piece up by freely admitting the article was a 'pro-AFL or NRL or ARU argument'. 'Soccer' you see, had to know its place. Working in football, it felt like the game was constantly under attack, and you were on the defensive, almost as a default position.

Frank Farina seemed to be in that state almost permanently, although not, I hasten to add, towards me personally. His moniker of 'Cranky Franky' was well earned, especially in his dealings with SBS. So when Andrew Orsatti asked him some pretty pointed questions after the 2–1 win over the Iraqis, Farina's mood was reflected by a succession of mainly two or three word answers. At the conclusion of a rather strained interview, there was a suggestion Orsatti, mistakenly or otherwise, called Farina 'Graham' as in, his assistant, Graham Arnold, which, if true, can't have helped.

Orsatti was a decent fella, and good at his job. Although his emotional nature sometimes caused him problems, on this occasion, I had sympathy for him. I felt that his questions had been fair, after a rather unimpressive display.

But the tension simmered for days afterwards and the 'Roos were back in action just three nights later in Perth for another friendly, this time against Indonesia. As we boarded the plane to Perth, the two parties remained at loggerheads, with Orsatti instructed to remain silent on the issue by SBS (and silence was not easy for him!). All in all, it had been some introduction into the ways of the national team, and while I didn't condone the tactics being used by Farina and others in the governing body, it was beginning to dawn on me just how much influence SBS had on football in Australia. The public seemed to worship SBS and its coverage, but the lack of interest from any other media outlets meant we were in danger of loving the game to death.

A few days later, the Socceroos defeated Indonesia 3–0. It had been a pretty routine win against average opposition, with the main talking points an excellent display by Ante Milicic (who scored twice), and the disappointing crowd of just 13,000. Australia wouldn't play another international in WA in more than a decade, with the low turnout that night regularly cited as being one of the reasons.

Even though Orsatti and Farina publicly apologised to each other a month later, the relationship was hardly repaired, and increasingly, it was me the Federation looked to, to conduct interviews, and host their events. Being an MC for press conferences, awards nights and major announcements was a departure for me, but I rather enjoyed it. As the only major football broadcaster in the country, SBS had provided MCs for this type of work for years.

Some thought my working for them was disloyal, given the recent history and list of grievances. So, when Stuart Hodge asked me to host some function or other midway through 2005, I turned them down, telling Hodge that until SBS and the Federation had a better working relationship, I was better off staying out of it. Except of course, that didn't reflect the view of SBS management and I was given a dressing down; they needed me to continue to have some sort of working relationship with the governing body. Increasingly, I was the only SBS figure they'd even contemplate dealing with. I couldn't win.

Thankfully, the tensions dissipated as 2005 wore on, essentially because the 'Roos didn't have another international pencilled in until the Confederations Cup in June of that year. This allowed me a few months to concentrate on my day-to-day work, and I was also trying to help Steph develop as a broadcaster, as any good boyfriend with media experience would. I tried to help by recording every piece of live TV Steph did. Later, we'd go through it, frame by frame, using some of the tips I'd picked up at the

BBC in particular. It worked brilliantly. Steph was a quick learner, and by mid-2005, she'd graduated to hosting the *Toyota World Sport* bulletins when Les was unavailable.

Both our stars were on the rise, and as news of our personal relationship spread at SBS, the head of publicity, Jo Parker, began pushing us both quite strongly in the media. Jo probably spotted an angle she could work with, to help her do her job in creating a few headlines for the network. She also became a good friend, to Steph in particular.

Television is a strange beast when accompanied by a certain amount of recognition. You can become quite oblivious to how the spotlight is making you appear to your peers. In retrospect, I can see that I was probably coming across as rather too cocksure, and the fact I was English probably wasn't helping my case either. Some professional relationships cooled – some my fault, some down to the infamous 'tall poppy syndrome' I'd heard so much about.

In June 2005, I headed off to Germany to cover the Confederations Cup for SBS. Perhaps wisely, the network had decided to leave Orsatti at home, where he helped present the coverage from the Sydney studio. On this trip, it was to be just me, and Melbourne-based cameraman Pete Healy. The two of us got along famously, and, with much less tension in the air around the Socceroos' camp, the tournament was hugely enjoyable, even if Australia's results weren't.

In fairness, the 'Roos weren't expected to achieve much in a group that also contained hosts, Germany, plus South American heavyweights, Argentina. They performed well against both those nations, losing the first against the Germans 4–3, and the second 4–2. John Aloisi hit a purple patch in the tournament, netting four of Australia's five goals, and it was plain to see that there was massive potential in the squad.

But it was in Leipzig where it all fell apart in the third and final group game against Tunisia – the game in which the Australians were expected to be the most competitive. Farina opted to give some of his fringe players a run (with qualification already impossible), but it backfired spectacularly. Playing a flat 4–4–2, Farina started Jason Culina in an unfamiliar right-sided midfield role, and Simon Colosimo at left full-back. The team looked unbalanced, and put in a suitably disjointed performance. Tunisia won 2–0, but had two more disallowed; it could have been seriously embarrassing.

Still, Germany had been a great experience. I'd snagged an interview with another childhood hero, Franz Beckenbauer, and at the conclusion of the tournament, I headed off to spend a few days on holiday in Berlin. As a keen student of the Second World War, I'd always wanted to visit the places made famous by history, and the German capital didn't disappoint. I stayed in trendy Charlottenburg, and took in the (now mainly dismantled) Wall, the Jewish Museum, the Olympic Stadium and the Sachsenhausen concentration camp – a fascinating, if rather sobering experience. Within 12 months, I'd be back in Germany.

From Berlin, I headed over to England for a brief trip home, where I became caught up in another terrorist attack, this time the London bombings of July, 2005. It was the day before my departure back to Australia, and I was in Bishop's Stortford, visiting my old Polytechnic and BBC mate, Ian Kemp. News came through of the dreadful devastation that had been wrought on London, and Ian was concerned about the welfare of his wife, Susan, who was at work in the capital. All the phone lines were busy, and it was only after two hours of trying that he got word she was okay.

Meantime, all train services into Liverpool Street had been cancelled, which gave me a problem – I simply HAD to get back to London, as my flight to Sydney was leaving early the next morning from Heathrow, and I had belongings I needed to pack at my apartment in Notting Hill.

Eventually, limited services were reopened back into Liverpool Street, but once I arrived, it was clear there would be no tube services anywhere across London for the rest of that day. So, I began to walk, along with thousands of others. I walked for hours, right across the city, before eventually, free bus services began springing up, and I was able to criss-cross back through various districts towards where I needed to go. London had been awarded the 2012 Olympics the previous day and had been celebrating. Now, 24 hours later, it was in mourning. The streets were crawling with police and security personnel – it felt like World War III had started. An eerie experience.

Back in Australia, Frank Lowy was rather more concerned by the Socceroos' performances at the Confederations Cup. With the all-important World Cup qualifiers looming, the performance against Tunisia had set tongues wagging, and it wasn't long before Frank Farina was removed from his post as national team coach. Farina, to his credit, took the news remarkably well.

The now renamed Football Federation Australia knew that a crucial few months were ahead for the game. The new A-League was set to start in October 2005, and national-team success was imperative to drive momentum for the relaunched domestic competition.

The name change from 'soccer' to football had been a particularly momentous one in 2005. Many, including me, applauded the switch, as it brought Australia into line with the rest of the world. Others resented it hugely, particularly when John

O'Neill used it to launch a catchphrase that would come back to haunt him, at the outset of the A-League. 'Old soccer, new football,' was O'Neill's line. Journalistic gold of course, but massively divisive for those who felt they – who'd kept the flame alive in the dark days – were being cast aside for this brave, new, and rather uncertain, world. It's an issue that still rankles with many, all these years later.

The Hyundai A-League was launched by Frank Lowy in August of that year, and he literally begged football fans to come and support the new venture. I was at the launch, notable for Andrew Orsatti's bold question to Frank about his potential conflict of interest as both Chairman of the Federation, and major stakeholder in one of the new clubs, Sydney FC. Again, it was a fair question, but at the time, there was little appetite for that sort of debate; the game was coming through the other side of a long civil war, and with few other investors keen to risk their dollars, Lowy's involvement in Sydney FC was seen as necessity.

Outside the football community, there was never any doubt that the switch to 'football' was going to be controversial. In a country where Aussie Rules in particular likes to commandeer the word, and where Rugby League and Union use it interchangeably too, the claim of 'soccer' was always going to put a few offside.

So it proved. A plethora of articles began appearing in the mainstream Aussie press, taking potshots at the name change, and, rather more predictably, the game itself. Some beggared belief in their use of stereotypes – the old sheilas, wogs and poofters that Johnny Warren talked about in his book. It was lazy, clichéd journalism, with many of the articles having little basis in fact. It was as if 'soccer' was waging cultural warfare against the nation, and had to be stopped at the gates. It was utterly absurd.

What sickened me most were the pieces containing nasty racial undertones regarding people of ethnic background. I'd had enough, and penned a piece called 'Can you smell the fear?' on the World Game website. It was deliberately provocative against the other codes in order to make its point. I belittled Aussie Rules and Rugby League as provincial games for simple minds, while defending the game from the tired prejudices; prejudices that were churned out so often, it seemed the writers suffered some form of football Tourette Syndrome.

The piece received a huge amount of feedback. Many were supportive; a minority were not, and were suitably riled by my ridicule of the other codes. Good, they'd taken the bait, and had received a small dose of their own medicine.

Such articles are still written today of course, but their frequency has stalled, and the journalists who write them are now held to account much more than ever before.

I like to think I might have played a small part in that, although I certainly wasn't the first to notice it.

Meanwhile, as Frank Lowy was busy launching the new domestic competition, and appointing Guus Hiddink to be Frank Farina's successor (more on which later), I was preparing for a challenge of an entirely different nature.

In a shock move, SBS had taken a punt on acquiring the rights to broadcast the 2005 Ashes series in England. The network had no history of broadcasting cricket, but Channel 9, the nation's usual service provider, had passed up on the opportunity, reasoning that England's competitiveness was far too flimsy (they hadn't won a series since the 1980s) to ensure bumper ratings during Australian primetime.

I was as surprised as anyone at this move, but with football occupying most of my energies, I took little interest as to the progress SBS were making in finding a team to present their nightly shows. That all changed one weekday morning when I took a call on my mobile from my boss who said they'd interviewed several potential hosts but hadn't really found anyone suitable for the head presenting role. Jo Parker had put forward my name, backing up her argument by saying it was good policy for SBS to promote their own internal talent, rather than employing outsiders. Was I interested?

I had to be honest, and my initial answer was not really. For a start, I hadn't covered cricket in any real shape or form since my days in BBC local radio – my knowledge was rusty to say the least. More importantly, I could only imagine the public reaction to an Englishman, a relatively unknown Englishman at that, getting the top gig on an Ashes series being broadcast in Australia.

I told them I'd think about it, but I wasn't overly keen. Steph and I were driving back from Canberra, where she'd been hosting a function, so we had plenty of time to discuss this new development. By the time we hit the southern suburbs of Sydney, she'd convinced me this was a chance in a lifetime, and that I'd be a fool to pass it up. So, albeit a little reluctantly at first, I accepted the gig. My first trip was to the bookshop, to stock up on a host of Ashes-related tomes – I was going to have to play catch-up on my knowledge of cricket, and the clock was already ticking.

As the first Test drew closer, my apprehension wasn't helped the day I was called in for a pre-series publicity shoot, alongside the two pundits SBS had employed to provide expertise. I knew all about Dean Jones and Greg Matthews's cricket histories of course – both former test players of some repute – but I knew nothing of their personalities. I was about to find out.

After saying 'Hello' to me in the studio, the pair ignored me for the next 20 minutes, reminiscent of my experience in Manchester, all those years ago. I thought I'd break the ice.

'So boys, how are you going to react on air when England win the Ashes?' I enquired somewhat provocatively.

'That won't happen. Three one to Australia, minimum. Trust me, we actually know about cricket,' replied Jones rather sniffily.

It was true that my lack of cricket knowledge presented something of a potential problem. But I decided to try and work with it, rather than try to con people. After all, for every aficionado watching our coverage, I reasoned there were bound to be many others – like myself – who weren't necessarily au fait with Jason Gillespie's averages, or didn't quite understand what a 'flying saucer' was.

So, I opted to play the dumb host in the early stages. I asked questions – lots of them – and the viewers seemed to enjoy the fact that a presenter was actually doing what he was paid to do: seek proper answers to legitimate queries, rather than merely opinionate.

Slowly, Dean and Mo started to realise what I was doing, and they grew into their roles of kindly teachers, with a fair bit of humour thrown in for good measure. That was exactly how I'd envisaged it. I knew I could never hope to wow the audience with my vast cricket knowledge, but I could try to make it an entertaining, and hopefully informative watch, to complement the live action.

We were helped of course, by what turned out to be arguably the best Ashes series in living memory. It didn't seem that way in the early stages. In the first test, Australia crushed England at Lord's by 239 runs, and Channel 9's decision to opt out seemed to be a good one.

As to where my allegiances lay? From day one, I was determined that I wouldn't give anyone a chance to make my nationality an issue, at least on air. Already, the pre-series publicity had gone exactly as I predicted it would. An interview with Sydney's *Daily Telegraph* had touched on all manner of subjects: my cricket background (or lack of), SBS's new venture, key men of the series, Dean and Greg, etcetera. The paper's headline? 'Pom to head up Ashes coverage'. Subtle as a sledgehammer.

I had been equally insistent to the show's producers, Noel Brady and David Tunnicliffe, that the daily discussion panels weren't just going to degenerate into a jingoistic slugfest, with me defending England, and the other two being pro-Australia.

On screen, Dean and Mo occasionally tried to goad me into retaliation when they'd say something overly jingoistic, or let the 'p' word slip (which I'd insisted was not to be used, as I wanted us to set an example to the rest of the media), always accompanied by an apology of course. But mainly, it was good humoured, and the chemistry seemed to be there from day one. Their coolness towards me evaporated, even as early as the opening link ahead of the first Test. I nailed a tricky opening sequence, handled the panel chat with ease, before handing over, bang on time to our reporter, ex-cricketer Michael Slater, in London.

'You've done this before haven't you?' said Jones.

The fact they could trust me to be a competent host seemed to relax both Dean and Greg, although, as is the case with any broadcasting team, both had their little nuances that needed taking into consideration.

Dean's self-confidence was legendary. As a fine batsmen for many years for Australia, he had probably needed all that belief to stay at the top for so long, but occasionally it was grating. On other occasions, it was downright funny.

One such incident happened on day two of that first Test. Knowing I was a football man, Dean proudly told me that he'd just completed a business deal that was going to net him thousands – if not millions – of dollars in the future. His purchase? He'd secured the rights to the term 'Soccer Ashes' which, in his opinion, was going to be the next biggest sporting event between England and Australia. This, sadly, was typical of the way some people I'd met in Australia viewed football. They only seemed able to rationalise a game that was anathema to them, by framing it in the context of their own sporting experience.

Needless to say, 12 years later, we are still waiting for the 'Soccer Ashes' to take off. I wonder why?

Greg, or 'Mo' to everyone who knew him, was a totally different kettle of fish. Mo, we quickly learned, only operated at two speeds. It was either 100 per cent or zero. In other words, if he was 'on' then you couldn't shut him up – he was full of ideas, jokes, weird seventies phrases such as 'you crazy cats', while physically, he was almost bouncing up and down inside (and outside) the studio. If you caught him on one of his 'down' days, then you could hardly get a word out of him. It wasn't always easy to work with, and I was no psychologist, so I just had to try and get on with it, and try to coax the best out of him and Deano.

But the cricket helped. Boy, did it help.

The second Test at Edgbaston was where the series really caught fire. The key was an injury sustained by Glenn McGrath as he was warming up ahead of the first day's play – inadvertently treading on a cricket ball and badly damaging ligaments in his ankle. It was enough to rule him out, and with replacement Michael Kasprowicz not nearly as effective, England smelt a weakness.

By day four, the hosts needed to take just the last two Australian wickets, while Ponting's team needed 107 runs. It looked England's Test for all money, but Brett Lee and Michael Kasprowicz put in a defiant stand that took the Aussies to the brink of victory. They were just two runs short when Steve Harmison let rip another short ball at Kasprowicz, who, in attempting to fend the delivery off, got a feather on the ball. Geraint Jones took the catch behind the stumps, and England had won by the narrowest of margins.

All the England players ran off to celebrate except one. Andrew Flintoff walked slowly to Brett Lee to offer a handshake and an arm across the shoulder. It was a moment that many agreed, encapsulated what sport should be all about. Replays later showed that Kasprowicz had only touched the ball with his glove AFTER his hand had come away from the bat – technically, he'd been not out.

We had only a four-day break between the second and the third Ashes Tests, and with the shifts starting at 7 pm (you can probably call that 4 pm if you include research), and only finishing at 4 am, the tiredness was starting to creep in.

I had a whole new respect for those who work day in, day out, covering cricket; it was almost like being an opener, who carries their bat throughout the entire day. Mental concentration and physical stamina were the key elements, and I longed for the day I could go back to my cushy life covering football, where the game was over in 90 minutes.

This being the infancy of websites, forums and social media, we were also asked to do web chats, Q&As, and write articles on the day's play. It was enjoyable, but full-on, particularly when the inevitable rain of an English summer meant being on standby, at a moment's notice, ready to pick up and talk informatively about what may, or may not be happening.

Channel 4, whose pictures we were relaying, did an excellent job with the coverage that (northern) summer. Not only was their commentary excellent, but in Simon Hughes, they had found a gem. Hughes's pieces on 'the analyst' segment were compulsive viewing. He clearly had a magnificent cricket brain, but he also had the gift of being able to deconstruct something complex, and translate it into basic English for us ordinary plebs to understand.

One such piece concerned England's use of 'Merlin', a machine designed to try and replicate the bowling action and variations of Shane Warne, a player the English had never really got to grips with. Hughes took us through all the gadgetry and theory behind its construction and use, in a fascinating three minutes of television, before handing back to Richie Benaud in the commentary box. After a suitably pregnant pause, the old master said, 'Hmmm…but has it got a brain?' Gold.

That third Test was to end in a draw, mainly due to the time lost for rain on day three, when only a handful of overs were possible. So, with two Tests to play, it was 1–1, and all to play for. Every day seemed to bring more controversy, and then in the fourth Test, England really pushed the boundaries (no pun intended), by bringing substitute Gary Pratt onto the field. Pratt was a specialist fielder, and he proceeded to run out Ricky Ponting, who made his displeasure all-too clear as he made his way back to the pavilion.

This was the sort of edgy cricket that had been missing from England's game, and Pratt had been brought on for legitimate reasons, after an injury to Simon Jones. The studio view was the complete opposite of course, feeling England had pulled a fast one – but I felt that this brinksmanship was the sort of stuff the Aussies had done without hesitation for years. Remember Steve Waugh's team, and their 'mental disintegration?' That worked a treat against fragile English minds. Now, the boot was on the other foot.

England needed just 129 to win by day four, but as was becoming customary, it became a nailbiter. Shane Warne took wicket after wicket, and it seemed England would crack – but they didn't, getting home by just three wickets, and taking a 2–1 lead.

It was fitting that this gripping series would go down to the fifth and final Test at the Oval; and fitting too, that right up until the fifth day, the destiny of the urn was still in the balance. A draw was enough for the hosts of course, and the English weather decided to lend a hand, with more rain delays edging Michael Vaughan's team closer to a first Ashes success in nearly two decades.

But the tension returned when McGrath (now fit again) and Warne, operating in tandem at either end, started to take wickets. I remember being sat in the studio midway through that morning session, and feeling rather sick at the prospect of having to go on air and look pleased about what looked increasingly like an Australian success! But a couple of uncharacteristic dropped catches swung the momentum back towards the hosts, and as the lunch break loomed, England could breathe a little more easily.

During the panel chat, I allowed myself one tiny moment of patriotism. I picked up on Glenn McGrath's usual pre-Ashes prediction of a 5–0 Australian success, saying it hadn't quite turned out that way. Dean responded immediately by saying, 'I said it would be 3–1!'

My response? 'It still might be Dean, it still might be, just not to Australia!'

Any lingering hopes Australia had of squaring the series and keeping the urn were wiped out completely by Kevin Pietersen in the afternoon session. His maiden Test century steered Andrew Strauss's team home, a magnificent 158 ensuring the final Test ended in a draw.

The scenes from the Oval made for great television, and the Aussies were magnanimous in defeat – with Dean jokingly throwing the replica urn we had positioned on our studio desk (as a prop) at me, the moment we came back on air, saying 'There you are, it's yours!'

I was pleased England had won, but more importantly, how we'd made people sit up and take notice of SBS as a competent, and hopefully unbiased broadcaster of cricket. The only glitch in our coverage had been the moment Glenn McGrath had taken his 500th Test wicket during the first Test at Lord's. SBS was also covering the Tour de France, and as the two overlapped, we had to perform a delicate balancing act by swapping around between the locations in the early days of the Ashes series. Our executive producer, Noel Brady, had taken the decision to stay with the Tour de France, as there was an exciting denouement to a particular stage in the race, thus, we inadvertently missed McGrath's big moment as he dismissed Marcus Trescothick. We received plenty of stick for that.

But generally speaking, most critics seemed to think the studio dynamic between myself, Dean and Greg had worked. SBS earned fantastic ratings (and apparently a fair bit of cash from advertising) for a memorable series, and I earned plenty of kudos for holding it all together.

When the series was over, Steph and I headed down the New South Wales coast for a few days rest and relaxation. I started to receive all manner of offers to speak at cricket clubs and MC cricket functions. It was flattering, but as much as I had enjoyed a different challenge, I was already itching to get back to what I knew, and loved.

CHAPTER TEN

10

BRITNEY, BAJO FLORES & MENTAL BLANKS

In fact, I'd already dipped my toe back into the 'real' world, even while the Ashes was still going on.

On 3 September 2005, just before that fateful Test at the Oval, football fans in Australia got their first glimpse of Guus Hiddink, the new coach of the Socceroos. Appointed amid much fanfare, the charismatic Hiddink had been charged with delivering the nation's first World Cup qualification in 32 years, and his first test was the two-legged Oceania qualifiers against the Solomon Islands.

The Solomons had, surprisingly, knocked out Australia's perennial regional competitor, New Zealand, but offered little resistance in the first leg in Sydney. Australia scored three good goals, including two utter peaches from Jason Culina and Mark Viduka. But the other four were gifts from a totally outclassed opposition, with goalkeeper Francis Aruwafu having a nightmare, in a 7–0 rout.

In truth, Australia hadn't played that well, and Hiddink knew there was still much work to do before the real test against the South Americans in November. But already, he was starting to work his magic, in particular, installing Viduka as captain. I thought this was a masterstroke, as Viduka had often been the subject of criticism for his rather lacklustre international displays, and especially his lack of goals. His debut as captain brought him a brace, and even given the low standard of the Solomons, something was stirring.

Viduka, incidentally, was and remains, one of my favourite-ever Socceroos. A man who had so much talent, yet he was the most down-to-earth guy, who always had time to stop and say hello. I always thought his decision not to return to play in the A-League was probably a wise move; it preserved his legacy, at a time when his body was probably beginning to struggle with the demands of full-time football. Many years later, I had a drink with 'Dukes' and Mark Bosnich in a Melbourne bar ahead of the 2015 Grand Final, and I enquired as to whether he was attending the day after?

'Nah, I don't have a ticket,' he said without any trace of humour. That was Dukes to a tee – and even after I'd suggested he might just be able to get one, he said he preferred to be with his kids. A terrific bloke with no pretension, and just quietly, what a player he was too.

Perhaps buoyed by my success that year, I had a little moment of pretentiousness myself following the Socceroos second-leg win over the Solomons, when I hosted Damien Lovelock's 'Fans' Corner' one weekend on *The World Game*. Damo's segment included a weekly question on a particular football topic. The answer (as decided by the fans who'd voted via the website) was revealed on the show the following Sunday. This particular weekend, Damo's question concerned the English Premier League relegation battle. Which clubs, he wanted to know, were going to finish in the bottom three. There were several choices, plus Damo's usual 'joke' option of Britney Spears. As we came off the back of the 'graphic' (the screen shot that shows the viewers the choices), Damo asked me my thoughts.

'I think we'd all like to see Britney Spears go down,' I quipped.

In 2005, I thought that was a funny line. In retrospect, I cringe when I remember I said it live on air. It was pub talk on television – the very sort of line I hated from others. Perhaps I'd become too Australian already?

There were one or two complaints, but thankfully, it didn't make much of a splash among the general public. Ken Shipp mentioned it to me in passing, remarking that it probably wasn't the smartest line ever, but that was the end of the matter. I got lucky.

But things were about to get a lot more serious, as Australia prepared for their four-yearly do or die World Cup qualifier against old foe Uruguay. FFA was determined that after the defeat at the hands of the same opposition in 2001, nothing was going to be left to chance this time. No expense was to be spared, no stone unturned, in the quest to give the Socceroos every chance of reaching their holy grail.

This meant, in the first instance, a camp of several days, to be held in nearby Argentina, ahead of the first leg in Montevideo. Four years prior, Australia had, somewhat naively, flown straight into the lion's den in the Uruguayan capital, leaving the airport via the usual passenger exit. There, they'd been met by a posse of Uruguayan fans, who'd jostled and (allegedly) spat at them as they made their way onto the team bus. Many believed they'd lost the tie, there and then, even though they'd taken a 1-goal advantage into the second leg at the Centenario.

This time, Australia would only fly into Montevideo the day before the game (as per FIFA protocol), after doing their preparation work in the relatively neutral territory of Buenos Aires. I flew into Argentina on the same plane as some of the backroom team, along with SBS unit manager, Jenny Hiscocks, who was designated to ensure everything ran smoothly with our host broadcaster, the infamous Traffic company, which, many years later, was to face serious allegations of corruption in relation to TV contracts awarded by FIFA. It was a lengthy journey: Sydney to Auckland, then Auckland to Santiago, and finally Santiago to Buenos Aires. But that last flight gave me my first glimpse of the Andes, a beautiful sight to behold, with the snow-capped mountains contrasting wonderfully with the dry, scrubby foothills below.

The camp was tough for the players. Hiddink – that wily old fox – wanted to prepare the players for some of the conditions Australia would face in Uruguay, so the training ground he'd chosen wasn't some opulent, state-of-the-art facility, but the rather basic Estadio Pedro Bidegain, home of San Lorenzo. The ground was situated in Bajo Flores, a particularly down at heel part of the Argentine capital, where poverty and crime was rife, and where mangy looking dogs roamed the streets. It was not a part of the city where you wanted to be alone during the day, and certainly not at night. Hiddink wanted to take his players out of their comfort zone.

Here, while Hiddink tried to whip his team into shape, I had the awkward task of attempting to create daily reports on the squad's progress – not easy when my camera crew consisted entirely of locals, most of whom spoke barely a word of English.

We employed a translator, a bubbly, attractive girl called Gabbi, but even her English wasn't smart enough for technical terms such as 'pan wide' or 'zoom', so every day was a battle to get the pictures we needed. It didn't help that the South American style of filming footballers seemed to be totally at odds from ours, with the lens constantly on the move, and rarely settling on the players face. Many of the rough shots, known as 'rushes', looked like they'd been filmed by someone who was drunk.

This being the South American summer time, it was also hot and sticky, and when a press conference or interview session per day was factored in along with the jet lag, the days were lengthy. In 2005, technology wasn't quite what it is today, so once the package was cut and voiced, we couldn't merely upload it digitally to be picked up by our people back in Sydney, we had to trek out to the Traffic studios in a different part of the city, for it to be fed via a satellite booking. In whatever time remained, I was also trying to do my research, in preparation for a hugely important commentary.

On the final day before our departure for Uruguay, I conducted a long interview with Guus Hiddink at the team hotel, which gave me an insight into the charisma of the man. With a World Cup qualifier just around the corner, some coaches would have been twitchy, irritated even, by having to do a lengthy interview for television. But I'd seen Hiddink in action before of course – at the 1998 World Cup – and he was just the same in Buenos Aires.

Breezing in airily, Hiddink shook the hand of every member of the camera crew before sitting down and jovially answering each of my questions. He was ultra-confident, without being arrogant, until a sudden gust of wind (we were filming in the hotel courtyard) blew over one of the lights. Gabbi, our vivacious young interpreter, retrieved it, and we set up to start again. Only this time, Hiddink flinched at my question. I wondered whether the incident had broken his zen-like state. Not a bit of it.

'Sorry,' said Guus in his thick Dutch accent. 'I am just now so mesmerised by this beautiful young lady, I am struggling to think of words!' he grinned as he gazed at Gabbi.

That was Guus to a tee. Always a charmer with the ladies, always very aware of his commitments to the media, but always in charge. His easy manner was disarming, and you wanted him to succeed because he seemed such a nice guy.

Some of the Socceroos didn't think so, however. Right from the outset, Hiddink had made clear that no-one was guaranteed a spot in his team. That didn't suit the players like Mark Schwarzer, who thrived on the security of knowing he was number one. Others, like Tim Cahill, Mark Bresciano and even Harry Kewell, would spend time on the bench during Hiddink's reign, and not all of them enjoyed the experience.

But against Uruguay, Hiddink had very little margin for error; he knew he had to get his tactics just right. Los Celestes were a dangerous team, full of brilliant talents such as Alvaro Recoba, Diego Forlan and Dario Silva.

FFA had pushed the boat out to provide assistance – or, in this case, the team bus. Anxious to avoid those airport scenes from 2001, the governing body hired two buses. The first, with blacked out windows, emerged from the private terminal where the 'Roos landed, and departed Montevideo airport in full view of the (relatively few) Uruguayan fans who had gathered to try and put the Australians off their stride. That bus however, was empty.

The real bus took a different route, thus bypassing the public completely. It worked a treat. The identity of the team hotel however, couldn't be kept secret, and the squad was mobbed upon their arrival, although the scenes were fairly good-natured.

We were due to be staying at a different hotel nearby, but when Jenny flew on ahead (to meet up with our South American correspondent, Tim Vickery, and executive producer Noel Brady), they found that the hotel had been rather economical with the truth in their advert. It was, by all accounts, a complete shithole. So, we were switched to the 'Roos' hotel – the only other establishment in town that had rooms free.

Les Murray (who'd flown in later to Argentina) and I received this news as we prepared to follow the team on the short hop from Buenos Aires to Montevideo. The plane we flew on however, looked like something out of the dark ages. An old Aerolineas Uruguayas Fokker, which had decor straight out of the seventies, and the noisiest propellers I'd ever heard. The 40-minute flight was the longest of my life, as the little 20-seater plane bounced up and down like a kite in the winds over the River Plate. I've never been so glad to be back on terra firma.

Come the day of the first leg, I was excited. This was a return to the big time, and I was looking forward to calling a game that really mattered. It was a bonus to have Tim Vickery along. Tim was someone who I'd helped give a break to many years previously. Then, he'd wandered into the BBC and asked to see someone from the World Service Sports Department – I just happened to be on shift that day. That was in the late 1990s, and he explained he was about to emigrate to Brazil, having met a Brazilian girl at the local theatre in London where he'd worked. Tim was football-mad, knew how to write, and offered his services as a stringer if we ever needed anything covered in South America.

As luck would have it, the BBC's South American correspondent, Wyre Davies, was just about to return to the UK after a long stint so Tim's timing was perfect. We took him on at World Service, and Tim has since forged an excellent career in broadcasting and written journalism. His knowledge of the game in the region is unsurpassed, in my opinion. His expertise with the Uruguayans was of invaluable assistance to me too, as he detailed everything he knew about Jorge Fossati's likely line-up.

As we made our way to the ground, I wondered where the Uruguayan fans were; it was deathly quiet, and there were only two and a half hours to go before kick-off (the timing of which had been the subject of much toing and froing, for reasons I'll go into later). But as we made our way into the stands from the bowels of the cavernous Centenario, it became all too obvious where the supporters were – they were already inside! The place was full to the brim, and the noise was phenomenal. There were 50,000 people, all bouncing up and down singing 'Soy Celeste!' ('I am sky blue') – it was an awesome sight.

My commentary box was quite a cramped affair, and fairly low in the stand – not the ideal vantage point from which to provide match commentary (and I was riding solo, in the days before SBS added a summariser). But that wasn't my only concern.

At the end of the match, I'd been slated to do a live two-way back to Sydney, which meant a cameraman had been helpfully placed in the doorway of my commentary box (there not being enough room for the two of us, plus the camera to fit inside), and when Uruguay scored what proved to be the only goal of that first leg, my Spanish-speaking cameraman couldn't help himself. At the very moment I called Dario Rodriguez's name (the goal scorer), I heard a loud 'Gooooooooooooooool!' behind me, as my cameraman celebrated his nation's strike. With a wave of the hand, I begged him to be quiet. He simply continued his scream and the next noise I heard was that of the door slamming behind him, and the camera (pushed forward because of the lack of space) banged into my chair behind me.

Now, it was vital Australia didn't concede a second; I knew that if Uruguay doubled their lead, it would be almost mission impossible back in Sydney four days later. The Uruguayans laid siege to the Australian goal late on, with Mark Schwarzer pulling off a couple of excellent saves. It finished 1–0 to the home team and Australia were in with a great chance of making the World Cup.

This is where Australia's planning really came into its own. The battle over the kick-off time in Montevideo was not just idle posturing, it was all about the flights back to Australia. The Uruguayans had tried to charter a flight for their team to make the dash to Sydney for the second leg, but failed in their efforts. The next tactic then, was to try to delay the Australians, by getting the kick-off put back. Originally, they wanted a 9 pm start, but FIFA intervened and set the time for 6 pm.

Australia were ready; they had chartered their own flight through sponsors, Qantas. As soon as the full-time whistle blew at the Centenario, the players were being hurried off the pitch in order to board the bus, bound for the airport. Unbeknown to all of us at the time, the Qantas plane had been reconfigured with massage tables, extra physios employed and the players' meal times and sleep patterns were all set to Sydney time. The plane even landed briefly in the Cook Islands, in order that the players might be allowed to get out and stretch on the airport grass.

Uruguay, meantime, arrived first in Sydney, but many of their players had been squashed into economy class at the back of a regular commercial flight. The 'Roos travelled in comfort with nobody but the players and staff on the flight.

The attention to detail was matched by Guus Hiddink. A good example was Hiddink's decision to leave Harry Kewell on the bench for the second leg. Many were surprised at this move, but as ever, there was method behind the Dutchman's apparent madness. Kewell came on early, and proceeded to have a hand in the all-important goal.

For the second leg, SBS had decided to give me a summariser. Craig Foster and I had worked reasonably well doing commentary together in previous internationals (along with Champions League games), although I felt he wasn't overly keen on the co-commentating gig – he much preferred to be in the studio alongside Les Murray (or Orsatti), where he could properly analyse games at half and full-time.

What people watching at home didn't know, was that Fozzie and I had already had a bit of a falling out, in the build-up to the qualifiers.

I'd queried Craig about his criticisms on *The World Game* of English coaches and he told me that the real object of his ire was the Australian Institute of Sport football programme, along with the National Training Centres (NTCs). Foster felt that they weren't producing the right type of player, and what Johnny Warren had labelled the 'Pommy mafia' (negative context again), who held most of the top jobs, was to blame.

While I didn't have enough inside knowledge to know whether Foster was right or not on the specifics, I did know that at least one Englishman who'd been central to the programme down the years, Ron Smith, was hugely respected in football circles, and that he'd helped develop many of the current Socceroos. I felt that Craig needed to go after specific targets, or else keep quiet. He was literally throwing a blanket over all English coaches, purely because of the colour of their passport.

Now, it's true that English-born coaches were (and still are) prevalent in Australia, and it's also true that Australia traditionally mimics England in terms of its playing approach. The old-style 'muscular Christianity' espoused by the English system was clearly outdated, and while I didn't disagree with Foster's sentiments in essence, in practice I thought he was being hugely unfair by using a group stereotype to get at certain individuals. Not every English coach is the same, and

Foster's old coach Terry Venables was hardly a long-ball, up and at 'em type of coach, thus proving the point.

Les Murray, in particular, had always been unflinchingly critical of anyone who used other sweeping national stereotypes, particularly against South Americans, and especially when they were labelled 'divers' on a football field. He felt such statements reinforced old prejudices, and were unacceptable on a multicultural network.

What really kicked things off was an article that appeared in the now defunct *Soccer International* magazine. It was a feature on coaching, and the way forward for Aussie football. In it, Foster was quoted extensively, and this one caught my eye immediately.

'Give me the keys to the NTCs tomorrow, and every English coach walks today. I don't care, I'll pay them out, they're gone. And I don't care about their tactical arguments. "Yeah, but we're coaching this and we're coaching that." I don't care.'

I thought that was a disgraceful thing to say. Substitute the word 'English' for any other nationality, and there would have been an outcry.

Trouble was brewing. Still, we were on good enough terms to work together at the Olympic Stadium that famous night, 16 November 2005, when 32 years of hurt finally came to an end for Australian football.

Right from the off, there was the sense that Australia knew exactly what it had to do. Even the fans played their part, drowning out the Uruguayan anthem with a chorus of boos. Some in the mainstream Aussie media didn't like that, feeling it disrespectful. In Montevideo four days earlier, the Australian anthem had been similarly silenced, but the non-football types who wrote the later articles probably hadn't watched that first match, given it had kicked off at 7 o'clock on a Sunday morning, Australian time. Those inside the stadium on 16 November – proper football fans, by and large – had, and they knew they had a duty to respond, by letting the Uruguayans know they were in for a game.

There's a key moment on the SBS coverage, which shows just how unnerved the Uruguayan coach, Jorge Fossati, looks as the anthem draws to a close. He's like a caged tiger, as he shifts from one foot to another, his bulging eyes glancing fearfully around the packed arena; he wasn't expecting the Australians to be such unfriendly hosts.

Aside of the big moments, I can't remember too much about the game itself – or the call. Of course, I remember that Hiddink made a change early in the game, taking off Tony Popovic, who'd just been yellow-carded, and replacing him with Harry Kewell, who then went on to tee up Mark Bresciano for the only goal, with the greatest miskick in the nation's football history.

I remember too, that Uruguay had a couple of fantastic chances to see Australia off. Recoba and Fonseca missing the target completely, when it looked easier to score. But it's what happened when the final whistle blew that lives long in the memory of every Australian sports fan. It also etched Craig Foster's (and my) name into the history books so far as commentary is concerned.

By the time extra time came around, Fozzie had, what we in the TV business call, 'gone'. He was so emotionally involved in the game. Applauding (literally in some places – I had to hold his hands together to stop him clapping more than once) every good Australian pass, and moaning at every mistake.

So when it came to the dreaded penalties, I thought I was more or less on my own. But in fairness to Craig, he gathered himself and came up with the goods in the shootout. Here's how it went out on SBS…word for word:

> SH: It's Harry Kewell who is going to go first for the Socceroos…and if you thought the 90 minutes and extra time brought drama, you ain't seen nothing yet folks! Here we go. It's Harry Kewell against Fabio Carini, first penalty Australia…GOAL! Beautifully put away by Harry Kewell.
>
> CF: Sheer class Harry…sheer class!
>
> SH: (Replay) Was it ever in any doubt?
>
> CF: No. Not with the game he's had tonight. You don't have the career he's had, with being a shrinking violet. You step up, and you get the job done.
>
> SH: 1–nil for Australia in the penalty shootout. Now next up is the man who scored the winning goal in Montevideo, it's the left-footed Dario Rodriguez. The benches, linked arm in arm. Rodriguez against Mark Schwarzer. SAVED by Schwarzer! He's done it again, in the shootout, Mark Schwarzer is the hero for Australia!
>
> CF: It's a massive save. It's huge. It is huge! He stood his ground beautifully. I liked it when Rodriguez stunted his run, not once but twice. Schwarzer's fast off his line, he's mobile. He didn't move early, waited for the kick. Mark, you've done it once son, you can do it again!
>
> SH: Nice height it had to be said. Listen, still a long way to go in this shootout. You still need nerves of steel from the spot. Next up is

Lucas Neill, who's had a great game. It's Neill. It's 2–nil! Australia 2–nil up in the shootout, and Lucas Neill was the calmest man on the pitch there. Pressure? What pressure?

CF: Two steps, thank you very much. Picked the spot, knew where he was going. Urging the crowd on Lucas!

SH: Oh it's tense. It's so tense.

CF: The guys on halfway, arm in arm. Team spirit for the jersey!

SH: And here's Gustavo Varela. Another save from Schwarzer and Australia are nearly there. It's Varela…ohhh…it's just underneath Schwarzer!

CF: It's too good. Again, he held his ground Schwarzer. He's reading them, he's not going early. It's worked once. Now Tony Vidmar… what a way to cap off a memorable career.

SH: Well Vidmar was the man who captained Australia to a famous victory over Brazil in the Confederations Cup a few years ago. He can draw on fourteen years' experience as a pro, but surely he's never had a kick as important as this.

CF: Well he's done it all – he has done it all. He's seen every situation, but he hasn't seen this. Just pick your spot.

SH: Come on Tony. It's Vidmar. And it's beautifully put away!

CF: Good on ya son!

SH: 3–1 Australia in the shootout! They are edging closer to the World Cup!

CF: Outstanding. He's the hero. Tony Vidmar is the hero tonight. Bresciano finished the goal, but Tony Vidmar's been a colossus, in the tradition of Yankos and the rest. He's been massive.

SH: Now, a lot of responsibility on a very young man's shoulders for Uruguay. Fabián Estoyanoff against Mark Schwarzer. Here we go… beautifully tucked away by Estoyanoff. 3–2.

CF: Yep, we must get this one. You must get this one.

SH: Have to score.

CF: You must go to 4–2, and put the pressure on this next kick, or you open the door for a possible 3–3. Mark Viduka, and rightly so.

SH: He's played the captain's role, Mark Viduka. Graham Arnold [assistant coach] can't look. Viduka…ohhhh, he's put it wide!! Would you believe it? Mark Viduka…who was enormous in the first leg.

CF: Mark Schwarzer now. Oh he's been enormous tonight as well. People miss penalty kicks…Roberto Baggio missed, Michel Platini missed in a World Cup. He's been a great captain, it's now up to Mark Schwarzer. This would be a great one to save. A great one to save.

SH: Schwarzer just, perhaps a little mind game with Zalayeta, asking whether the ball is on the spot. Here is Zalayeta…ohhhh great save again by Schwarzer!

CF: It's a huuuuge save!

SH: Wonderful save!

CF: It's as big as we've ever seen in Australia! I'm sorry, I'm sorry it is! It's as big as we've ever seen under pressure! It's the sort of heart you need to make World Cups. Mark Schwarzer, you are a champion!

Now, here is where it got interesting. Amid the tumult of Schwarzer's save, I had to gather my thoughts and focus on the scenario, which wasn't easy. In the pandemonium, my mind went blank, and I grabbed our assistant producer, Nick Christou, who was with us in the commentary box, and going as wild as everyone else. I needed confirmation that what I was about to say next was the correct information.

SH: [Slowly, and looking directly at Nick] Now, that means, that IF John Aloisi can score this goal, Australia will be there. [Nick was now frantically trying to do basic arithmetic!]

CF: [Totally gone] Are you sure?

SH: I'm trying to do my maths, I can hardly stand it! [Quick nod from Nick for confirmation.]

CF: It's 4–2. It's 4–2. Who wins it for us? John! John, you win it for us!

SH: Here's Aloisi for a place in the World Cup…he's SCORED! (CF: Yeeeeeeeeeeeaaaahh!)

SH: Australia have done it! (CF: Come ooooon!! Come on!!! Come on my son!)

SH: John Aloisi, the Confederations Cup hero, has done it in the biggest game of all!

CF: Come on Australia! Johnny Warren!

SH: At last! At long, long last! Thirty-one years, four months and twenty-

> four days have passed since Australia ended its campaign at the '74 World Cup, and now, finally, belatedly, wonderfully and joyfully, Australia is back on the biggest stage! What a night! What drama, what tension, but its ended in success, and Guus Hiddink is a legend!
>
> CF: Ah, he's a freak, he's a genius! And his legend grows…

He was indeed. To turn around a team which looked in disarray only a few months beforehand, into World Cup qualifiers against a gnarly outfit like Uruguay was some achievement – even if they had a bit of luck along the way.

The joy in people's faces was incredible. All the pain Australian football fans had experienced seemed to melt away that night, and even though I am English, I'm not ashamed to say I was ecstatic the 'Roos qualified, especially in such dramatic circumstances.

One question I'm asked time and again about that night is where I went to party afterwards. The truth is fairly dull unfortunately. I was utterly shattered, and went straight back to Steph's house, and was in bed by 1 am!

Besides, I was more concerned with how our call would be received in the morning because, to tell the truth, I wasn't convinced it had been all that great.

Fozzie's emotional outpourings had daubed the commentary canvas that night like splodges of randomly thrown paint. I was excited too, but in a different way, and kept trying to deliver decent lines (known as 'sound bites' in the industry), while reflecting the excitement in a more controlled manner. But Craig was just too invested in the outcome, and there was no rhyme nor reason as to when his next yelp into the microphone was coming. It was, in many ways, one of the more difficult nights of my commentary career; but most people don't remember it that way of course, only the result.

As it turns out, Foster's commentary has become an iconic part of the moment, and whatever differences we had before (and particularly since), I am pleased about that, because his passion was genuine, and heartfelt.

There were elements of my own commentary that didn't especially please me either. In particular, the line about John Aloisi being the 'Confederations Cup hero' was a weird thing to throw in, although in fairness, in 2005, his performance in that competition had been relatively big news.

The problem with those moments of course, is that you only get one shot at them and when they are as big as a first World Cup qualification in 32 years, they get replayed over, and over, and over again. So, I've had plenty of years to pick holes in my call of that game, and many others. I guess most commentators would tell you the same thing – you're never satisfied.

I had been booked to MC the Socceroos' celebration party down at Tumbalong Park, and that was the cue for another incredible day, as thousands turned up to serenade the nation's new sporting darlings. One guy even walked across the grass in a hospital gown, attached to a saline drip with his nurse alongside him. It was 24 hours that no-one associated with Australian football will ever, ever forget.

CHAPTER ELEVEN

BERLIN, BLOW-UPS & BREAK-UPS

For me, 2005 had been a huge year professionally. I had gone from being relatively unknown to being front and centre in the broadcasting of two major sporting events. That day with the Socceroos in Tumbalong Park, I seemed to sign almost as many autographs, and pose for as many pictures as some of the players. A few weeks later, this elevated status was underlined as Steph and I were invited to attend the annual 'Logies' TV awards ceremony in Melbourne, where we sat through an interminably long and boring night, punctuated only by the razor-sharp wit of Joan Rivers, who memorably quipped 'I don't know who any of you fucking people are!'

It was recommended that I seek a pay rise at SBS, but in the meantime, I had a call from someone who was about to take my professional life in a very different direction.

The guy at the other end of the phone introduced himself as Leo Karis, a talent agent whose name at least, I vaguely recognised. He wanted to know if I had any representation. I'd never had an agent in all my years in the media; in truth, I'd never really needed one. The closest I'd come was with Jonathan Marks in London all those years ago. Had my career at ITV taken off, I'm sure I'd have signed with Marks, but that scenario had never eventuated. Leo wanted to meet, so a week after the Uruguay game, we had coffee across the road from the SBS offices in Artarmon. Leo thought I had potential to do more with my career in Australia, and said he had heard there was interest in my services from Fox Sports.

This was certainly something worth considering. At that time, Fox were nowhere near the major sporting player they are today, but the A-League had just kicked off (in October 2005), and I liked the way the channel had freshened up the look of domestic football in Australia. Their style of covering sport reminded me of Sky in the early days of the Premier League. Although clearly, their budget wasn't as big, the coverage was fast moving, made decent use of technical gadgetry, and their complementary magazine programme (*Total Football*) gave you all the relevant information without trying to be too high brow. I liked it.

But while the idea of working at Fox appealed, it seemed to me to be a non-starter. The reason was, that after two years in Australia, I had just acquired my permanent residency, and in achieving that, I'd needed SBS's help. Initially, I'd tried to pursue my permanent residency myself, figuring that SBS had been good enough to get me Down Under in the first place, so I wouldn't trouble them for further assistance. However, it quickly became clear that SBS would not only be useful, but absolutely necessary. Getting into Australia to live and work is tough in the first place, but staying there takes it to a different level. I had to undergo police checks in both Australia and the UK, health checks, an interview process, and finally, I needed the guarantee of a three-year contract from my employer.

SBS had been gracious enough to offer me that, so I figured leaving them just a few months after signing that deal, wouldn't have been the nicest thing to do. I put the Fox idea on the backburner, although I did sign up with Leo, who has been my agent ever since.

But as 2006 dawned, it became increasingly clear that Fox wasn't just a long-term possibility, it was my only short-term Australian option, thanks to a combination of events that happened over the next few months.

Before that all started to unfold, I had a trip to – of all places – Bahrain.

Frank Lowy had done a magnificent job in persuading the Asian Football Confederation to finally accept Australia as a member in 2005. This, for me, was, and remains, the biggest achievement in the history of the game Down Under, as it secured the nation's long-term future in a hugely competitive environment – a world away from the backwater of Oceania. Quite how he managed it, I've no idea. After 50 years of trying to get access to the AFC, Lowy's negotiating skills acquired the golden ticket from (then) AFC President, Mohamed bin Hammam, whose cajoling got Australia over the line with enough support from the other 50-odd AFC nations – though some were hugely sceptical, and remain so to this day.

Mike Cockerill memorably quipped in the *Sydney Morning Herald* that after half a century of effort, it had taken 'A Jew to befriend an Arab, to make an Anglo-European nation part of Asia.' I wish I'd written that!

As a result, Australia would now have regular competitive international football, and soon enough, at club level too, via the Asian Champions League.

The Socceroos' first test was a qualifier for the 2007 Asian Cup, against Bahrain in Manama. I flew to the Middle East along with SBS cameraman/editor, Jorge Lazo, and apart from having a minor car crash, and Jorge being thrown out of a TV studio because his shorts showed rather too much leg (this being a Muslim country of course), the trip passed by without incident. Australia won their first-ever competitive game as part of the AFC, 3–1.

Back in Australia in February, Aimé Jacquet, the former World Cup–winning coach from France, arrived in Sydney to conduct coaching courses and a speaking conference. This development was to become hugely significant in my career.

The relationship between SBS and FFA remained tense, despite the removal of Frank Farina as head coach. The reason? Les and Fozzie were pushing for significant change to the entire structure of youth coaching.

This put them on a collision course with CEO John O'Neill, who, in their view, wasn't moving quickly enough to make the necessary changes. The SBS pair felt the technical standard of the new A-League was poor (they may have had a point), and that this was reflecting the type of player being produced at junior level. O'Neill felt that SBS were overstepping the mark, given their commercial relationship with the governing body.

Against this backdrop, SBS were attempting to tie up a new TV deal for broadcasting the Socceroos matches. With Fox holding the A-League (and EPL) rights, the 'Roos were all we had left, and I was increasingly worried all the bad feeling would spill over into the rights negotiations.

But disagreements are one thing, direct action quite another.

So I couldn't quite believe my ears when I heard that there was a move to bring legendary French coach, Aimé Jacquet, over to Australia to conduct a course and a speaking conference for any interested coaches here. This was, in my opinion, an unnecessarily inflammatory move – not because Jacquet didn't have plenty to offer, but because SBS promoted the events relentlessly through the *World Game* programme and other outlets, and passed his coaching course off as a 'PFA initiative'.

Jacquet's credentials weren't in question. He'd won the World Cup in 1998, and was instrumental in setting up France's famed youth academy at Clairefontaine. That wasn't the issue – the real problem was SBS's attempts to run the game, when, in my opinion, as a TV network, its only role should have been to cover the sport, however critically, from a distance.

The SBS crew of course, disagreed; they were 'helping the game'. My arguments about us working in broadcasting – not football – fell on deaf ears, and, as the coaching conference loomed, it was clear I was going to be left holding the baby, hosting the six-hour *World Game* show on my own.

But that was only part of the story.

Earlier that week, I'd been at a press conference at North Sydney Oval for some FFA announcement or other. John O'Neill had been in attendance, and, mischievously, I'd thrown in a question during my interview with him, regarding the Jacquet coaching conference. O'Neill was only too happy to unload, and he gave me two minutes of pure broadcasting gold, reminding the PFA that their role was to look after the needs of their players, not organise coaching courses.

I brought the tape back to SBS HQ in Artarmon, and said I thought we should run the O'Neill quotes on the Sunday show, in order to prove that we were balanced in our coverage. I was told no. I knew at that moment I would be leaving SBS.

The O'Neill grab, I was told, was not for broadcast. Instead, we were to run a 20-minute one-on-one interview with Jacquet (with subtitles, Jacquet didn't speak any English), regarding his coaching 'philosophy'. I've always hated that word incidentally – it makes football sound like astrophysics.

In my opinion, not only was this broadcasting suicide, it was picking a fight deliberately with the FFA. With the negotiations for the new broadcasting deal already in play, this was a risky strategy.

I called Leo, and asked him whether Fox Sports were still interested. He assured me they were, but to sit tight for the time being. Leo knew the World Cup wasn't far away, and felt that the right time to make my move would be after the tournament in Germany.

One of the more enjoyable projects I worked on in preparation for the World Cup however, was a documentary detailing Australia's journey to reach Germany. Unfortunately, it was to bring me into conflict with the FFA myself, and the Socceroos assistant coach, Graham Arnold in particular.

As part of the material-gathering for the doco, I went out to Manly to interview 'Arnie' about his memories of the journey to Germany. Graham was brilliant, waxing lyrical about how he'd missed part of the penalty shootout against Uruguay because he was desperate for the toilet!

When we'd finished the main part of the chat, I threw a couple of supplementary questions at him for other stories we were working on, one of which was about the next generation of players, and the youth development structures currently in place (no prizes for guessing who wanted those particular answers).

Arnie gave some very honest replies, saying he'd warned his employers that there was a black hole about to appear once the 'golden generation' headed off into retirement. As things turned out, they proved to be very prescient comments, but as soon as the interview stopped, Arnie got nervous about what he'd said. I told him not to worry because his comments had been perfectly fair, but Arnie suddenly became very twitchy indeed, saying he needed 'permission' from FFA before it could be broadcast.

Furious, I returned to SBS and relayed the details to Les, who wasn't best pleased either. We decided to wait it out. Eventually, John Boultbee, FFA's Head of High Performance, came into the SBS studios a full week later saying calmly that FFA were 'happy with the content'.

I flew into a rage, saying I didn't give a flying fuck whether FFA liked the content or not. It was not their right to have editorial control over interviews once they had been recorded. I couldn't figure out which was worse – SBS or FFA. It was mind-boggling the way the two parties behaved. One TV network who wanted to run the game, and one governing body who wanted to control the TV network.

In May 2006, after a wonderful send-off match at the MCG, where 90,000 attended the friendly against Greece, Australia were preparing to depart for Germany. My participation, incidentally, had been in doubt right up to the last moment. News had leaked – via the *Daily Telegraph* – of Fox's interest in me, and I had been forced to deny the speculation.

The day before we headed overseas, I acted as MC for another Socceroos function – their departure to Germany, in a hangar at Sydney airport, where a specially configured plane, complete with Socceroos livery, had been commissioned for the flight. There was a wonderful sense of pending adventure. But on my return to Artarmon, Les called the entire sports team together in the office for a special announcement. He looked ashen-faced. What on earth could this news be?

Les announced that SBS had lost the broadcast rights for the Socceroos, with the FFA signing a deal with Fox Sports to take over the coverage of the national team exclusively from 2007. As a further blow, the nightly *Toyota World Sport* show was to be axed, leaving the futures of many in the department up in the air.

Whether the ructions between SBS and FFA had played a part in the broadcasting deal I can't say with any degree of certainty. It's also clear that FFA needed the extra money that Fox promised to invest in a joint agreement that included an extended deal with the A-League (worth around $120 million). SBS's days of being the premier football broadcaster in the country were coming to an end and with Fox having signed a whopping seven-year deal, those days weren't about to return any time soon.

My hunch is that Les hoped his personal friendship with Frank Lowy, and the network's past history of football coverage, might just win the day for SBS regarding the national team. Les and Frank had known each other for many years, but times were moving on, and Lowy, an astute businessman, sensed a better deal for the game.

I didn't have much time to digest the news however, as I was off to Germany, where I would be based in Stuttgart, just down the road from the Socceroos' camp in Ohringen. Before that however, we headed to the Netherlands, where Guus Hiddink was holding a pre–World Cup camp for his charges in the city of Mierlo, a short hop from Eindhoven. Our location wasn't ideal; we were holed up in Rotterdam, which meant a 90-minute drive every morning to reach the camp. Inevitably, on occasion we were late, and many weeks later, cameraman Ryan Sheridan's mad driving (as we tried to make up time), came back to haunt me. I received a letter from the authorities (all in Dutch) that, once translated, informed me that I, as the registered driver of our vehicle, had been fined for speeding!

In trying to clear this up, I called SBS, who told me not to worry, as they would pay the fine. I then called the Dutch authorities, and spoke to an administrator to give her the details. Except she wasn't interested in hearing about SBS, or the fact that I hadn't been the driver. The only thing she kept repeating was that if I didn't pay the money, I was liable to be blacklisted by the Dutch police. Time and again, I tried to convince her that it was a case of mistaken identity, and that the money would be coming via SBS but something was being lost in translation.

'SBS will be paying the money. It will come from them,' I said.

'No, if you don't pay the money, then the Dutch police may arrest you,' she said.

'I wasn't the driver, I don't live in Holland, and I have no intention of returning to Holland!' I said in exasperation.

'Oh, didn't you like it?' said the lady, suddenly changing tack, and sounding almost hurt that I'd disrespected her nation! Eventually, SBS – I think – brought in a Dutch translator to help resolve the matter. Anyway, I digress.

Hiddink really put his squad through the mill those few days in Holland. Mark Viduka in particular had been targeted by the Dutchman, who'd hinted his skipper was a little overweight. By the end of one session, Viduka collapsed in exhaustion and lay prone on his back for more than five minutes, gasping for air. It was brutal but Hiddink was clearly determined that, if his team weren't going to be the best team in Germany, then at least they would be the fittest.

By this time, Hiddink had already announced he wouldn't be staying on as Socceroos coach post-Germany. This was disappointing, but no surprise. Guus didn't really do long-term contracts, especially in faraway countries like Australia. The question on everyone's lips was, who was going to replace him?

Hiddink's number two, the legendary Johan Neeskens, put his hand up immediately. Neeskens loved Australia, it being one of the few countries in the world where he could wander around freely, without being stopped every five minutes for an autograph. But he wasn't the only Dutchman interested in the gig. With Hiddink the flavour of the month, it seemed he'd started a trend. I interviewed 1974 (and 1978) legend, Ruud Krol, who intimated he'd like the role. Then I had a call from an agent putting me in touch with Gerard van der Lem, an old acquaintance of Hiddink's – he too wanted to throw his hat into the ring.

During an interview, I asked Hiddink whether he'd like to endorse Van der Lem's candidacy, as his compatriot had made it sound like they were good friends. Hiddink sounded almost bewildered.

'Oh, that's a surprise. I mean, I know him. I know him. But that's a surprise!' he said.

It was one of the few occasions I caught Hiddink off guard. By the next day in Mierlo, he was back to his more usual form. A Korean journalist was conducting a private interview with him in a corner of the team hotel, and asked him whether he'd ever consider a return to coaching with the Taeguk Warriors. Hiddink replied loudly (making doubly sure we Australian journalists could hear him), 'Maybe…but first, I have to get these Skippies to the second round!' He winked at us as he delivered that line, and it showed he had every faith in his own ability to create history for Australia at the World Cup.

The squad then tapered off their preparations by going on a fishing trip off the coast of Zeeland. It was supposed to be a few hours relaxation for them after the rigours of Hiddink's training regime. They hadn't banked on us media types spoiling it for them. We, of course, needed pictures and stories every day of that trip. So the (by now sizeable) Australian contingent decided to follow the 'Roos on their angling expedition, on the back of a hired trawler. They didn't catch much fish that day, probably not helped by the trawler scaring them off by constantly circling their boat. They looked thoroughly miserable at our presence, and I could hardly blame them.

After a low-key friendly against local club side, Kloetinge, a beautifully picturesque Dutch village, the entire operation then shifted north. There, the 'Roos underlined their potential and new-found fitness, as they played a friendly in Rotterdam against Hiddink's home country, the Netherlands, earning a 1–all draw in a bruising encounter at De Kuip, the magnificent ground belonging to Feyenoord. The big event wasn't far away.

From Holland, it was on to our base in Stuttgart, where we quickly settled in to our new, rather cramped, quarters above the old railway station, a far cry from the plush digs in Berlin where the rest of the team had been billeted.

My first commitment in Germany was to call the pre–World Cup friendly between Australia and Liechtenstein in Ulm, a small town a few hours' drive away from Stuttgart. The Socceroos won this game 3–1, and a young, relatively unknown, striker called Josh Kennedy hit the headlines, scoring a goal just 15 minutes after coming off the bench on his international debut.

Kennedy hadn't been part of the 2005 qualifiers, and he was a shock selection for the World Cup party, but at 6 foot 4, and naturally dangerous in the air, he looked handy. With long straggly hair, and a beard to boot, he also looked very much like Jesus, a nickname he quickly acquired.

Here, Hiddink showed all his experience. Almost immediately, a clamour started for Kennedy to play a big role in the World Cup, but when training resumed the next day, Hiddink had a different plan for big Josh – and the watching media.

As the squad were put through their paces in Ohringen, Hiddink targeted Kennedy, berating him at every opportunity. Every one of his touches was poor, none of his movements good enough. Hiddink was making his point, both to the striker, and the press – only Guus picked the team. When Hiddink did eventually pick his 11 for the opening World Cup game against Japan, Kennedy was on the bench. The surprise was the inclusion of Luke Wilkshire, a largely unheralded lower league defender from Bristol City, whom Hiddink had taken a shine to, mainly for his ability to play to a system, along with his non-stop energy.

I didn't see the Socceroos' final training session however. As part of my duties in Germany, I was in Berlin. Once a week, I was standing in for Les as the presenter of the daily World Cup show in the German capital. The studio was set in beautiful surrounds, in the park opposite the imposing Reichstag building, and the accommodation was several levels above our rather shabby apartments in Stuttgart. But it was the SBS team's mode of transport to get from Berlin to Kaiserslautern for the opening game that was to become the cause of consternation.

Les was eager for the team to return straight to Berlin after the game. I presumed we'd get the train (as that was the only option – Kaiserslautern doesn't have an airport), but, for whatever reason, Les wasn't keen on that idea. Instead, it was in a private plane – a Lear jet. Upon our return to Australia, the story leaked (not from me, I hasten to add), and there was a fair bit of grumbling at such a perceived extravagance.

That day in Kaiserslautern will live long in the memory of every Australian fan – and this commentator too. It was a hot, sticky afternoon, and the walk up the steep Betzenberg hill to the Fritz-Walter Stadion left us sweating and out of breath at the top; especially cameraman Ryan Sheridan, who'd remained in Stuttgart, and had to park the van, before carrying the majority of his equipment up there too.

Australian fans were everywhere, and I remember shaking my head in bemusement at the sight of so much green and gold, recalling the sight of that lone Australian girl at Sydney airport just over 12 months earlier, ahead of the Iraq game.

I was as nervous as a kitten pre-game, but once the anthems were out of the way, I paid homage to Johnny Warren to the listening millions at home, and settled into commentary. Football is football, whatever the occasion, and it's strange how you find a rhythm, whether it's a World Cup, or a windswept Wednesday in Wigan.

Australia had good early chances through Mark Viduka, and then Mark Bresciano, but couldn't find a way through. Then disaster struck. Shunsuke Nakamura swung in a cross, into what in cricket would be called the corridor of uncertainty – right in the zone between attackers, defenders and goalkeeper.

Mark Schwarzer came to punch, but got a nudge from a Japanese attacker, enough to put him off his stride and miss the ball, which floated gently into the net. Later, many viewers complained I'd made too much of the alleged foul, and that my commentary had been 'biased' (that word again). Replays showed Guus Hiddink asking similar questions of the fourth official, and trying to crane his neck towards a TV monitor to check whether his suspicions were correct. Phil Dowd would have hated that!

The scoreline stayed the same until half-time, and as the second half wore on, it seemed Australia would be unable to find a way through. But Hiddink was bold. He threw on three attacking players – Tim Cahill, Josh Kennedy and John Aloisi – and his bravery was to reap big dividends.

With just six minutes to go, the score remained 1–0 to Japan, when Australia won a free kick. Aloisi blasted it towards goal. It was beaten away by goalkeeper Yoshikatsu Kawaguchi, and the Samurai Blue scrambled it away for a throw-in. Here's how I called what happened next:

> Neill's long throw, goalkeeper has come, hasn't got there…Harry Kewell…and then poked home by Tim Cahill! Australia have done it! Six minutes to go, and it's a landmark moment for Australian football. Tim Cahill has scored the nation's first-ever World Cup Finals goal!

From that moment on, Japan became more expansive as they sought a winner themselves. In doing so, they left big gaps defensively, although it should be pointed out, Australia were lucky to get away with a mistimed lunge by Cahill inside his own penalty area, which really should have resulted in a Japanese penalty. Not for the first time in the game however, referee Essam Abd El Fatah got it wrong.

But with just two minutes to go, Australia seized their chance. Here's how it unfolded, with my commentary on SBS:

> You just wonder whether that extra fitness training that Australia have done may pay dividends in the final moments, especially as they have the impetus. Aloisi…Cahill…CAHILL…Tim Cahill has done it again! What a goal by Tim Cahill! 2–1 Australia! Ohhh it's a wonderful moment in Kaiserslautern!

As we moved into stoppage time, Japanese resistance was finally ended:

> Cahill…Aloisi…Viduka's in an offside position, Aloisi might go on his own…ALOISIIII…3–1! It's all over! Three points for Australia! What about that? Japan have collapsed in the closing moments, and John Aloisi, who wrote one chapter in Australian football history back in November 2005, adds a little postscript for the Socceroos. It's a sea of green and gold around the Fritz-Walter Stadion. Hey, and this is a great finish from John Aloisi. Brilliant stuff by Australia!

At the end of the game, I made my way down to the press conference, only to be lifted off the ground in a huge bear hug by FFA Press Officer, Stuart Hodge. If anything, this topped the qualifier against Uruguay. As with the Uruguay game, I've heard the call of those goals many, many times in the years since, and I've always felt much more satisfied with that particular effort.

A nice spin-off from that game came much later. During the match, I'd made some reference to Tim Cahill's sponsorship with a popular cereal as he'd come off the bench. For those unaware, Weet-bix adverts make great play of sporting prowess being enhanced by eating their brand of breakfast biscuit – so, as Cahill got ready to come on with the Socceroos still trailing, I made a remark along the lines of 'I hope he had his Weet-bix!' I repeated this after his first goal, saying 'He DID have his Weet-bix this morning!'

Some later accused me of promoting a brand deliberately, but that wasn't the case – I just felt it was a good line. But Sanitarium (who make Weet-bix) were obviously delighted, so much so, that post-Germany, they got in touch to ask whether I'd record a spoof commentary to run over pictures of Tim eating his Weet-bix! The ad ran for a good 12 months, and while it was a nice association to have, there was certainly nothing intentional on my part.

Meantime, back in Germany, Australia were preparing for their second group game against world champions Brazil. Here, the brilliance of Hiddink's nuanced football mind became the story itself, both before and after the game.

For two days, the Australian squad played full 11 v 11 training games on a pitch with full-sized goals, but on a playing area only a third of the normal dimensions. The reason was to put the players under pressure, to teach them how to retain possession under the kind of duress the Brazilians would put them under.

'Ten seconds, TEN SECONDS!' Hiddink barked relentlessly throughout the sessions. The players' target was to keep possession of the ball for a full 10 seconds on that tiny pitch, under extreme pressure. Not everyone managed it of course, and the growl that emanated from the Dutchman whenever the ball was turned over, told you all you needed to know about who was going to be playing in that second game in Munich.

When people look back now at the 2006 campaign, few remember in any detail the match against Brazil. It's an indication of how much our views are coloured by the end result. But I remember that performance as being Australia's best, even though they ultimately went down 2–0.

For long periods, Australia dominated possession (which would have delighted Hiddink, no doubt), created chances, and generally gave Brazil problems they didn't expect. In the end, only that extra bit of quality saw the Seleção home at the magnificent Allianz Arena.

The only other sour note – aside of the result – was a spat involving Harry Kewell and the match referee, Markus Merk, after the full-time whistle. Kewell protested, fairly forcefully, about some of the decisions during the game, which led to a final foul count of 25–9 in favour (if that's the right word) of the Socceroos. It later transpired that Merk had told Kewell his World Cup was over.

But Merk's words – overheard by several Australian players – did him no favours, as they were seen as pre-empting any FIFA enquiry, and Kewell was ultimately deemed free to play. But none of the world's press knew that at the time, and as we wandered into the post-match press conference, that was the topic that was most definitely up for debate. But once again, Guus Hiddink showed all his experience in handling a potentially difficult situation. Whether he pre-planned what happened next, I can't be absolutely sure, but it was just the sort of ruse he'd use to get the upper hand.

As Hiddink sat down in preparation to answer the inevitable barrage of Kewell questions, his mobile phone rang. Hiddink excused himself for a moment, then in full view of the media, he said 'Hello Mum! I'm a bit busy right now, can I call you back?'

Cue gales of laughter, as all the tension evaporated. Hiddink smiled and charmed his way through the questions with ease. He was a master at playing the press, and humour was one of his chief weapons.

My feeling is he asked someone to wait until he'd sat down, and then ring his phone. Maybe it was Pedro Salazar, his media guy, but I don't know for sure. Sadly, Pedro died tragically young a year or two ago. Rest in peace my friend.

The other group game had ended in a goalless draw between Japan and Croatia, which left Australia needing just a point against the Croats to ensure qualification for the last 16. That was, unless Japan somehow beat Brazil by a decent margin, and no-one really expected that to happen.

However, the pace of work had begun to catch up with me in the build-up to the final group game in Stuttgart. The day before the Australia/Croatia game, I came down with the flu. My duties in Germany didn't just extend to commentary, reporting on the 'Roos, and presenting in Berlin. I probably hadn't done myself any favours by also agreeing (through Leo) to host a function for NAB in Munich, several days before the Brazil game. That meant yet another flight which, on a stormy night in Stuttgart, led to the plane being delayed. The skies were so threatening, the pilot told us via the intercom that he was going to make the short hop across southern Germany at a lower altitude, staying beneath the clouds and attempting to avoid the regular bolts of lightning.

Upon my return to Stuttgart the following morning, I knew my body was starting to complain, so it wasn't a surprise that the sniffles and the shivers began a few hours later. As Australia's day of destiny arrived, I felt lousy. Staying in bed as long as possible, I tried to dose myself on Lemsip and attempted to get some sleep. When it was time to leave, I didn't feel much better. It was going to be a long night with the kick-off scheduled for 9 pm. But my evening wasn't to feel as lengthy as a certain Graham Poll's – my old acquaintance from that controversial game in Hitchin, 12 years earlier.

The Croatians were still in with a chance of qualifying as well but they needed to win, and they made the perfect start. Darijo Srna curled in a wonderful free kick from long range after just two minutes, only for Craig Moore to equalise in the 38th minute with a penalty kick, after Poll spotted a handball by Stjepan Tomas. It was to be Poll's best moment of that particular evening.

Guus Hiddink had stuck by his earlier pledge that no-one was guaranteed a spot in his team, and had handed a shock start to Zeljko Kalac in goal, in place of Mark Schwarzer. But the gambler's plan, for once, backfired. Already, Kalac had spilled a routine corner under no pressure, but what happened next was far, far worse.

In the 56th minute, the elegant Niko Kovač picked up the ball a fair way out from the Australian goal, but when his shot failed to pack much of a punch, there seemed little danger. Wrong.

'Ohhh, and Zeljko Kalac, an absolute howler, and Croatia are back in front!' was my call of Kovač's goal.

Zeljko had inexplicably allowed the ball to roll over his prone body, and into the net. Australia were on the brink of going out with just 11 minutes remaining. It needed something – or someone – special. Fortunately, the 'Roos had just the man.

'Bresciano, towards Kennedy. It might drop for KEWELL! Harry Kewell has done it! Australia's golden boy, has come up with a golden goal! And we're back tied at 2–2!'

The replays showed Kewell may have been marginally offside, but Graham Poll hadn't seen it. Perhaps that was payback for what appeared a certain penalty in the first half, after Josip Šimunić had rugby tackled Mark Viduka inside the penalty area. Poll had missed that too.

But as the game drew towards a dramatic conclusion, Poll really got involved in the thick of it. After issuing Dario Śimić with a red card in the 85th minute, and then Brett Emerton in the 87th, Šimunić (who'd already been booked) was bizarrely given a lifeline, as Poll completely lost the plot.

Šimunić committed a blatant foul against Josh Kennedy, and Poll brandished a second yellow. Here's my description of what happened next:

> That is, is it not, his second yellow card? [The caption then appears on screen showing the two yellows turning into a red] It is! They are down to nine! [Pause] Now, Šimunić has stayed on the park. I'm absolutely convinced that is his second yellow card, the caption confirmed it, but he is still on the park for Croatia! This has been a quite extraordinary game, and FIFA will surely look into that.

Amazingly, Šimunić was to receive a third yellow in stoppage time, when he finally admitted defeat by wandering off. By then, there was utter chaos on the pitch, with nobody quite knowing whether Poll had also blown the full-time whistle or not. When the mayhem subsided, the Australian bench swarmed the pitch and celebrated a first-ever qualification through the group stage.

I wasn't joining in however; I was concerned that it had been me who'd made the mistake with the card situation regarding Šimunić. Thankfully, it wasn't long before I found out that it had indeed, been Poll's error, and I breathed a sigh of relief. Apparently, Poll, tired and a little confused by Šimunić's Australian accent (he'd grown up in Canberra before switching allegiance), believed he'd booked Craig Moore instead – Šimunić's opposite number on the Australian team. It was a bad mistake, and it cost Poll any chance of refereeing the World Cup Final.

I thought of the similar chaotic scenes at Hitchin a decade or so before, and his cocky manner that day at the FA at Lancaster Gate. What goes around, comes around.

With Brazil accounting for Japan, that draw in Stuttgart earned Australia second place in the group behind the Brazilians, and a crack at Italy in the Round of 16 back in Kaiserslautern.

Before that however, I was on duty in Leipzig for another Round of 16 encounter, between Argentina and Mexico. Another flight, another hotel, but well worth the trip, if only to call Maxi Rodriguez's sublime strike, which won the game in extra time for the Argentines.

More importantly, while in Leipzig, I'd stumbled across a potential scoop. The Australian press were starting to speculate that Guus Hiddink's replacement could be Liverpool's former manager, Gerard Houllier. As luck would have it, Houllier was commentating for French television, and I clocked him, just a row behind me in the commentary area.

I approached Houllier, and asked whether we could conduct an interview with him. He said he'd be happy to but he was busy with his commitments at that particular moment. Could we catch up with him in Kaiserslautern, where he was also scheduled to cover the Australian game with the Italians? I agreed, sent word to Ken Shipp (now in Berlin with the rest of the team), and made my way back to Stuttgart, satisfied that I had a little exclusive in the bag. Almost.

The day of the Australia/Italy game was where the Socceroos' World Cup road came to an end. It was also the end of the road for me and SBS.

My plan on 26 June, the day of the game, was to arrive early at the Fritz-Walter Stadion with my cameraman, Ryan, to conduct the interview with Houllier, before he got busy with his TV commitments. That also left me plenty of time to prepare mentally for another huge game commentary-wise. Sadly, all those best laid plans foundered thanks to the politics of the SBS football department.

On the morning of the game, I received a phone call from Ken. He apologised before he even told me the gist of his story. Ryan was needed elsewhere that day, and therefore couldn't film the interview with Houllier. What? What on earth could be more important than getting an exclusive with a man who, potentially, was about to become the Socceroos' new coach?

The answer was that SBS wanted to conduct another interview with Aimé Jacquet. Interestingly, there was history between Jacquet and Houllier. Jacquet was the man who'd been Houllier's number two, when France's bid to qualify for the World Cup in 1994 had ended in acrimony.

On SBS, Craig Foster had been lukewarm regarding the plan, saying he believed there were 'better people than Houllier' for the job. Not exactly the perfect build-up to a vital World Cup knockout game. But Australia, in my opinion, were below their best in that game anyway. They'd achieved more than they ever dreamed possible, but even when Marco Materazzi was sent off after 50 minutes, the Socceroos rarely threatened the Italian goal.

No team defends quite as well as the Azzurri, and after they'd allowed the Australians to punch themselves out, the late penalty, controversial as it may have been, had a certain air of inevitability about it. True, Fabio Grosso made the most of minimal contact by Lucas Neill (who otherwise had a magnificent tournament), but any Australian player would have done exactly the same. Francesco Totti tucked away the penalty, went off sucking his thumb, and it was over.

Australian heartbreak was understandable, as was the reaction towards Grosso's theatrics. But this was football at the top level, in some ways, I thought it was good that the 'Roos now, finally, had a meaningful narrative on the world stage. Tales of joy, misery and controversy, are what every nation with a proper football history has at the World Cup.

Some of the anti-football media back home didn't see it that way of course. They saw Grosso's 'dive' (a theory I never bought into) as further evidence of how the game was not for them, nor Australia. How cheating was rife…sheilas, wogs, poofters…you know the drill.

As Australia headed home, I was en route to Hamburg to call the quarterfinal between the Italians and Ukraine. Not much of a contest that one, with Italy easing into the last four with a 3–0 win, Luca Toni scoring twice. A day later, I was in Frankfurt to call Brazil/France, won by the French thanks to a lone Thierry Henry strike.

I had one more commentary commitment – the third/fourth place play-off back in Stuttgart between Germany and Portugal, and this proved to be hugely enjoyable (as these games often are), with the Germans setting the seal on a very impressive tournament by claiming the bronze medals.

After that, it was back to Berlin for the final few days of a memorable month. But I was in no mood to celebrate after all that had happened. I was determined to use my time there to set the ball rolling with Ken Shipp regarding my departure from SBS.

The SBS team all had tickets for the final between Italy and France and the day after Italy had secured the crown (after the infamous head butt had seen Zinedine Zidane sent off), I began to prepare the ground for my departure from SBS. I was tired of the way the department was run according to specific football agendas, and the tension it produced. It was time to go, and a chance meeting with Fox Sports Executive Producer, Murray Shaw, at one of the Australian games, had confirmed that they were still interested in my services.

However, SBS weren't going to accede to my demands that easily. I was reminded that I was under contract – a long one at that. I was also reminded that SBS saw me as a valuable asset, which I appreciated, but I told them it wasn't going to make any difference. Privately, I'd already made up my mind that if SBS wouldn't release me to sign for another network in Australia, I was going to return to the UK.

Upon my return to Australia, I wasn't the only one with my future up in the air. Steph's contract was almost up, although, after the axing of *Toyota World Sport,* she had been offered the role of sports host on the revamped *World News Australia.* Steph had interest from Fox Sports too, and was on the verge of accepting the role at Fox, when another offer came in from Channel 9. Eventually, she opted to go to the free-to-air network.

Meantime, I was in a holding pattern. I'd spoken to Leo, who repeated his mantra that I had to be patient. There were a few things that needed sorting out, but he remained confident I'd get my wish and move to Fox Sports. A few days later, I wasn't feeling so bullish. I was frustrated but SBS had me over a barrel. I was under contract, and they didn't have to let me go.

In a bid to try and resolve the situation, SBS laid out the network's plans over the next two years, but when you have to include the Beach Soccer World Cup and futsal on your list of properties, you know it's not a hugely impressive portfolio. Fox had taken most of the better football rights, and they and I both knew it.

I was offered a pay rise, but it wasn't about money, nor even SBS's lack of football rights, although that was a factor. This was about professional relationships, and the way the department worked – it was a model that, in my opinion, was broken, and there seemed to be no quick fix.

In secret, Leo opened talks with Fox, and in scenes more reminiscent of cloak and dagger thrillers, we'd meet in coffee bars well away from SBS, where we'd discuss various details of the proposed deal. I wasn't convinced SBS would play ball, but Leo stayed calm, and did his best to reassure me.

Finally, after what seemed like an age of waiting, Leo came up with the goods. He called me to say he had the piece of paper that confirmed my release from SBS. What on earth had he done, or said to make the difference? I still don't know the answer, and Leo has never told me. But I didn't care. I was free.

The very same day, I put pen to paper on a three-year contract with Fox Sports, after a meeting with Head of Programmes, Tony Sinclair, at Leo's house in Woollahra.

I was hugely indebted to SBS for bringing me over to Australia in the first place, and I was grateful they'd given me so many opportunities to build a profile in my new country. I felt I'd let Ken Shipp down in particular, after he'd shown so much faith in me; I was truly sorry about that.

Many people believe that it was Les who brought me over to Australia, and while it is true he (as then Head of Sport), had to make the final decision, the person I had all my dealings with was Ken. Of course I respected the fact Les had lots of skin in the game, but the fact was, the failure of football to break through into the mainstream of the Australian sporting landscape had given SBS almost unfettered influence. Most of the time, they used that power for good, but there were few checks and balances in the system, because so few people – SBS bosses included – really knew, or understood the game.

My final show for SBS in 2006 was a rather stilted affair, with everyone aware of the circumstances.

I was off to become what one of my old BBC colleagues had once labelled rather disparagingly 'one of Murdoch's minions'. Whatever. It sounded pretty good to me.

Before we move on though, a postscript to my time at SBS.

While I absolutely stand by my comments on how the department was run, it should be said that, at times, I overstepped my remit. In fact, most people recognised the anti-English agenda, without my having to become so entangled in the debate, thus leading to unnecessary conflict, and a feeling from many that I was merely 'protecting' English coaches because of my own background. That wasn't true at all – I couldn't have cared less whether they succeeded or not. It was a point of principle, however, that you can't apply a 'one size fits all' approach when dealing with individuals. I'd have done the same with any other nationality; as indeed, I did to a point, when the 'Dutch coaching mafia' became the next target, some years later.

The reality was that some of my co-workers, to a degree, were correct in their assumption that Australian football needed to move in a different direction. They were also correct in feeling that coaches from other parts of the world needed to be given a chance, or indeed, prioritised. I also sympathised with the fact that the only form of 'soccer' the mainstream Australian public seemed to understand originated in England, and therefore that culture dominated. But that didn't make their crusade to try and run the game, or the vendetta against ALL English coaches right or proper. If they'd framed their arguments in more reasonable terms, then a proper conversation could have ensued. In the event, their dogmatic approach only divided the football community – and their own department.

CHAPTER TWELVE

12

FOX, FIREWORKS & 'FUCK YOU!'

Three years into the Lowy revolution, and football had made great strides in Australia. A new domestic league, World Cup qualification, and a move into Asia. Things were looking good.

But mainstream acceptance was still a challenge, and even after my high-profile role at the World Cup in Germany, my initial contract with Fox wasn't exclusively tailored towards football. One day a week, I presented on the fledgling Fox Sports News channel, a concept clearly modelled on the Sky equivalent in the UK.

The fact was however – and it remains the case to this day – that football just didn't generate big enough ratings to justify big numbers of full-time staff. Other areas of the football media had similar problems, with only a handful of written journalists (Tom Smithies, Marco Monteverde, David Davutovic to name three of the News Limited stable), able to earn a full-time living from the game of football.

To Fox's eternal credit however, they have continued to invest in the game, and today I, along with many others, ARE working full-time in our chosen sport. In fact, Fox rarely gets the credit it deserves for its role in the football revolution. Then CEO, David Malone, took a huge punt in agreeing to broadcast the new A-League when it started in 2005. The money paid for the initial contract was miniscule by today's standards, but Fox were, essentially, backing an unknown, and unproven product, in a sport that had been almost dead in the water, domestically at least.

Fans, of course, rarely see things that way. They always want more. In the early phase, supporters grumbled about having to pay to watch their chosen sport. Many still do. But what is the alternative for a game that needs finance, not just to grow, but survive? I knew for a fact that the only other player in the market in 2005 – SBS – had even less money to invest. Only Fox were (and are) prepared to put its money where its mouth is.

I joined Fox on the same day the network announced Andy Harper would be part of its football stable. Andy and I have worked closely together ever since. We don't always see eye to eye, but we have a fairly solid professional relationship, and I think our partnership works reasonably well. I have a straighter style of commentary, while Andy provides the flowery language, befitting of an intelligent man who has a background as a teacher, as well as a player with Marconi Stallions, Brisbane Strikers and others.

But in the early days, my regular co-commentary partner (and TV analyst) was Robbie Slater, the former Blackburn Rovers winger, who'd been at Fox since the start-up days. We made our debut working together on the opening night of the 2006/07 season, as Melbourne Victory defeated Adelaide United 2–0 at the old Olympic Park. I was a little nervous and probably 'over' commentated, if that's the right word. But the experience of calling football on a weekly basis again after so many years away from that sort of environment, gave me immense satisfaction. Plus, the A-League was clearly a competition on the up.

But my association with SBS wasn't quite over yet. As part of my 'release' SBS had insisted I call their remaining Socceroo games in 2006, until the contract transferred over to Fox at the outset of 2007. Eventually, SBS hired David Basheer to take over commentary duties, but at this point they either hadn't yet made their choice, or he was unavailable to start for some reason. So, I had the rather bizarre situation whereby I had to work for another network on a temporary basis. Also, given the manner of my departure from SBS, the communication between the two companies was rather strained.

I had just four games to call before I could finally bid 'adieu' to SBS, and although they passed by without incident, it was an odd experience. Two of the matches were 'home' games, and I stayed in separate hotels to the rest of the SBS team, and the only time I ever heard from them was when Les handed over to me in the commentary box after the national anthems, pre–kick off. Otherwise, never the twain did meet.

The two 'away' games meant I had to call off-tube from the SBS studios, which presented even more of an opportunity to cross paths with my erstwhile colleagues.

Again, the admin staff did their duty, and kept the two warring factions apart, ensuring a day pass was left for me at SBS reception in Artarmon.

At the end of my four-game stint, Australia had secured qualification to their first-ever Asian Cup in 2007. But another national team hadn't been quite so lucky, and their coach was about to pay the price, in part courtesy of my old network.

In November of 2006, SBS caused an almighty stir, with an interview screened on *The World Game,* involving Craig Foster and national youth team coach, Ange Postecoglou. Postecoglou had just seen his junior team knocked out of the Asian qualifiers for the FIFA World Youth Cup. Foster suggested Postecoglou resign, accusing him of hiding behind his players.

In some ways, I could understand why Foster had gone on the offensive. In the absence of any commercial constraints due to their lack of broadcasting rights, SBS were now totally free to opinionate in any way they liked, while at the same time, keeping their coverage relevant to the general football discussion.

As the only other network broadcasting football, we had no choice but to cover the story, and we did so by inviting Ange to appear on our *Total Football* show the following week. I hosted the programme only occasionally, with Andy Harper the regular presenter, but on this occasion, I happened to be in the chair.

We gave Postecoglou a platform to talk, but as we closed the chat, I – unprofessionally – allowed myself to get caught up in the emotion of the debate, particularly given my history with SBS. Stupidly, I said something along the lines of, 'Thanks Ange, hopefully you feel you had a chance to have your say, more than you did last week. In any case, by all accounts not many people were watching that show.'

Having a dig was an unnecessarily inflammatory thing to say, and even Steph wasn't impressed. Nor was my old producer, who texted me afterwards, telling me to 'pull my head in'. I apologised. The last thing Fox wanted was a broadcast war.

The battle was to rumble on for many more years yet and, even though I learned from that mistake, I was utterly determined to play my part in making people feel Fox was the proper home of the game.

We got some vindication for that point of view at the end of my first season, when the Fox football department won the Australian Sports Commission Award for best coverage. SBS meantime, won a Gold Logie for the World Cup coverage in 2006. I got a text from Noel Brady saying 'congratulations' after the announcement, but somehow, I didn't feel as though I had anything to celebrate, after the way it had all ended.

SBS were at it again as the 2006/07 season got underway – Sydney FC's appointment of Englishman, Terry Butcher, as their new coach, being akin to flying a red rag in front of a bull.

Butcher was no Pep Guardiola, it's true, but some were sticking the knife in, even before he landed on the tarmac at Sydney Airport. While the brand of football his team played may have underlined their point, the truth was, he'd already been judged before Sydney had kicked a ball. I was no particular fan of Butcher, or Sydney, but I believed integrity had again gone out the window – especially as he had mitigating circumstances.

For example, after just one game of the new campaign, Butcher lost his biggest star, Dwight Yorke, who departed to join Sunderland. Butcher was also refused permission, due to the club's financial situation, to bring his own assistant. Furthermore, during his entire spell at the Sydney Football Stadium, Butcher was allowed to sign only one recognised first team player, the Italian Benito Carbone, who was a big hit, until injury brought his stint to a close. Finally, after Butcher had led the Sky Blues to a respectable third place, the club were docked three points for salary-cap breaches in season one, relegating them to fourth. He was let go shortly after they were dumped out of the play-offs by Newcastle.

After that defeat, Butcher walked across to the Sydney FC fans to applaud them, and they returned the compliment. Aside of a few refuseniks, there was little evidence of a major campaign to oust him, yet SBS acted as though he was constantly on the verge of dismissal – though there may have been some currency in their allegations of player dissatisfaction. Butcher was even criticised for wearing tracksuit pants to games and accused of dressing like a hobo.

Some of my new Fox colleagues joined in the criticism of Butcher – Mike Cockerill in particular, who penned a vitriolic piece when Butcher eventually returned to the UK. I wrote a piece on the Fox website, remarking that, had Butcher's name been Thierry Boucher, he'd have been cut a lot more slack.

A similar thing happened when Jim Magilton was appointed coach of Melbourne Victory in 2012. The vitriol was astonishing, with Foster calling for a ruling that would disallow any imported coach not demonstrating success in a league with a 'high tactical level'. He went on to claim that the English Championship would 'clearly not comply'.

Yet two years later, there was barely a squeak when Josep Gombau was appointed at Adelaide United – despite the Spaniard's only tangible success being in the world-renowned Hong Kong First Division!

Anyway, back in 2007, the anti-English brigade all got their wish, when one of their favourite coaches, Branko Culina, got the Sydney FC gig in succession to Butcher. Mike Cockerill stated in *The Sydney Morning Herald* that the players had been 'liberated' by Culina. But he couldn't buy a result in season three if his life had depended on it. His reign was even shorter than Butcher's, and he was moved on after just six months. Poetic justice, some might say, although I had nothing personal against Culina.

In February 2007, we got a glimpse of what the A-League could possibly become, as I called my first Grand Final since the 2004 NSL decider. It was also a repeat of my first-ever A-League commentary on Fox.

Melbourne Victory had overcome a poor inaugural season, and won through to host the final against cross-border rivals, Adelaide United. The two had finished first and second in the regular season, but it was Victory's enormous potential for drawing crowds that had left many observers open-mouthed; after all, this was a club, or 'franchise' that was only a year or so old.

Following that opening night success for Victory over the Reds at Olympic Park, Victory had gambled on moving their next fixture – against Sydney FC – to nearby Telstra Dome. The Dome held well over 50,000, and some felt it was a case of attempting to run before you could walk. But Victory, who drew nearly 16,000 for that Round 1 clash, felt it was worth the risk, and they were rewarded by a crowd of nearly 40,000 for the meeting with Sydney. Later on that season, they drew a staggering 50,333 for the return home game with Sydney FC, and had decamped permanently to Telstra Dome from that moment on.

The other sports, of course, didn't like it. Articles began reappearing in the Melbourne media, focusing on 'trouble' in the crowd. Three fans had been ejected from that second meeting with Sydney, but the minor issues in no way reflected the celebratory atmosphere of that particular night. Yet again, football's growth was worrying the sporting establishment.

By the time Victory hosted the Grand Final, excitement was at fever pitch. The year before, Sydney FC had pulled a crowd in excess of 41,000 for the decider with the Central Coast Mariners, but this was set for a sellout.

Just on that 2006 Grand Final – although there wasn't any crowd trouble on that occasion, it didn't stop a writer from penning a most astonishing piece in the aftermath. Here's a few examples from the *Sydney Morning Herald* article of his razor-sharp 'wit' while talking about that 41,000 Grand Final crowd:

'That was a colourful crowd holding hands on the Flinders Street footpath outside the Captain Cook last weekend. Don't think I've seen so many poofters prancing about on one corner of this city in my life.'

'Being on television does not make something wrong, right. And just because all of a sudden everyone is getting off a ferry, doesn't mean it's manly.'

'The season seems to have run fairly well from my reading of it, but football's impact on my consciousness has, in fact, probably gone backwards in the absence of crowd violence, ethnic tension and maritime flares.'

This was the sort of bullshit that was starting to reappear in the wake of the A-League's early gains, and although I was, by now, well accustomed to the ingrained prejudice against the game, that horrible blending of football with blatant homophobia was shocking.

Gibbs's day job was that of a crime reporter. So why the hell was he writing about football? That's a question I've asked many times down the years in Australia – because every single one of these articles comes from someone I've never, ever seen at a football ground, training session or press conference.

Anyway, I needn't have worried about fan behaviour on the day of the 2007 Grand Final – the only brutality was from Victory, as they put Adelaide to the sword, winning by six goals to nil, with Archie Thompson incredibly netting five of them.

The Reds' day started off badly, with Ross Aloisi getting sent off, and ended in humiliation, and then bitterness, as they accused the match officials of having 'cheated' them out of silverware. It was nonsense of course, but their behaviour did leave something of a sour taste in the mouth – more on that shortly. But otherwise, the occasion was overwhelmingly positive. A record crowd of 55,436 packed out the Dome, swelled by several thousand Adelaide fans who came to support their team in vain. Evidence of the competition's growth was the appearance of the (then) Prime Minister, John Howard, to present the trophy and medals. Kristian Sarkies planted a kiss on the top of his bald pate as he received his, and it seemed football had truly arrived.

Yet just a week or two later, the old bile re-emerged, this time in *The Adelaide Advertiser.* An ABC radio presenter – with no obvious links to the game of football – was strangely given a platform in the local rag to pen a piece entitled 'Soccer – why I can't stand the game'.

Now, I have often thought of asking the local papers in Sydney whether I can write a column on topics such as 'Tomatoes – why I don't like the taste' but, given I have no Gordon Ramsay-type background, I don't think they'd take me seriously. So, why was this given valuable editorial space in order to antagonise people about football?

> 'Soccer is a stupid game, riven with ethnic division and violence between supporters. It gives multiculturalism a bad name. It's un-Australian, and it suits more passionate nations...We're lumbered with Adelaide United, perhaps the worst team ever to supposedly represent our state in any sport. It's unworthy to be called South Australian.'

And that's after they reached the Grand Final!

In June 2007, we were off to the Asian Cup, another new experience. This tournament was unique, in that it was going to be the first to be held in four separate countries: Indonesia, Malaysia, Thailand and Vietnam.

The Socceroos were based in Thailand, so after a routine 3–0 friendly success in Singapore, they – and we – flew into Bangkok. The Fox Sports team in Bangkok included myself, executive producer Murray Shaw, and Robbie Slater. As Murray and I busied ourselves making pre-tournament packages on the local culture for the producers back home, Robbie was at a bit of a loose end. We assumed he was busy doing research for a competition that contained plenty of unfamiliar names but it turned out he'd been sampling the local nightlife a little too much instead!

As the opening game of the tournament drew closer, Murray had us record a two-way (presenter and expert chat) for Fox Sports News. Murray wanted us to focus on the opposition, and perhaps investigate just how much research Robbie had done on Australia's first opponents, Oman. Whatever the reason, it worked. I asked Robbie what we could expect from the Omanis, and he looked blank before offering up the only piece of information he (and everyone else) already knew, regarding Oman's most famous player, 'Well, they have Ali Al-Habsi (the English Premier League goalkeeper), and as we know, he's big, and he's good.'

The rest of the chat wasn't much better, and in fairness, Robbie was clever enough to realise it too. As soon as I wrapped up the interview and our cameraman had said 'That's a take,' Robbie exclaimed, 'That's it, my holiday is over. I've got to go and do some work!' We didn't see him for the next two days, but he got his prep done.

Robbie's big mate from his playing days, Graham Arnold, had some preparation problems too. He'd actually wanted to use this Asian Cup as a testing ground for the next generation of Socceroos, but that plan had been vetoed by FFA, who were keen to be competitive on their regional debut. So, Arnie was instructed to call up all of his big-name European-based stars. But like Slater, they'd left their preparation late, and they were also clearly struggling with the heat, even in the environs of the team hotel. Several players would routinely wander around the lobby area without their tops on, and while in most Thai tourist resorts this wouldn't normally be a problem, SBS journalist Scott McIntyre in particular, thought this disrespectful in the lobby of a city hotel, in an otherwise conservative country.

Now, I consider Scott a friend. I like his quirky personality, and I have huge respect for his football knowledge of Asia, a region whose football he has covered in great depth for many years. But he does have a certain knowledge of Asian culture, and he regularly unloads on his fellow countrymen for their lack of understanding, or appreciation of, regional nuances.

Anyway, McIntyre made mention of this 'topless wandering' in his SBS reports, which brought him into direct conflict with Graham Arnold. Arnold felt he was making a mountain out of a molehill, and I was inclined to agree with him. But instead of ignoring it – as Guus Hiddink would undoubtedly have done – Arnie couldn't resist becoming involved.

This is where I thought he struggled a little under the demands of a high-profile job. No-one likes being criticised, especially if that criticism is perceived to be unfair. But when you are in a top job, it does somewhat come with the territory, and you need to develop a strategy to be able to deal with it – as Hiddink had done in 2006, with his 'phone call' from his mum in Munich. Arnie regularly attached his ethos to that of Hiddink, yet he seemed to have learned little of the master's psychology. Instead, in this vital area of media relations, he would have very public disagreements, all of which gave the impression of a man under pressure, and not entirely in control. When results go south as well, then you are in big trouble and that's what happened at this Asian Cup.

Before the Socceroos got their campaign under way, Robbie and I had to call the opening game at the Rajamangala Stadium on the outskirts of Bangkok. The match pitted the hosts Thailand, against Iraq. Both teams were in Australia's group, so it was a good chance to see what the 'Roos would be up against, but it was a game that almost didn't happen.

Bangkok in July is hot, steamy and monsoonal, and the storms that blow across from the turbulent Bay of Bengal can be vicious. This was one such storm. With an hour to go before the opening ceremony, the skies first turned grey, then black, and then, the rain came. Oh blimey, did the rain come. I have never seen a storm so intense as that one. We were at the back of the empty stand (underneath the roof in the broadcast zone, the only area which had any cover provided, in what was a rather antiquated arena), and thank God we were. So much water poured down from the skies that it actually broke through certain areas of the roof, and was cascading down the steps of the stand around us in torrents. We couldn't even see the far side of the ground for the deluge and the claps of thunder and shards of lightning sounded and felt like the apocalypse was only moments away.

When we heard an almighty bang, I thought doomsday was upon us. But when the storm started to subside a few minutes later, our field of vision began to improve and it was then we saw what had happened. Behind the goal away to our left had stood a huge tower of scaffolding, holding tons of fireworks, all in place for the opening ceremony, ready to go off in celebration of the start of the Asian Cup. But the wind, rain, general instability in the skies, or perhaps even a lightning strike, had somehow destabilised the tower, and it had come crashing down – falling over 50 feet onto the unprotected area below, with debris being scattered everywhere.

The only saving grace was that the storm had hit just before people began to enter the stadium to take their seats. Otherwise, there would have been casualties to rival the Bradford fire, or even Hillsborough, I'm sure of it. Stadium staff scurried around like ants trying to recover the fireworks, removing twisted pieces of metal and broken seats, and we wondered whether the ceremony – even the game – could possibly go ahead. But to the organisers' credit, within half an hour the clean-up operation had been deemed a success and, as there had been no casualties, a rather damp and low-key ceremony went ahead with just a short delay.

That night, Iraq recovered from falling behind to an early Sutee Suksomkit (later to play briefly for Melbourne Victory) penalty to earn a 1–1 draw. They would concede just once more in five matches, en route to a most unlikely triumph a couple of weeks later.

Twenty-four hours after that encounter, we were back at the Rajamangala for Australia's opener against Oman. Well, 22 to be precise, because the 'Roos' game kicked off a bit earlier, in the stifling heat of the late afternoon, and that proved to be a key factor in a rather limp display by Graham Arnold's team, with only a last gasp equaliser from Tim Cahill preventing an embarrassing defeat.

If we're being honest, Australia looked woefully underdone. They'd admitted they knew little about Oman, and the conditions left them unable to press the opposition. Mark Viduka was too often isolated, Harry Kewell marked out of the game by Ahmed Mubarak, and Oman looked the fitter, better organised team.

Robbie and I then started a marathon phase of commentating 10 matches in as many days – in two different countries. With other commentary teams located in (much further away) Indonesia and Vietnam, we needed to cover the group based in Malaysia, in addition to our commitments in Bangkok. This meant crisscrossing the Gulf of Thailand on a plane, from Bangkok to Kuala Lumpur and then back again, with two games in each city in between. It was a punishing schedule, not least because both airports are located quite some way from the city, and we were travelling on tourist visas only. I'm sure some of the airport security thought we were trafficking drugs, so often did our passports get stamped on those frequent trips, but no-one ever questioned us.

We were not only providing commentary for the folks back home in Australia, but also for the 'world feed' too. In Bangkok, we had got to know the various fixers, movers and shakers at the stadium by virtue of having been in the city for a couple of weeks prior to the kick-off. But in Malaysia, we had no such luxury, arriving only on the day of our first scheduled game between the hosts and China. To say they were unfriendly wouldn't quite be the right description. The truth is, they utterly ignored us after vaguely pointing us in the direction of the commentary box. With language barriers a problem, we had little choice but to just get on with it.

After finding our way, we called a fairly straightforward Chinese win (by five goals to one, against a Malaysian team that were quite the worst I've ever seen at international level), and were expecting to continue into our 10-minute post-game analysis, a procedure that was routine for world feed callers in all games such as these. To do this, we switched our gaze from the field of play to the TV monitors in front of us, and reacted verbally to the pictures that unfolded in front of us, cut by the director and his team in the truck back at the TV compound, in the apron of the stadium. Except this time, the TV monitors went black almost immediately. I was perplexed, and continued unaided for two minutes, Robbie and I both shrugging our shoulders, believing it was a technical fault that would soon be remedied. But when an engineer appeared and started to unplug the cables around us (quite nonchalantly ignoring the fact we were still talking), I could only presume that Malaysia had a different setup to that of Thailand.

Robbie and I downed tools, picked up our bags and made for the exits, believing the broadcast had finished. Except it hadn't. Haring towards us was a producer, bellowing at us in broken English to get back inside and keep talking. It transpired later that the engineers elsewhere in the stadium had acted unilaterally in switching off our monitor feed. The world must have heard me and Robbie saying 'Oh well, that must be it then. Let's go!'

It just goes to show that without preparation – and in this case, the world feed crew had been negligent in their lack of communication – you can be made to look utterly stupid when you are live on air, even if you think you aren't!

A day later, we were wiser (and so were the engineers), as Iran won a much closer game against Uzbekistan by two goals to one – a game memorable for Robbie's pronunciation of the Iranian striker, Iman Mobali, which came out as something resembling 'mobile home'. I could barely call the game for laughing. But it still doesn't come close to his best-ever mispronunciation, which was heard on Fox during an Asian Champions League game involving Adelaide United and the Korean team, Seongnam. Robbie called their flying winger Choi Sung-kuk 'Chasing Chuck!'

Robbie's incorrect use of the English language has become legendary at Fox down the years. Perhaps because he is also a fluent French speaker, he occasionally bastardises English words and comes up with something entirely new. In no particular order, we have had:

'Relegable' to describe a team that is in danger of being relegated.

'De-flammatory' meaning inflammatory.

'Secretarian violence' talking about the Celtic/Rangers Old Firm rivalry.

It's a language we've come to call 'Robbish' – an apt mix of Robbie, and rubbish!

Back in Thailand, Australia were preparing for their now vital encounter against Iraq at the Rajamangala. It was another blisteringly hot day, and another early kick-off – and the shit was really about to hit the fan.

The Socceroos were run ragged by an excellent Iraqi team, whose pass and move game revolving around the brilliant Nashat Akram, tore them to shreds. Late in the game, my bonhomie with Robbie started to sour, when I invited him to pass opinion on what had been an utterly abject Australian performance, for the listening audience back home.

Robbie looked a little awkward, and then shook his head. He wasn't prepared to hammer his mate. In some ways, I could understand his inner conflict given his friendship with Arnie, but at that moment, it really needed to be put to one side for the sake of honesty. In fairness, down the years Robbie has tempered that approach. But not on that day in Bangkok.

Instead, I got stuck into them to a certain extent – I felt I had no choice. But what happened next meant that whatever either of us said, didn't really matter. The Socceroos' coach was about to make a rod for his own back. On the back of the 3–1 loss, Murray Shaw interviewed Arnie down on the sidelines, with the exchange going live back to Australia. Murray asked the coach what he thought had gone wrong. Arnie passed the buck, saying that he thought some of the players 'didn't want to be there'. It was a surprising remark, even if you take into account the emotion of the moment.

When Murray then spoke to Mark Viduka, and repeated Arnie's accusation back to the Australian captain, Viduka was incredulous. 'He said what?' was Viduka's response. Worse, Lucas Neill had capped a rather petulant display by getting himself sent off, and he would now miss the decider with hosts Thailand.

When the *Daily Telegraph* then ran a story alleging Lucas had been banished to train alone in the wake of his red card, it looked increasingly like the Socceroos' debut at the Asian Cup would end in disaster, and recrimination. The Neill story however, proved to be untrue, which didn't exactly endear another section of the media entourage to Arnie and co.

Not that Robbie and I had much time to digest that performance – we were back on the plane bound for Kuala Lumpur, where the locals it seemed, had already given up on their pitiful team. For the opener against China, 21,000 had attended the enormous Bukit Jalil Stadium (capacity 100,000, and purpose-built for the Commonwealth Games of 1998). Against Uzbekistan, only 7000 braved another thrashing, this time by five goals to nil.

The only impressive thing about Malaysian football was their snazzy yellow and black striped shirts, and when the game finished I bought myself one from a stall outside. I had plenty of time to admire it. With so few potential customers, the local taxi companies hadn't bothered to send large numbers of cars for pick-ups. The Bukit Jalil was miles outside the city centre, which left us with a problem, as we searched for a lift back to our hotel. With no official transport booked, we had to wait over an hour for a cab to pick us up and transport us back to KL. Malaysia were out of the Asian Cup, and we were almost out on our feet.

Back we zigzagged to Bangkok for the decider between Thailand and Australia. There was no margin for error for the 'Roos now, they needed to win to edge out the Thais, who'd beaten Oman 2–0 in their second game. They were also hoping for an Oman win in the other match in the group against Iraq. If that happened, and the 'Roos could stick a few past the Thais, then they had a chance of staying in Bangkok for the quarterfinal. Otherwise, they'd have to travel to Vietnam, for a potential meeting with Japan, who'd already won Group C, defeating the Vietnamese earlier that day.

With Lucas Neill suspended, and Patrick Kisnorbo having had a pretty ordinary game against Iraq, Arnold had a new central defensive pairing in Mark Milligan and Michael Beauchamp. He also handed a Cup debut to David Carney at left-back, with Luke Wilkshire restored to his more favoured right side.

The changes worked a treat, with Milligan in particular outstanding. In front of 46,000 expectant Thais, the Socceroos ran out fairly comfortable winners, although the scoreline may have flattered them. The other game finished goalless however, so the quarterfinal would be in Hanoi, against one of the tournament favourites, Japan. The 'Roos had improved, but they would surely need to take their game to a different level, if they were to stand a chance.

The change of destination was problematic because no-one in the Australian camp expected it. Most thought the group phase would be a breeze, with the real tests to begin at the quarter, or even semifinal stage. Now, there was a rush to get to Vietnam – and for us, it meant getting visas. Not as easy as it sounded.

Many Australian fans had the same idea of course. Storm the Vietnamese embassy in Bangkok, and sort out the precious pieces of paper needed for entry. Except, being far away from home (where Vietnam were en route to a quarterfinal berth themselves), the embassy was largely unaware the Asian Cup was even going on. Publicity for this competition had, in truth, been fairly sparse. Even in the streets around the stadium, questions about the Asian Cup were met with quizzical looks, although many wore the tops of their favourite English Premier League club – a familiar refrain in Asia, as in Australia.

In the meantime, the Asian Cup was being played out in front of mainly empty stadiums. Only the four hosts were managing to pull any sort of a crowd – reminiscent of the African equivalent I'd witnessed back in 1998. The marketing was poor, tickets were pricey for the locals, and once their national team had gone out (as in Malaysia), they moved onto other things.

So, the poor official whose job it was to sort out tourist visas in the Vietnamese embassy had no clue as to what was about to hit her. We arrived one morning, only to find a queue of around 30 sweaty Australian fans, stinking in their polyester Socceroos jerseys, ahead of us – and the administrator losing patience with it all. By the time we got to the front of the queue on another oppressively hot Bangkok day, she had clearly had enough.

'No visa! No visa! Only visa next week! No more visa today! You organise weeks ago, not today!' she bellowed at us in broken English. After calming her down, we tried to persuade her to push through the paperwork, having explained – as best we could, given the language barrier – that we were official media, and simply couldn't wait until next week. Finally, she relented.

Hanoi turned out to be quite the experience. Still technically a communist country, it nevertheless seemed to have a thriving economy, and beautiful architecture, courtesy of first Chinese, then French colonial rule in the mid-nineteenth century. Relics of the Vietnam War were proudly displayed in many places, and the drone of motorbikes followed us everywhere – everyone in Vietnam it appeared, used this as their method of transport. All except me, that is.

In the build-up to the Japan–Australia quarterfinal, I decided to do a spot of sightseeing. In particular, I was intent on taking a glimpse inside the Ho Chi Minh Mausoleum, where the embalmed body of the former communist revolutionary is kept on display. Unfortunately, after finding the imposing building, I was informed that the mausoleum was closed for cleaning that particular day. While I was pondering my next move, a rickshaw driver pedalled up to me, stopped, and asked me did I want to go on a tour of the city?

I was keen, but my potential courier had a problem. He only had one arm, his left arm, as he later explained, having been amputated after being shot during the Vietnam War. While that clearly didn't stop him cycling around a busy city, I wondered how he coped with making hand signals if he needed to turn left in Hanoi's heavy traffic?

No matter, he wouldn't be deterred, and eventually I succumbed to his offer, asking him what price I would have to pay for the journey? He waved (figuratively speaking of course, he needed his only arm on the handlebars) my questions away, saying we could decide a price later, and that he was very cheap. And that I was his friend. Hmmm.

To be fair to my one-armed companion, he was an excellent tour guide. He took me to several sites of interest concerning the Vietnam War, including a river which still contained the upturned fuselage remains of an American fighter jet, shot down by the Viet Cong in that brutal conflict. I also visited a torture chamber (nice), temples, beautiful parks and various government buildings, before I signalled to him that it was probably time I made my way back to my hotel. This is where my previously good-natured driver turned tail, as I suspected might be the case.

After pulling up outside my hotel, we discussed a price. He wanted 100 American dollars, but I only had the local currency, the Vietnamese dong, of which I had the equivalent of roughly 50 American dollars. Having assured me all afternoon that he wasn't in the least bit tired, despite the lack of one of his upper limbs, the driver suddenly became very agitated, saying he was exhausted from driving me around, and that I needed to compensate him commensurately, as he couldn't now work again that day, due to his tiredness.

I opened my wallet, and showed him all I had – then offered it to him. He snatched the money off me, and as I walked off he shouted at me in perfect English, 'Fuck you! Fuck you! I only have one arm, I drive you round all day – fuck you!'

'And fuck you too!' I responded, smiling as I made my way into the hotel foyer. Had I underpaid him? I didn't think so, but I wanted to make sure, so I told the English-speaking receptionist my story. Was $50 fair?

'Fair? That's about a month's salary for him!' she said. I retreated to my room giggling that he'd tried to drive such a hard bargain. Mind you, three hours pedalling with one arm and a tourist on your bike can't have been easy – perhaps he did deserve double?

That little contretemps wasn't the only one I had in Hanoi. Robbie and I also fell out, which, given the schedule and the heat, perhaps wasn't too surprising. The altercation happened during another trip to the aforementioned Ho Chi Minh Mausoleum, which we wanted to use as a backdrop for a two-way for Fox Sports News. Our cameraman set up the shot, but as we started talking, I became aware that menacing-looking guards were moving quickly towards us. This was a special site for the Vietnamese, and of course, we had no permission from the authorities to be there, filming for television.

One of the guards walked into shot and put his hand over our camera, instructing us to stop. We had little choice but to comply, and he'd ruined the take anyway. I tried to ask him whether we could film in a different location, still using the mausoleum as a backdrop. With the liberal use of sign language, I pointed to various vantage points, each of which was met with a firm shake of the head and a wag of the finger. He just wanted us out of there.

With no mausoleum shot possible, we were limited for options. We had no transport, and there was no other fitting backdrop within walking range. It was a baking hot day, and we had heavy camera equipment with us. The only option, in my mind, was to get a taxi, seek out another location, and, if all else failed, head to the My Dính Stadium (pronounced Mee Din), which would at least give us an identifiable location. At this point, Robbie – tired and irritable no doubt, like the rest of us – exploded.

'I'm not fucking going to the stadium. It's miles away, and I have a massage booked this afternoon,' he ranted.

'I don't give a shit what you have booked Rob. We have to do this, so do your fucking job!' I responded.

The two of us squared up for several seconds, while Adrian, our cameraman, stood there agog, before the two of us collapsed in a fit of giggles, realising we were just edgy due to tiredness.

'Phew,' said Adrian, our lensman. 'I thought I was going to have to referee a boxing match in front of Ho Chi Minh for a minute there!'

Eventually, we sidled off round a corner, and found a different angle of the mausoleum, and just about got our two-minute chat recorded before the guards started to move in again, with their hands moving twitchily towards the guns stored in their hip pockets. Yep, it's all glamour, is television.

Australia's quarterfinal with Japan was arguably the Socceroos' best performance of a disappointing campaign. In the end, Japan won on penalties after a 1–all draw, with Vince Grella receiving Australia's second red card of the tournament after 75 minutes. Australia battled manfully with the reduced numbers throughout extra time, but perhaps the man advantage, along with the travel, was the difference. Japan had by that time, spent the best part of three weeks in Vietnam.

Ultimately, Australia paid the price for poor preparation, a selection policy that was wrong, underestimating the opposition, and struggling to cope with an unfamiliar climate. They would learn from those mistakes, and so would Arnie. He would become a much better coach over the next few years.

The Aussies made their way home, but it wasn't the end of our sojourn in Hanoi. We were staying on to call Japan's semi with Saudi Arabia four days later. This gave us the chance of a bit of down time, and while Robbie and I were happy to rest and wander around the city, Murray was keen to sightsee further afield. In particular, he wanted to experience the stunning Halong Bay. Ordinarily, I'd have jumped at the chance to go with him, but after all our travel, a day-long excursion just seemed too much effort, and I declined. Besides, I needed to do some research on the Saudis, who I hadn't yet called at this Asian Cup.

The first semifinal saw Iraq prevail on penalties over South Korea after a goalless draw – a major surprise. That meant whoever managed to win through the second semi, would be clear favourites to lift the Asian crown itself.

The match was a classic. An end-to-end encounter of punch, and counterpunch. The Saudis struck first through Yasser Al-Qahtani, nicknamed 'the Sniper', before Japan equalised through Yuji Nakazawa. Malek Mouath restored the Green Falcons' lead, only for them to be pegged back again thanks to Yuki Abe's strike.

Mouath eventually won the game for Saudi Arabia after a mazy dribble ended in a futsal-style toe-poke which caught Yoshi Kawaguchi by surprise and slammed into the roof of the net. It was a goal worthy of winning a semi, and the Saudis were through to an all Middle Eastern Final.

Our long month in South-East Asia ended in the Indonesian capital, Jakarta, for one of the most romantic stories in sporting history. Iraq, a nation torn apart by war, had given their troubled people something to cheer by winning through to the final against the odds. They were everyone's second favourite team, and their run to the decider had captured the imagination of the world's press.

Steph had flown over for our impending holiday in Cambodia, and I managed to get her a ticket for the game, at the majestic Gelora Bung Karno. There was Australian interest on the field too, with referee Mark Shield chosen as the match referee, and he was heavily involved in a tense final, issuing seven yellow cards, with six of them coming in the first half.

Younes Mahmoud netted the winner to ensure this particular piece of sporting romance had a happy ending, and aside of the Saudis, 60,000 inside the stadium stayed to applaud their unlikely success.

Afterwards, we were having a drink at the hotel bar, when Shield walked in. He told us that, at one stage, Mahmoud (the Iraqi captain), had threatened to take his team off the park in protest at the number of yellow cards being issued. Shield's response?

'Okay, off you go, see you later!'

Shield was one of the better refs Australia has produced, and in contrast to the popular view, I've never thought the refs who have officiated in the A-League down the years were as bad as some fans (and media) made out. That view has been backed up by the AFC, who have consistently chosen Australian referees to take charge of their bigger matches.

The A-League has now embarked upon the era of full-time referees, but it's my view that, while it may make a slight difference, the complaining will never stop. As a community, football fans have become obsessed by incorrect decisions, and while it's understandable if a big decision goes against you, it is, in my opinion, all part of the game.

The only area where I have ever wanted to see improvement in is goal line technology. After all, goals are the most important bit. Thankfully, FIFA, after fighting hard against its introduction for quite some time, has now agreed, and at the top level at least, the technology is utilised to help the refs and linesmen.

Football, as a sport, needs a cultural change in its approach to officialdom. Other sports, such as Rugby Union, manage to accept decisions without much complaint, yet in football it has become a case of mob mentality, with players herding around referees to make their protest.

This behaviour came to a head in the A-League the following season, when Joel Griffiths aimed a punch in the direction of a linesman's groin in protest at a decision that had gone against him. Joel became universally known as the 'sack whacker' among A-League fans, and later that season, Danny Vukovic got himself into hot water by slapping the arm of Shield in the Grand Final between Central Coast Mariners and Newcastle Jets. But while Griffiths escaped punishment, Vukovic's was severe, a lengthy ban which saw him miss the 2008 Olympics.

Generally, FFA has been very good in trying to curb player excesses – a necessary approach, in a country where football remains under the microscope for any hint of misbehaviour, on and off the pitch. A good example of this is the fact that diving, or simulation, is theoretically punishable under the FFA's disciplinary policy. This was hugely controversial at the time, and remains so, but diving is one of those acts that is an instant turn-off for non-football people in Australia, so I applauded the FFA's stance. I still do. It's rarely been used, but Patricio Perez of Central Coast Mariners was once banned for simulation, an act which earned his team a penalty against Sydney. Sydney FC themselves fined one of their own players, Shannon Cole, for taking a dive against Gold Coast United, and I think that course of action is even better. Club culture is paramount in stamping out this sort of nonsense.

Many years later, I wrote an article on the Fox website regarding the amount of abuse refs were having to put up with, and while doing the research for it, the stats shocked me. Ben Wilson, the current Head of Referees at the FFA, told me that over 50 per cent of young refs give the game away before they reach adulthood, in the main, down to the abuse they suffer on the playing fields of Australia, up and down the country. That's just plain wrong, and A-League clubs being at the top level of the game, have a responsibility to set the right example.

As the 2016/2017 season drew to a close, video assistant replays were given an airing on a trial basis. Many feel they are overdue, and will help the refs. I disagree. Although their scope is limited in the initial phase of testing, it surely won't be long before we have fans (and coaches) screaming for every decision to be reviewed. That will suit TV of course – more stoppages, more chance for advertising – but I think it will ruin the flow of the game. Far better to instigate a 'respect' campaign to help the officials; but will the 'mob' accept that?

CHAPTER 13 THIRTEEN

FOUR WEDDINGS & A FUNERAL

With the Asian Cup over, Steph and I were about to embark upon a well-earned holiday in Cambodia, where we toured the spellbinding temples of Angkor Watt, sailed down the Tonle Sap floating villages, and visited the killing fields and the Tuol Sleng genocide museum in Phnom Penh.

Our first flight en route to the Cambodian capital was back to Bangkok, to catch our connection, and as we boarded the plane in Jakarta, I was delighted to see the joyful Iraqi players, along with the Cup, were on the same route as us. As we disembarked in Thailand, I chatted briefly to their genial coach, Jorvan Vieira, who was almost overcome with the emotion of it all. He did, however, let slip that he wouldn't be continuing in his role with the Iraq FA, and that he was due to speak to the FFA with regards to the coaching job with Australia. I immediately relayed this back to the producers at Fox Sports News – the hunt was on to find a full-time coach, with Graham Arnold set to be relieved of his duties as interim.

I felt sorry for Arnie. I liked him as a bloke, and I think he's a good coach but much of the Asian Cup experience had been a disaster, and I wrote an article saying FFA should never make the same mistake of appointing an interim coach again. This wasn't intended as a dig at Arnie in isolation. In many ways, he was in a no-win situation. The good news for Graham, was that FFA found him alternative employment, leading the Olympic team towards the Beijing Games. He would also be back with the senior team as assistant to the new coach, Pim Verbeek, who was not FFA's initial choice. Arnie's last game in charge of the national team was a friendly at the MCG against Argentina. The South Americans won the game 1–0, and the only reason I remember this game at all, is because of an exchange in the players' tunnel with a certain FFA Board Member.

Fox, at the time, had just taken on Spencer Prior as a pundit on our English Premier League coverage. Many people thought he was my 'friend' (the mates culture once again), but I'd only ever met him once, on the day Manchester City had won promotion at Blackburn, all the way back in 2000. Some even believed Prior's appointment was my doing but the truth was, I didn't hold that sort of sway at Fox, and still don't.

Anyhow, the FFA Board member and I were chatting about various things as we waited for the players to come out and do their pre-match routine, when he asked about Prior (of whom, he clearly wasn't a fan).

I explained that Murray Shaw had taken a gamble on him, and that he had a decent pedigree as a player. My friend concurred, but then offered this opinion, which rather typified the whole debate surrounding Australian football at the time.

'But why has he got the job, when we are trying to get rid of the English out of football here?'

I raised my eyebrows at him, inviting him to continue to talk. Realising his faux pas, he tried to backtrack.

'Well, I don't mean you obviously. Anyway, you've been here ages.'

The old 'I'm not racist, some of my best friends are black' type argument. That was the level of debate we were now having. I was considered an Aussie because I'd been there four years – so I got a pass. I was eager to know where the cut-off point was, but he couldn't tell me.

As if to underline the ridiculousness of this love/hate relationship with the 'mother country' barely two weeks after that game, 80,000 people turned up to watch a game set up by FFA – Sydney FC against Los Angeles Galaxy in a glorified friendly, mainly on the strength of the presence of an Englishman.

David Beckham's arrival in Sydney had people scrambling over themselves for tickets; it was extraordinary. I was asked to MC the Galaxy's pre-game press conference (although the rights to broadcast the game itself were held by Channel 10), which naturally enough, included the main star, Beckham himself.

I only spoke to David for a few moments back stage, and while he was typically polite and friendly, it was obvious he was tired after his long flight, and perhaps rather weary of the constant attention that followed him, wherever he went.

Case in point, the pre-game function – a lavish party, thrown at the Museum of Sydney which had a red carpet entrance, lined with barriers to keep the public at bay, and which was akin to attending the Oscars. Beckham spent the entire night holed up in a corner, flanked by security, as one-by-one, the Sydney social set tried to get a photo with him. It was all rather laughable in a country where 'soccer' encountered such hostility. The clearest sign of the shallowness of the occasion was when Steph and I clocked the legendary Ruud Gullit (then the coach of LA Galaxy), standing alone – totally unrecognised, and unmolested by the fawning hordes. We went over for a chat, and he seemed grateful for the company, making us smile by telling us he'd said to Beckham, 'This used to be my life. Now it's yours, and you are welcome to it!'

Anyhow, Beckham certainly delivered in the game, scoring a trademark peach of a free-kick, causing 80,000 to swoon. The game must have made a fair few dollars from that single night. Not bad for one of those 'poms' people didn't want anywhere near Australian football.

There was one more international to be played in the calendar year, a friendly against Nigeria in London in November. I was sent across to cover the game, and interview the new Socceroos coach, expected to be named as Dick Advocaat. Except, by the time I got to London, Advocaat was having second thoughts, and eventually refused the job. Still, the trip was worthwhile if only to meet the infamous Mark Bosnich for the first time. Bozza had been brought out of his self-imposed exile for this match, to co-commentate with me. No-one knew what to expect – few had sighted the former Aston Villa, Man United and Chelsea goalkeeper, since a failed drugs test ended his English Premier League career in 2001.

I called Bosnich upon my arrival into London, just to check that he was au fait with the preparations, and what we had to do. Mark wanted to come and meet me at my hotel in Paddington, and then travel with me to watch a Socceroo training session. Half an hour later, in he breezed, looking a million dollars in a snazzy suit and overcoat, topped off with a huge Cuban cigar – he looked like a fifties film star!

I'd actually met Bozza once before, very briefly, during my BBC days. We'd arranged to interview him just after he'd signed with Manchester United. Given the Beeb's rather prickly relationship with the club, we'd checked everything very thoroughly before I got the go-ahead to travel up north. But when I spotted Bozza coming off the pitch at the end of a training session at the Cliff (then United's training ground), and told him who I was, he shook his head and said he wouldn't be doing any interviews that day.

Later, Bozza would tell me the interview had been blocked by Alex Ferguson, who of course had a long-running feud with the Beeb that dated back to an article written by broadcaster, Pat Murphy, in the *Match of the Day* magazine. The end result was that Fergie refused to countenance any interviews with the BBC for years, and this incident with Bosnich took place right in the middle of that ban. I had to interview Phil Neville instead, who incidentally, was very good value!

Anyway, back in London ahead of the Nigeria match, Bosnich accompanied me to the Socceroos training session at a small, non-league ground in West London. When he walked through the gates and took his place in the small stand, even some of the players couldn't quite believe it.

I heard Mark Schwarzer exclaim, 'Is that Mark Bosnich?' and as he sauntered across curiously, I told our cameraman to get filming, as this was our money shot coming right up. Sure enough, Schwarzer and Bosnich embraced and chatted for several moments before Schwarzy resumed his duties on the field. One by one, others then briefly ran up and shook hands, or high-fived their former colleague – and Bozza was loving it, as you might expect of a personality the size of his.

As was (and is) typical of Bozza however, as Schwarzy ran back to his drills, he asked if he could see him after the session. 'Sure, I'll be here,' said Bozza.

Ten minutes later, and with the cameras switched off, Bozza shouted at Schwarzer again. 'Schwarzy – I'm off son! Got to go. See you soon!' And with that, he was gone, leaving Schwarzer shaking his head and smiling. He knew Bozza only too well.

Australia won the game 1–0 with Rob Baan taking charge temporarily. David Carney scored a belter of a goal. Bosnich? He did reasonably well behind the mic, although he consistently referred to Carney as 'Scott Carney' and insisted on saying 'back to the action' as he finished a point and handed back to me in commentary!

However, it was to be the start of a long and fruitful relationship between Bosnich and Fox – he is now arguably the most-loved member of our on-air team, and his views hold huge sway among the public. In fact, so much so, that Robbie Slater, only half-jokingly, refers to him as the 'Minister of Football!'

After the shock of Dick Advocaat's about turn, Pim Verbeek was appointed Socceroos coach on 6 December 2007, and no-one quite knew what to make of FFA's selection. He had a fairly lengthy coaching career behind him, but most of his more recent roles had been as a number two. Perhaps crucially, one of those was under Guus Hiddink, always the two magical words in an Australian context.

In his most recent senior role, with South Korea, he'd hardly pulled up any trees, with their third place finish at the 2007 Asian Cup coming on the back of several dull displays, featuring precious few goals. A quick check of online articles concerning his time at Omiya Ardija in the J-League, confirmed that supporters of that club quickly tired of long balls being aimed in the direction of the club's (then) centre forward, Jeroen Boere. I wrote a piece on the Fox website giving only a cautious welcome to the appointment.

Robbie Slater meantime, was more critical, perhaps understandably, given his connections to Arnie. His piece in the *Daily Telegraph* carried the headline 'Who is this Neville Nobody?' So, it was somewhat embarrassing for him to be asked to sit next to Pim, when he was invited onto *Total Football* the following week.

I was on the panel too and Harps tried to throw a curve ball right from the start on that particular show – challenging both Robbie and I to justify our stance on Verbeek, with the Dutchman sat there, right next to us. It was an awkward moment, but I tried to explain that, as members of the football media, our opinions on football matters were sought on all sorts of issues, and therefore we were obliged to have a view. I added that, if Verbeek was successful, then we would be delighted, and gladly eat our words.

Thankfully, Pim understood what being in the media meant, and he didn't take offence. In fact, Pim and I would go on to have a fantastic working relationship – without doubt the best I have ever had with a coach, either at club or international level.

He even took a faux pas made by Robbie and I in good spirits, when the power of modern technology left us with our pants down, one night in Newcastle. That night, we were in the Hunter for a routine A-League game, and preparing to go on air to do our pre-game show. The cameras were panning around the stadium, trying to get some interesting shots for us to talk over. Pim appeared in the director's box, with his trademark comb-over. Robbie and I were messing about a bit – we were still not on air for a good 10 minutes – and so we started to imitate Pim's Dutch accent, playing on stereotypes of the Netherlands as a nation, for good measure.

'Going to the coffee shop?' I said in jest to Robbie.

'Yah, and going to shee the shexshy girlsh!' said Robbie in response, both of us in a faux Dutch accent.

There was more too – all good fun, or so we thought. Until the next day, when some techno geek, who'd been recording our 'off-air' coverage via some glitch in the system, decided to put the whole thing up on YouTube.

I had a call from a friend who warned me it was up there, so I had little option but to ring Pim, and tell him that he may well hear about a video that was doing the rounds, in which Robbie and I were utterly taking the piss out of the national team coach. Pim was brilliant. In Hiddink-esque fashion, he told me, 'Simon, I'm not worried. I know you, I know you. I know you wouldn't do such a thing to hurt me. Don't worry about it.'

If it ever bothered him, he never let it show. That really was Pim to a tee – or perhaps he just had a good tutor in Guus.

Pim was in attendance the night I co-hosted the AFC Annual Awards night in Sydney too, in November 2007. The other compere was a very pretty Malaysian girl called Paula Malai Ali. She was an excellent host, very professional, and the two of us hit it off straightaway. But Paula was tiny – only around 5 feet 2 inches – and with me being nearer 6 feet 3 inches, we looked ridiculous stood next to each other at the podium in rehearsals. The problem was solved by the use of a curtain, judiciously draped in front of the lectern, which did the job of hiding an upturned beer crate, upon which Paula stood for the duration of the ceremony!

That ceremony was also a little lesson into how the world of football politics operated at the highest levels. The auditorium at the Hordern Pavilion had been arranged in such a way that the members of the AFC Executive Committee sat in a long line of chairs, with their individual tables facing the front stage. Everyone else was situated further back, sitting around circular tables. The ExCo members were mainly Princes or Sheikhs from the Middle East. Not only did that region dominate the AFC, but their representatives were clearly used to this sort of preferential treatment. Several of them worked their way through so much food and drink that they were asleep in their chairs well before the main trophy was presented, only waking up in time for their limousine to take them back to their plush hotel suites.

It had been another good 12 months professionally, but as the end of the 2007 approached, I had some bad news from back home in England.

My sister Fiona, who had been in remission for several years after her cancer scare, was unwell. Within days, our worst fears had been confirmed – the breast cancer had returned, and she was to start chemotherapy almost immediately. This, sadly, is a regular feature of breast cancer, and the earlier in life you suffer from it, the higher the chance it will recur.

Fiona got all the 'nice' genes in our family. She was a stay-at-home mum, who never moved far away from my parents' house. Family was very important to her, and she lived a frugal life, ensuring any money she and husband Mike had, went on their three subsequent kids, Philip, Thomas and Kathryn. Fiona didn't smoke, rarely drank, and was a well-known and popular member of the village community, where she'd always lived. She was a regular church-goer and generally saw the best in people.

By contrast, I was the hell-raising, smoking, drinking, womanising, career-chasing, argumentative, complaining brother. We'd always been poles apart. And yet the cancer chose Fiona.

I sought permission to take a short period of leave to travel back to the UK and visit her. I figured she needed all the strength she could muster from her family. It was a dark time, and I discussed the situation with my parents, asking them whether they thought me moving back would be a good idea. They said no, I had a life to lead, and for the moment, that was in Australia. So, after a week in England doing the best I could, in encouraging Fiona to take up the fight for a second time, I returned to Australia. Fiona fought her battle stoically, but tragically, there was to be no happy ending.

I'd literally been off the plane 24 hours before I was back on one, flying to South Australia to take up my duties as commentator at Adelaide Oval, where a wonder goal from Brendon Santalab helped Sydney FC to a 3–1 win over Adelaide United.

As 2008 dawned, and perhaps with the old maxim 'life is short' at the forefront of my mind in the wake of Fiona's illness, I made a big life decision. Steph and I were planning to buy a house in Sydney's inner west and when her birthday (in January) came around, I thought it would be a nice idea to have a surprise party, with a few close friends. I organised a meal at Wildfire, the restaurant at Circular Quay, sending out invitations to some of our closest friends. I asked them to keep it a secret, for no other reason than I wanted Steph to have a nice surprise when we turned up at the restaurant. But when I got a message back from two of our best friends, Simon and Lineka (Lineka was Steph's old partner in her naturopathy business), jokingly asking whether the 'secret' element was due to the prospect of me proposing, it set me thinking.

Why not? I purchased a ring, and proposed with a poem that only revealed my true intentions in the very last line. We hoped we could – finally – make a marriage work between us. Steph had been married twice before, me once…all had failed. Now you know the reason behind the 'Four Weddings' part in the title of this chapter. Collectively, this is our fourth go at it!

While we househunted and set in motion plans to get married, the Socceroos began their World Cup qualifying campaign under new boss, Pim Verbeek, defeating Qatar 3–0 in Melbourne.

Meanwhile, I'd also rekindled my interest in music. Although I'd had to sell my old acoustic drum kit, a chance conversation with a former SBS colleague (director, John Firth), led to me purchasing one of the new-fangled electronic kits. It was fairly basic, but it got me back into the old routine of hitting the skins (or in this case, pads), and John and I had the occasional 'jam' in the front room of his house, which must have delighted his neighbours.

Within a few months, we'd been joined by John's friend, Kylie Gass, who was then just learning to play bass, and afterwards, by former ABC journalist, Mark Chester on vocals. With the addition of his daughter, Greer, on keyboards, all of a sudden we had a band, and were rehearsing regularly with a view to playing gigs and going in the studio.

We've been at it ever since, and even had a nice article written on us by Aidan Ormond of Australian FourFourTwo website, with whom I was a columnist for many years. It's one of the great joys of my life, and I've since progressed to playing in a metal band, Green Manalishi, which of course, was my ultimate musical dream.

Back in Socceroo-land, Australia were preparing to play their next World Cup qualifier in China, arranging a friendly in Singapore as a warm-up. I was on a whistlestop tour of Asia that would also take in a few days in Bangkok to call the Asian Champions League game between Chonburi and Melbourne Victory. I was flying solo in this game, working without a co-commentator, and this was the first real indication that the ACL was going to be tough for A-League clubs, even against supposedly 'lesser' opposition.

Chonburi won the game 3–1 in stifling conditions, and Victory, who were expecting their other group opponents, Gamba Osaka and Chunnam Dragons, to be their main threat, were left a little stunned.

From Bangkok, I flew onto the city-state of Singapore, expecting a rather celebratory affair, as the Singaporeans had announced this would be their last-ever game at the old Kallang venue, before it was knocked down and replaced with a more modern structure. In the end however, just 6000 turned up, perhaps in part due to a big rock concert going on over the road; or perhaps they had read the weather forecast, which had predicted a storm. Certainly, the game itself was a damp squib. Literally. In addition, the technical side of things were the worst I'd ever experienced, before or since.

The local company looking after the broadcast had, bizarrely, forgotten to book any crew, such as cameramen, editors, producers, engineers etcetera. Realising their mistake just a couple of days before the game was scheduled to take place, they had hurriedly recruited staff who were double-booked to work on the Malaysian Grand Prix.

This meant they had to fly back from Kuala Lumpur on the day of the game, before heading back north after the match. Their flights were delayed by the weather, and with just an hour to go before kick-off, almost nothing was in place. The engineers were working like stink to get things up and running, but there was nothing ready for us to broadcast with in our tiny commentary booth.

The heavens helped us, thankfully. A tropical storm, the likes of which we'd seen in Thailand the previous year, descended over the Kallang Stadium and drenched the place so thoroughly, that kick-off was delayed by a quarter of an hour. Those 15 minutes saved our bacon, allowing the engineers to apply the finishing touches to their work, and set up our commentary position properly. Even then, it was a close run thing, with the final cables being attached as the teams stood in line for the national anthems.

As a commentator, these sorts of technical issues can really throw you off your game – you are focusing on other things, rather than the game. It takes you out of your 'zone' when TV directors are constantly asking for sound checks, and there are technical people scurrying around you looking panicky. It was one of my worst calls of a Socceroos game.

The match itself was utterly spoiled, the pitch suffering as a result of the now abated storm. The long and spongy South-East Asian grass, sodden with water, held the ball up so much that it was almost impossible for either team to play any sort of a passing game. It finished 0–0, and not many of Verbeek's experimental 11 had the chance to make much of an impression, and force their way into his starting team for the qualifier a few days later.

The following day, we flew into Kunming. It was my first trip to China, and I can't say I was much impressed by the city they had chosen to host the qualifier. It was busy, dirty, our hotel had a knocking shop on the second floor, and to make matters worse, I fell ill. I wasn't the only one.

In fairness to the Chinese, they'd opted for Kunming with good reason. The city lies at an altitude of 1900 metres, and taking the game there was an attempt to put the 'Roos off their stride. It didn't help that Verbeek lost seven of his players through various, unrelated injuries. The Chinese tried every trick in the book to upset the Australians.

Verbeek had to cancel a training session one day, when the police escort failed to turn up. Australian fans meantime, were being charged 444 yuan to buy a ticket, more than double the price being asked of the locals. The number four, incidentally, was no accident either; it is considered to be very unlucky in China, as it sounds like the way their word 'death' is pronounced. It was gamesmanship, pure and simple.

Verbeek himself was under the weather. During a pre-game press conference, Pim had mistakenly called Bruce Djite 'Bruce Willis', much to the hilarity of the gathered media, but when he ventured towards us to conduct one-to-ones, it was clear that his mistake was not just absent-mindedness. As the cameras started to roll, all of a sudden he swayed, and almost fell over, before steadying himself by grabbing a chair.

'I'm sorry, I need to take a small break, I don't feel very well,' said Verbeek.

The 'Roos coach recovered after a few minutes, joking that the media now 'had their headline' but the gastric bug gave him a ghastly pallor. It had claimed one of his backroom staff too, who would spend most of that trip in bed. I was suffering from it too, a mixture of diarrhoea and vomiting that threatened to take me out of the commentary box.

Salvation came in the shape of the 'Roos team doctor, Peter Brukner, who gave me some pills that got me – just about – through the game. At the full-time whistle, our producer Gary Burchett asked me if I wanted to do some interviews. I declined, saying I had more urgent requirements. That was the cue for a sprint back to the hotel, ready for another lengthy session in the bathroom. Such is life on the road with the 'Roos!

With only 48 hours acclimatisation time, and so many key personnel missing, Australia had sent out a team for that particular game with a rather odd look about it. Robbie remarked that it was probably the first time he'd ever seen a 4–6–0 formation, with Archie Thompson the player given the most licence to roam forward. He, however, was substituted after just 10 minutes due to injury, and the rest barely got over the halfway line until the last half an hour.

For all that, China didn't have the quality to threaten the Socceroos, and even when they won a late penalty, Mark Schwarzer again performed heroics from the spot to ensure the scoreline stayed blank. All in all, a very good point away from home in such trying circumstances – and David Carney had a great chance to win it near the end.

In July 2008, I became an Australian citizen. Surprised? I suppose you'd have every right to be, given some of the stories I've recounted so far in this book. But as is the story with many immigrants, mine is not a tale that is simply black and white.

For all the cultural problems I'd had in Australia, there was no doubt there were (and are) many positives of living in such a fantastic country. I'd quickly learned that while certain aspects of the culture were frustrating, others were a breath of fresh air. Certainly, the old Aussie adage of a 'fair go' (English football coaches being the clear exception) most certainly applied. If you were prepared to work hard, then the system would reward you – I thought that was a fantastic scenario, and much preferable to the class-based hierarchy I'd been used to in the UK. Australia is clean, prosperous, safe (by and large), and the climate is a big attraction.

In addition, I felt that if I wanted to have my say on the things I didn't like, I had better sign up to being a fully-fledged Australian, rather than throw hand grenades from the outside. I know many British people who've had the same cultural issues as me, and who refuse to get an Aussie passport (even though they are entitled to apply for one) because of it. I think that is the coward's way out, and ultimately, counterproductive. Especially as you can hold dual passports, which is what I have done since that day in 2008.

The 2007/08 A-League season had ended with Newcastle Jets winning their first championship, and there were tentative plans to expand the competition for the following season. North Queensland Thunder and Gold Coast Galaxy were both issued with provisional licences, but just a couple of weeks before that qualifier in China, they were revoked due to financial concerns, and expansion was put on hold until the following campaign. Eventually of course, both North Queensland and Gold Coast were admitted – with the suffixes of Fury and United instead. Neither would last longer than a few years, which I thought was a huge shame.

Expanding a fledgling league is a tricky business, especially in a country the size of Australia. The distances, time differences and varying climates of the states means bringing in new clubs is always going to require a lot of careful thought. But I felt – and still feel – that FFA gave up too early on both clubs. With only a few major cities in Australia, the game can ill afford to throw the towel in, after having gone to a particular market. The Gold Coast in particular, had major problems with the global financial crisis hitting tourism in the area, and Clive Palmer's rather prickly relationship with the local population.

In North Queensland, there seemed to be a passionate, if smallish, fan base, who wanted to support the club, and make it work. Don Mathieson didn't have the cash to keep the club going, but I felt with a little perseverance, FFA could have grown an important market, one which gave the league an important geographical foothold in the far north of the country.

The Fury have now been reborn as Northern Fury, and Chairman Rabieh Krayem and his team continue to try and fly the flag, in the new National Premier Leagues set up. A year or so ago, I went up to Townsville, to have a look at their 'new' facility but sadly, it is little more than a park with a porta-cabin for dressing rooms. It's such a shame that all that initial work went to waste, and many people feel North Queensland was merely 'used' as a potential venue for its World Cup bid for 2022. I hope they can rise again, but it will take a lot of time, and work.

In my opinion, the tendency in Australia is to want to rip up clubs and start again when things go wrong. I hear the same thing even now with Melbourne City, Central Coast Mariners and Wellington Phoenix. 'Get rid of them' is the cry. This is one of the biggest problems of the game in Australia – longevity, or the lack of it. How can we possibly hope to entice generation after generation of supporters to watch the A-League if the clubs are constantly going out of business, only to be replaced by new ones?

As I said at the outset of this book, I was brought into the Manchester City fold by my dad, because he was a fan. In turn, my dad was a City fan, because his dad was – and so on. Football teams are precious family heirlooms, handed down to the next generation in most cases – you can't do that if your club doesn't exist.

Fans of NSL clubs will no doubt scream blue murder, opining that their clubs were thrown out of the top competition, and dispensed with. Yes, but they do still exist – and that was a peculiar set of circumstances, in which the league itself was broken, and the clubs themselves had 28 seasons in which to embed themselves in their local communities, and broaden their base accordingly. Few of them did with any great success, in terms of support, either at the gate, or commercially.

Football in Australia had to start again and by and large, the A-League has worked brilliantly. But the 10 clubs that now make up the elite competition must survive, and put down long-term roots. Perhaps eventually, some of those former NSL clubs can return to the top flight, when circumstances and times are different.

Talking of which, in mid-2008, Steph and I put down some roots, buying a large family house in the inner-west of Sydney. We got a bargain with the seven-bedroomed, corner plot with plenty of space for us, the kids and our lovely dog, Othello. But it desperately needed some renovation, so we lived in the upper part of the house for the first month, while workmen drilled, banged and chiselled away beneath us, knocking the bottom half of the house into some sort of shape.

As we moved into the latter part of the year, Steph and I started to put plans into place for our wedding. But by now, my sister was seriously unwell. The cancer had really taken a hold. Even though the doctors kept going back to their medicine cabinet and producing new drugs, the outlook seemed bleak, as every test confirmed that the cancer was still there, and starting to spread.

Steph and I made a decision that we were going to get married in Europe at the beginning of 2009. There was no way Fiona was going to be well enough to travel all the way to Australia, and in any case, Steph's grandma (Oma-Oma in Dutch) was about to celebrate her ninety-fifth birthday in February 2009. It was an ideal time for Steph and the kids to visit their elderly relative, perhaps for the last time. Hopefully both could come to our wedding.

Except yet again, the Dutch authorities made simple plans look like a proposition from Wittgenstein (in the words of Basil Fawlty). We'd opted for Den Haag (where Steph's family were celebrating her grandmother's birthday) as the city where we would like to wed. Some investigation told us that civil celebrations were allowed at the Oude Stadhuis in the middle of the city – a beautiful old building.

We set about trying to get the paperwork in train for our big day, settling on 20 February 2009 as the date. This was harder than it sounded. The Dutch authorities wanted document after document after document, and all of them had to be signed and sealed ('apostilled') by the Department of Foreign Affairs and Trade. It cost a fortune, and every time we sent another one of these documents over to the Netherlands, back it came a fortnight later with 'errors' ringed in red pen. Something was always wrong – a date wrong, a signature missing, an erroneous stamp, or some such.

We had to start over again so many times it become hugely frustrating. Steph spoke some Dutch, and her parents, of course, were fluent, but mainly, the problem was plain old cultural misunderstanding. In particular, the Dutch authorities just couldn't fathom why an Australian girl (albeit one with a Dutch passport), was marrying an English boy in Holland. I suppose that was a fair question. But even when we explained it to them, something was still being lost. They kept asking where our intended address in the Netherlands would be. We told them we didn't live in the Netherlands. They asked us where we HAD lived in the Netherlands. We told them we had NEVER lived in the Netherlands. Then, they asked us why we were getting married IN the Netherlands. And round and round we went. For months.

Eventually, we solved each of these problems – at a cost of thousands of dollars

– before we hit upon one main snag, with just a week to go.

Apparently, the birth certificate I had been given by my parents years and years ago was not the original, it was merely a short-form copy! The Dutch needed a better, more detailed, copy of the original and the only office where such information is housed in the UK is in Milton Keynes. With such little time left, I needed the form as quickly as possible. We'd booked the Oude Stadhuis, an English-speaking celebrant, a restaurant in Den Haag for the reception (thanks to help from Mario Van der Ende, the Dutch former head of referees at FFA), and invited all our guests. But if we didn't get this paperwork sorted, the marriage couldn't go ahead.

So, my dad – bless him – drove down to Milton Keynes on a bitterly cold winter's day, to try and get the form for me. We were now almost at the cut-off point for the wedding, so Dad couldn't take any chances. He booked a room for the night at the Travel Lodge in lovely Milton Keynes (that's sarcasm by the way), ready for when the office opened at 9 am the next morning, and after getting the precious document, posted it off to the Netherlands.

Now, it was a race against time; the form was on its way, but it had to be there by the close of business on the Friday, the week before we were due to leave for Holland. If not, the wedding would be off. Dad had sent the document recorded post, so we kept track of it, and it finally arrived at lunchtime on the Friday. The offices in Den Haag however, closed early on Fridays, so we must have phoned five or six times, checking whether they were in possession of our crucial piece of paper.

At 2.50 pm (Dutch time) – 10 minutes before they were due to close for the weekend, we received confirmation they had everything in order, and that we could marry. Phew! All that work over so many months, and we'd made it, by the skin of our teeth.

I flew into Holland from Japan, where I'd called the Socceroos' goalless draw with the Samurai Blue – a very good point, considering most of the Australians had only flown into Tokyo 48 hours beforehand.

Both families were due to meet up at a holiday resort just outside Den Haag, called Kijkduin, but Fiona's attendance wasn't guaranteed. She'd now become so ill, that even flying the short distance between England and the Netherlands was out of the question. But she was so determined to make our big day. So husband Mike booked them on the ferry to Zeebrugge in Belgium, whereupon he would drive the rest of the way to Den Haag.

It was the first I'd seen of her in months of course, and it was clear she was very sick. Fiona was a bag of bones, and so weak she was no longer able to walk. Mike would bathe her, dress her, and push her around in a wheelchair all day – he was truly a saint. The best brother-in-law anyone could wish for his sister in her hour of need.

Before the wedding, we had Steph's grandma's ninety-fifth birthday celebration, which meant meeting the Dutch side of Steph's family. The Brantzs are actually two countries blended into one – Steph's dad was born in Indonesia, so half the family are small, Asian-looking, with lovely olive skin. Her mum is full-on Dutch, so the other half are all giant, Nordic-looking types with names like Joop and Wout.

They were all very friendly, and we had a lovely day, meeting and greeting new family members – many of whom would attend our wedding. On the actual day of our marriage, Steph's Uncle, formerly on the Dutch Flower Board, stopped by at our holiday apartment and gave Steph a posy to bring to the wedding. The posy was tulips – of course – all wrapped up with the national flags of Australia, Britain, and the Netherlands. It was a lovely gesture.

Still, our wedding day seemed cursed. First, Steph and I had decided we would make our own way to the Oude Stadthuis via taxi, which proceeded to be more than half an hour late, leaving us looking like prize lemons, waiting by the side of a road in a suit and bridal dress near a holiday beach resort.

Then, once we'd arrived, there was no sign of my family. We'd given them a map with directions, but they had somehow got lost, and parked up at another similar building elsewhere in town. So, with 20 minutes to go before we were due inside, I was racing around Den Haag in my best suit and buttonhole, desperately scouring the streets trying to find them. Other members of Steph's family joined in – we must have looked a bizarre sight, dressed up to the nines, running through the streets in panic!

They arrived of course, just in the nick of time. After all the problems in the build-up, it was almost a relief to finally become Mr and Mrs Hill. Our witness book was signed by Fiona and Steph's grandma – it was to be almost the last thing they ever did.

With the Grand Final of 2008/09 scheduled for 28 February, there was no time for a honeymoon for the newlyweds. I was back on a plane the day after the wedding, arriving in time to call Melbourne Victory's second title win, as they defeated Adelaide United by a goal to nil.

A couple of days later, Steph had a phone call from Holland, informing her that Oma-Oma had died. She'd had a stomach problem, and needed major surgery, but had refused, believing it was her time. Steph was very, very upset. She idolised her grandma.

Steph couldn't fly over for the funeral, but soon, I was returning to Europe. I received a phone call one Saturday night in mid-March from my dad, telling me that if I wanted to see Fiona, I had better come home immediately. She had taken a turn for the worse, was in hospital on breathing apparatus, and they weren't sure if she'd survive the weekend.

I hurriedly booked a ticket back to the UK – the last seat on the plane, which meant a 24-hour journey squashed into a middle seat on the back row.

By the time I arrived in England, Fiona's condition had been stabilised somewhat, and she'd been found a place at St Rocco's Hospice, a wonderful organisation that ensures people with terminal illness get to see out their final days peacefully, in a tranquil, caring environment.

Knowing what to say to a sibling who is about to die is not easy. Fiona and I would talk (as much as she could – she was starting to drift in and out of consciousness, and her breathing apparatus made chatting awkward) about our past life together. I asked if she was scared or in pain – she said not much, no, and she wasn't scared, as she had made her peace. She also hoped that it would be over quickly. She didn't want it to be drawn out and painful for her husband, kids, or us. That was typical of her.

Fiona wrote all of us letters, thanking us for our love and asking us all to take care of each other. She signed birthday cards and wedding cards for all her kids for years hence; occasions she wasn't ever going to see or experience. It was heartbreaking, and to this day, I have only read that letter once – I cannot bear to even look at it.

After nine days at St Rocco's, Fiona died peacefully during the night of 25 March 2009. Mike called us in the morning to tell us the news, and it was almost too much to take in. There were tears of course, but we knew it was coming. The nearest word I can find to describe the feeling is 'numbness'.

My parents and I then went in to St Rocco's to see Fiona for the last time, her lifeless body, now thankfully shorn of the tubes and machinery that had kept her alive. I was stunned at the damage the cancer had done to my sister.

The days that followed were tough for all of us. With my parents beside themselves with grief, I tried to take on some the manly duties, helping Mike do the practical stuff. I went with him to register her death with the local authorities, which seemed horribly clinical, but had to be done. Next, we returned to St Rocco's to remove her belongings, an especially tough task. Finally, I helped with some of the funeral arrangements, even offering to read the eulogy if Mike didn't feel up to it. However, tough old cookie that he is, Mike insisted he'd get through it – and he did.

The funeral, as you might expect, was a very sad affair. Fiona was just 46, younger than I am now, and she was laid to rest in the little church where she'd worshipped all those years, in the same grave as her daughter, Beth – reunited at least.

Steph tried her best to make it over for the funeral, but her connecting flight got delayed due to bad weather in London, and she missed the ceremony by a couple of hours. Later, we moved back to London to have some time together, and I stayed on afterwards, trying to make sense of my loss, and how my world had changed – because changed, it most certainly had.

A death in the family, particularly one who passes before their time and is a close relative, leaves a gap that is never filled. Life takes on a more uncertain hue, and awareness of mortality becomes even clearer. As I write this, it has been eight years since Fiona's death, and I'm still not sure I have processed it. Do you ever?

Aside of my memories, my only reminder is an orchid that Steph buys me every year on the anniversary of Fiona's death. It is supposed to represent her life, and it lives in my office. Not for long though – like the letter, I struggle to look at it as the memories of her last days are too painful, and by the time the next year comes around, it has normally died of neglect.

My loss, of course, pales into insignificance when compared to Fiona's children. To lose your mum so young is a terrible shock. Mike also took his loss particularly badly. Thankfully, he had plenty to live for with three children, and I think that kept him going. Today he has remarried to the lovely Leanne, who also suffered the loss of her partner, and they have relocated to the coastal English town of Southport. The kids are fond of her, and he has – finally – found some happiness after losing both his wife, and his daughter.

My parents have struggled on, but I often feel terribly sorry for them. They are now in their eighties, and have spent the last few years being surrogate parents to children all over again. They had two kids: one died, and one went to Australia – not how they envisaged their old age I imagine.

People in Australia were very good about Fiona. I had lots of messages of support, from Murray Shaw at Fox Sports in particular, and even a message of sympathy from (then) FFA CEO, Ben Buckley. My absence meant I had missed the vital World Cup qualifier between the 'Roos and Uzbekistan, where Australia's win put them on the brink of a second successive World Cup Finals appearance. A small price to pay.

I was back on board however, for the match that confirmed the Socceroos' qualification, a goalless draw in Qatar in the stinking heat of the desert. Strangely, although this had been a much more difficult achievement, the moment of triumph was almost an anticlimax in comparison to four years earlier against Uruguay. The game being in the middle of the Australian night didn't help, and nor did the fact that only a few hundred Australians were in the stands to help the players celebrate.

We had a strange night work wise in the Middle East too, this being the first time I had ever called a game in a commentary booth situated behind the goal. The Qataris had shifted us there because the main stand had been exclusively reserved for VIPs. As our spot was bang in front of a major thoroughfare in the stand, we spent most of the game waving idling spectators away, so we could have some sort of view. Still, no matter; Pim Verbeek had done his job. Australia were going to South Africa in 2010.

CHAPTER FOURTEEN 14

DURBAN, DUDLEY & THE DIRTY GAME

Things at Fox began to change a little in 2009. Tony Sinclair moved on from his job as the head of programmes, and in his place came Soames Treffry, promoted from within the company after being involved in setting up the Fox Sports News Channel.

I had a decent relationship with Soames, and when he started talking about the place needing a shake-up, I was excited. The Fox football team had done well in establishing the A-League as a staple of the network's output, but we were all keen to take it to the next level.

Soames talked in very modern business speak, all jargon and catchphrases such as 'It's all a game of rats and mice' (the TV industry), and 'We have to move to the noodle' (increase ratings). Much of it was lighthearted gibberish, but he seemed to have a plan, and I was all for innovation if it meant moving the game further forward.

The plan was to increase ratings, and Soames felt the way to do this was to entice a mythical viewer, a viewer he liked to believe was the archetypal Fox subscriber. 'Trevor from Rydalmere' needed to be catered for at all times, and to do this in football, we had to make football appeal more to the mainstream. That was fair enough in my book. But not this opinion that followed soon after: 'The problem with football, is that it's not Rugby League.' Uh-oh.

This conflation of the sports is rather typical of many Australian sports TV executives. Lacking any real knowledge or understanding of football, they make the not-so-subtle connection between what works in Rugby League or AFL, and think it should automatically apply it to football.

Soames wrought big changes in the football department, and unfortunately, I was one of the fall guys, losing my role as host (initially co-host), of the successor to *Total Football* (*Fox Sports FC*), and being removed from my presenting gig on the English Premier League coverage.

Instead of the standalone Premier League hosting, there was to be a new show, *Hyundai Matchday Saturday,* which would encompass the Saturday A-League games, AND the late-night Premier League matches.

In fairness, *Matchday Saturday* was a good show, full of fun and invention – I liked it, even though the emphasis moved slightly away from football and more onto 'celebrity'. The only thing that rankled was the press release that went out stating that the move would 'allow Simon Hill to focus on more commentary duties'. I didn't do any more matches that season than I'd done in any other.

The fact of life in the media, is that things move on, quickly. Nothing stays the same for long, and I've always accepted that – worked with it, embraced it, used it for motivation, and to push my career along. But I didn't like deception. Even all those years ago when I'd ended the careers of those two freelancers at BBC Hereford & Worcester, I told them straight – face-to-face.

Later in 2009, another change was made, when Andy Harper replaced Robbie Slater as my co-commentator for the Socceroos. To be fair, Robbie didn't much enjoy the international travel. One of his last trips with me was in 2008, when we travelled to Tashkent, for Australia's World Cup qualifier against Uzbekistan. It was a fascinating trip to the former Soviet republic, a part of the world I'd always wanted to visit.

On our arrival in the capital, we were told the visa office was shut for the night, which presented a problem for us, and many other travelling Australians. The visa officer had to be called – out of his bed it seems – and he arrived an hour later, still in his pyjamas underneath his overcoat, cursing in the local language.

When we finally ventured out of the airport, it was gone midnight, and there were only a few taxis milling around, waiting to pick up the late fares. We had little option but to go with whatever was on offer, if we wanted to reach our hotel. For me and Robbie, that meant squeezing into the back of what looked like a death trap.

The driver's tiny Fiat had seen better days – I was sharing the back seat with the car's spare tyre and my suitcase (there being room only for Robbie's in the tiny boot), and our cabbie was driving with his head stuck out of the window to get a clear view, with his windscreen having more cracks in it than a batting strip at the WACA in midsummer. We trundled through the streets of Tashkent, with our driver desperately trying to make small talk with us in limited English. Eventually, he found a phrase we understood:

Driver: 'Which country?'

Us: 'Ah, Australia!'

Driver: (thinking to himself) 'Australia, Australia…hmmm…'

Driver: (hitting upon the only Australian names he knew) 'Harry Kewell!'

Us: 'Yes, Harry Kewell!'

Driver: 'Tim Cahill!'

Us: 'Yes, haha, Tim Cahill…'

Driver: 'Mark Viduka!'

And so on, and so on. He named virtually the entire team. That's the power of football. A man for whom Australia was probably no more than a dot on a map – but he knew the Socceroos, that's for sure. I tried to respond, offering up the local Tashkent teams name:

Me: 'Pakhtakor!'

Driver: (scowling) 'Bunyodkor!'

I'd picked the wrong one!

Our next trip (and Robbie's last), was to Seoul for a friendly between South Korea and Australia. This was a four-day stopover, and the 'Roos were training up at the Korean FA's official training base in Paju, about an hour's drive away from our hotel. It was right up near the border with the North (the DMZ) and was a venue Pim Verbeek knew well from his days with South Korea. He once regaled me with the tale of how he was instructed to stay in his room at the base and take cover, as there was a rumour the North Koreans were about to launch an offensive!

One training session in Paju was on a very hot and humid day, and there was precious little shade at the training ground. The South Korean team were in before the Aussies, and so we took the opportunity to watch their session. The local Korean journalists were very welcoming and friendly, and they brought drinks over for us, to help us cool down.

When the Koreans finished their session, two players were brought over to speak to the press, including Park Ji-Sung, then the Koreans' biggest star, who played for Manchester United. Park's English wasn't brilliant, but the Korean journalists asked whether he'd answer a couple of questions for us on camera in English. He was happy to do so. It was a fantastic gesture, and one we really appreciated.

When the Australians arrived, the Koreans naturally hung around to watch the Socceroos' session, and once it had finished, a couple of players were designated to come over and talk to us. We promised we'd try and repay their politeness in kind. But barely had we started our first interview, when Gary Moretti appeared in the background, tapping at his watch and gesturing to FFA Media Officer, Adam Mark, to wrap things up so the players could get on the bus and return to their hotel. We told Adam our story, and asked if there was any chance we could return the goodwill the Koreans had shown us. But with Moretti getting increasingly agitated, the answer was a very firm no. Australian journalists were the only ones getting interviews; the Koreans were getting nothing. It was cringeworthy, and all we could do, was offer apologies to our gracious hosts.

This, sadly, was typical of the culture at the time. Pim was friendly enough and happy to chat to the media, but Moretti ran the timetables, and Verbeek didn't argue. He took his lead from the guy who probably ensured everything ran like clockwork for him. But I thought Moretti constantly overstepped his remit.

In Europe, football is front and centre. It dominates the sporting landscape, and the media are ever-present. Whether players or coaches talk to the press, or treat them well, is actually of little relevance – the game is going to be back-page news anyway. When arriving in Australia, the landscape is totally different, and it's easy to look down your nose at how the media operates, focusing (as it does) on seemingly rather meaningless and parochial sports like Rugby League and AFL. It takes a while to understand that, beneath the media veneer, lies a fan base that, while smaller than in Europe, is no less passionate. The professional end of the game, therefore, has a duty to try and connect, in what is a very hostile environment. In Europe, you may be able to get away with ignoring the press, or treating them with disdain, but in Australia, all it does is hurt football, because the media is quite happy to move onto other sports. Eventually, it hurts your own job prospects, through the lack of coverage.

Thankfully, things have changed these days under Ange Postecoglou, who recognises only too well the value of the media, having worked in it himself. But for many years the way some of the Australian staff (not, it must be said, the majority of the players) behaved, beggared belief.

Pim Verbeek, however, was great with me personally. Perhaps because I had a wife of Dutch heritage, or because I was also from Europe, he seemed to feel a connection with me, and I was able to forge a very good working relationship with him. Verbeek isn't remembered too fondly by Australian supporters, but I think that's a harsh assessment – and yes, I might just be a little biased on this occasion. In my opinion, he only made two mistakes during his entire time with the 'Roos. The first – the obvious one – was selecting the wrong team for the 2010 World Cup opener against Germany, a topic I will touch upon later.

The other came rather earlier in his tenure. When choosing one of his squads, he made a casual remark that came back to haunt him. He was asked about Michael Beauchamp, whom he'd selected, despite the defender not playing regularly for his (then) German club side, Nuremburg. There were other candidates playing in the A-League, who some members of the press believed were more deserving cases. Pim's response was that 'training with a Bundesliga club was preferable to playing in the A-League.' Ouch. Talk about putting your foot in it.

It was clumsy and not very diplomatic. Pim really, was only guilty of speaking his mind in the way many Dutch people do; and some in Australia, incidentally, agreed with his assessment. But it was a brutal insight into the disdain the European coach had for the local competition – and it didn't go down well. Some in the press (and the public at large) were openly hostile towards him after that. It was the turn of the Dutch to get 'the treatment', especially with compatriot Han Berger succeeding Rob Baan as the FFA Technical Director.

You couldn't fault Pim's results however. I labelled him 'Pragmatic Pim' because he had a knack of obtaining results in tricky conditions, often with only a minimal build-up. He remained loyal to his senior European stars which caused some consternation but, at the time, I felt he was within his rights to try and fulfil his mandate – to qualify the team for major tournaments.

As 2010 dawned, the Fox football boys headed off to another new and unknown destination, Kuwait, for an Asian Cup qualifier, this time with Andy Harper in tow as my new co-commentator. We also had a technician with us for the first time. Todd Procter was on the trip due to the problems we'd had in the return fixture in Oman, Australia's last international of 2009.

Oman was quite unlike many of the other Middle Eastern nations we'd visited. With its pretty harbour and more moderate version of Islam, Oman was much more western, and the locals were very glad to welcome tourists. During our trip, we'd gone on an excursion to Nizwa in the interior, supposedly the birthplace of Islam, and where there was a huge marketplace every weekday, full of local tribesmen, attempting to sell their goats, cows and other wares. We walked high up into the Al-Hajar Mountain range too, offering stunning views of the barren rocky landscape below, and ate the local produce at a fine restaurant on our way back to the hotel.

But all that good cheer fell flat on match day, when the Army, fearful of terrorist attacks, acted as security around the Sultan Qaboos Stadium, creating a very tense atmosphere, and frisking everyone thoroughly on their way into the ground.

That was nothing though, to what awaited us in our rather Spartan commentary booth. Murray (Shaw) had booked the full broadcasting set up – or so he thought – but the only hardware in the room was two sorry looking wires, hanging limply out of a prehistoric socket. This is what can happen on overseas trips in unfamiliar parts of the world. Often, there are cultural or language misunderstandings; on other occasions, the local broadcaster with whom we liaise, just doesn't want to (or can't) provide the equipment we need. It can be hit and miss – and this was most certainly the latter.

Murray spent an hour running up and down staircases in hot conditions, desperately trying to cobble together bits of equipment, in order that we could broadcast the game back to Australia. In the end, we had a rudimentary broadcasting kit, patched together with masking tape, and one pair of ancient headphones with a tiny microphone attached to them. This was patently unsuitable for two commentators, but there was little we could do but make the best of it.

I simply had to hold the headset in my hands, and point the microphone hopefully either in front of my mouth, or alternatively (when he was speaking) Andy's. The quality was reportedly woeful, and I'm not surprised. The headset was falling to pieces, but the Omanis couldn't have cared less – they insisted that was all they were obliged to provide.

Sometimes in Australia, we are too nice to the opposition. Pim Verbeek noticed this too. He'd highlight the fact that opposition fans – always numerous in multicultural Australia – were often situated right behind the goal, thus giving Australia's opponents an advantage when kicking towards that particular end of the field. Verbeek took it upon his shoulders to inform the FFA that he wanted them shifted to a different part of the stadium. Higher up, and at an angle, where their noise couldn't have as much of an impact.

So, when the trip to Kuwait City came around, Murray wasn't taking any chances. Technical guru, Todd Procter, came with us, complete with a full set of equipment. He was at the ground 24 hours before kick-off, rigging the set-up we needed, and liaising with the local broadcast crew. Knowing exactly what was needed, he wasn't afraid to knock a few heads together either. I can't tell you how much of a difference his presence made, our jobs were made that much easier for him being on that trip.

Both Oman and Kuwait put up stiff opposition. The heat hindered Australia in Muscat, but they came away with a rather fortuitous 2–1 win, before drawing 2–2 in Kuwait City with a mainly A-League based squad. The Kuwaiti crowd were loud and passionate, and their team played with pace and verve. Australia were becoming used to this. As one of the 'big fish' in Asia, they were a scalp every team wanted to have, and when the European-based stars were unavailable, the odds of a shock were dramatically improved. Perhaps Pim was right?

Back in Australia, a narrow win over Indonesia in Brisbane ensured Verbeek a little place in history – the first coach to have qualified the nation for two major tournaments. After that, the focus was very much on the forthcoming World Cup in South Africa.

Unlike in 2006, when I'd commentated all the Australian games at the finals, I went to South Africa purely as a presenter and reporter. SBS had the rights to broadcast the tournament again, and Fox weren't 100 per cent sure they were even going to send a team to cover the tournament. Eventually, sponsors provided the necessary finances, and it was decided we would broadcast a daily news and highlights show. I was the host, and a revolving team of pundits would assist me on the half-hour programme, to be broadcast from the official host broadcasting site in Johannesburg.

We were billeted at a holiday apartment complex in Sandton, the posh (mainly white) area, in one of the most dangerous cities in the world. But danger wasn't to be as big a foe for us as the weather. This being June/July in the Southern Hemisphere, it was winter in southern Africa, and it was bloody freezing!

We were the some of the first broadcasters to arrive in the country, simply because Australia were the first team to set up camp in nearby Ruimsig. We also had to call the team's two friendly matches there (being part of our broadcast remit) against Denmark and the United States.

By the time the World Cup Finals kicked off, we were already tiring of our lodgings. The local hoteliers had, as they always do in a hosting country, bumped up the prices in anticipation of overseas visitors, and the top hotels (where we normally stayed), had been completely booked up by the various FIFA bigwigs. That meant we were in a place where making money was the primary object – and fair enough too, you might think. But in the middle of winter, our apartments had no heating, and temperatures were regularly dropping to close to zero at night. Small bar heaters were located and distributed, which helped a little, but the bare floors were clearly designed for summer, and didn't trap any sort of warmth. We requested electric blankets, which were provided, at a cost of several rand per night. The food menu was bland, and room service stopped late at night. No good for us when we had to be out broadcasting the show until well after midnight.

In fact, by all accounts, we had it rather better than some of our media colleagues. Later, I found out from Peter Wilkins that the ABC accommodation was so cold, they resorted to leaving their electric cookers turned on all night, to try and take the edge off their icy apartments.

During the day, this wasn't a problem of course – often, the brilliant winter sun gave us sunburn, but the mercury dropped alarmingly once dusk fell. It was on such a sunny, cloudless day on 11 June, that we attended the opening ceremony of the 2010 World Cup at the splendid Soccer City Complex, known locally as the Calabash. Steph had also flown over; she was doing a bit of work for the FFA, and was part of their official touring party. We were sat with Ben Buckley and his wife, Sarah, along with Fox Sports CEO David Malone (and future CEO, Patrick Delany) and David and Patrick's wives for the ceremony, which included a breathtaking fly over from the South African Air Force. Disappointingly, Nelson Mandela wasn't there, but the notorious vuvuzelas were. They sounded like a swarm of bees swirling around the stadium, and they were to become a feature of this tournament.

The opening game was the hosts, South Africa, against Mexico. To give you a flavour of this wonderful event, the South Africans, known as Bafana Bafana (the Boys!) didn't just walk, or run out for their pre-match warm-up, they danced out, with that wonderful African rhythm on full show. I've seen this before and since with African teams, and it is mesmerising. Not only is it impressive musically (they are all in perfect time), but it looks like a real team-bonding exercise, a celebration of their heritage, culture and togetherness. I love it.

The Mexicans were the favourites, but I desperately wanted South Africa to win to get the tournament off to a positive start for the hosts. This was crucial for the locals, who had invested a lot of money (too much, as we later found out), and emotion into this first-ever African World Cup. It didn't quite work out that way, but it seemed as though the fairytale might be on when Siphile Tshabalala gave South Africa the lead on 55 minutes. We were on our feet cheering with the rest, as he slammed the ball into the top corner. But Rafael Marquez equalised with just 11 minutes remaining, and it finished in a 1–all draw.

As the crowd of 84,000 dispersed, I had to make my way across the fields at the back of the Calabash to broadcast the first *World Cup Show* on Fox Sports. The broadcast position was situated on a golf course, adjacent to the Soccer City Complex, and the backdrop of the Calabash (lit all through the night during the World Cup) was spectacular. Clearly however, in a city like Johannesburg, there was no way we could entrust our safety to local taxis in the wee small hours. So Fox had organised two 'minders' to look after us. Dudley, and his sidekick, Alan, were tough, grizzled South Africans, who were well used to looking after naive tourists conducting business in their troubled nation.

Dudley was a veteran of the Angolan war, and he still had the bullet holes in his body to prove it. Bald as a coot, he looked like a smaller version of Rambo, and his temper had a hair-trigger, although fortunately, never towards us – that would have been bad for his business. The pair of them were brilliant with us. Wherever we needed to go, they were there, be it first thing in the morning, last thing at night, or even at weekends. Their job was to keep us safe, and they took it very seriously. Anyone who got in our way was quickly dealt with – not that we had many of those incidents, thankfully.

Dudley took to calling me the 'Silver Fox' due to my greying hairline, and he had an excellent sense of humour. He also seemed to be on first-name terms with every single person in the country – he knew every restaurant, every bar, and everyone who worked there. No building was off limits to us, no stadium security too tough to bypass after a word from Dudley, which normally started with the Afrikaaner greeting 'Howzit?'

The flip side to this, was Dudley's short fuse, and we saw flashes of it occasionally; to be honest, it scared the shit out of me. One night, after a particularly late shift doing the show in front of the Calabash, Dudley drove us back to our lodgings as per usual. The complex, as with all the others in Jo'burg, was locked behind a security gate, with a guard on duty outside, 24 hours a day. He was the only man who was allowed to let our vehicle pass through.

This particular evening, the temperatures had dipped well below zero. We (myself and Paul Trimboli on this occasion), had presented the show (on a rather exposed platform, with the wind howling through) in beanies and scarves. I seriously thought we were going to get hypothermia. So, when we arrived back at the complex, the guard was tucked up under a blanket, trying to keep warm inside his tiny sentry post. With his bar fire on full blast, he had inadvertently nodded off however. Dudley peeped his horn gently, but there was no response from the guard, who was fast asleep. Dudley immediately flew into a rage, storming out of the minibus, and flinging open the sentry door. Before the guard had time to react, Dudley had ripped the heater out of its socket, shouting profanities towards the guard as he did it. The guard recognised him, apologised, and pressed the button to open the complex gate. But Dudley's anger hadn't subsided yet.

'If you EVER fall asleep on duty again when I'm around, I'll rip your fucking head off!' said Dudley to the stunned guard.

Paul and I sat open-mouthed on the bus, and when Dudley sat in the driver's seat, adrenaline still coursing through his veins, we didn't dare speak. He was not a man to be messed with, and like most South Africans, he was fully armed, every moment of the day.

The day after that opening match in Johannesburg, we joined the FFA party (non-playing) on the flight to Durban, ahead of the Socceroos' opening game against Germany. We were hosting the show from the Green & Gold Army headquarters, and there were thousands in Australian colours, enjoying the festival in the city.

We were rather glad that the weather was more temperate in Durban. Our beachfront hotel was relatively safe, but we were warned not to stray, even a couple of streets further back, where mugging and other crime was rife. Still, what did we care? We had Dudley with us, and I reckon he could have taken out every criminal in the city on, one by one!

The 13th of June 2010 will go down in history as perhaps Australia's worst-ever World Cup day. It didn't seem that way as we snaked our way to the stadium, however. It was a warm night, and the fans clad in green and gold were in good spirits, expectant of a positive result for Pim Verbeek's team.

Earlier in the day, I'd spoken at a NAB Function in the city, to a group of Australian fans, many of whom were at their very first football tournament. Leo had organised three of these functions – one each ahead of Australia's group games, and my brief was to discuss the possible team line-ups, deliver a bit of analysis as to where the game might be won and lost, and answer whatever questions the supporters had.

It's probably fair to say that whatever line-up I put forward as being the 'likely' Australian team that day, it didn't include Richard Garcia. I don't think anyone expected that. In fact, as we took our seats in the refurbished Moses Mabhida Stadium along with 62,000 others, we thought his inclusion was a misprint on the team lists, being widely debated among the Australian fan base.

I was concerned, not because Garcia was a bad player by any stretch, but because Pim looked as though he'd panicked in the face of a very competent looking German team. By leaving out several of his big stars – Harry Kewell, Josh Kennedy (who was bang in form) and Mark Bresciano, in particular – Verbeek looked as though he was packing the midfield in the hope of snatching a draw. Garcia was starting on the left hand side of the 4–2–3–1, but the Germans, Philip Lahm especially, simply played around him, and his teammates.

This was probably the first real evidence that the Australian team was starting to creak. At 28, Garcia was the youngest player in that starting 11, and the defence – Schwarzer, Wilkshire, Neill, Moore, Chipperfield – had an average age of 32. Craig Moore, who'd by then ended his A-League career, went straight from training with a state league club in Queensland, to facing the likes of Mesut Ozil and Thomas Muller.

Tim Cahill's red card didn't help, but by that stage, Australia were already 2–0 down, and staring down the barrel of a bit of a mauling. Steph was sat on the opposite side of the ground to me, and I remember texting her saying 'this could get seriously embarrassing'.

The final 4–0 score line however, was a good enough reflection of how the game had played out. It was Pim's biggest mistake during his time with Australia, and his worst result by far. The criticism was brutal from the press, and from our own Mark Bosnich and Robbie Slater, who ripped into Pim's tactics on our show that night. I felt sorry for him, but I couldn't offer any defence. As good as the Germans had been (and they went on to dismantle both England and Argentina by similar scorelines at that World Cup), the Socceroos' coach had got things badly wrong.

I was mystified as to why he had done this. All through qualifying, his team had virtually picked itself, then, in the biggest game, it appears he got spooked. Afterwards, Pim said he'd been trying to protect some of his other stars for later on in the group stage, but that didn't really wash with the public. They were angry at a rather spineless collapse, and rightly so. During qualifying, Australia had kept 12 clean sheets, and although the football wasn't pretty, Pim could always point to his results. Now, the pressure was really on, against a much higher class of opposition.

SBS took the criticism to a different level – as was their want during this period – calling for Verbeek's immediate removal, to be replaced by a panel of former captains to select the team. You could understand the emotion, but sacking a coach after one game at a World Cup?

The following day, we flew back into Johannesburg, where Ben Buckley held an impromptu press conference to discuss the fallout from Durban. He was asked point blank whether Verbeek would be removed – proof of how the mainstream media (not football-savvy for the most part) could also be manipulated editorially.

Buckley of course, vehemently denied Verbeek's position had even been discussed. Pim by this time, had already announced he wouldn't be staying on post-World Cup anyway, so to my mind, there wasn't much to be discussed on that score. What was clear, however, was that big changes would be required for the second game versus Ghana.

Ben Buckley was another who received a bad rap from the Australian media. In some ways, I understood that point of view. Ben wasn't a great media performer, and at times, he seemed to struggle with the nuances of the game – in public at least. But Ben's capabilities as a CEO were being stretched by the World Cup bid, being run concurrently alongside Australia's finals campaign.

At the time, we in the football media were solidly behind the World Cup bid. It seemed like a golden opportunity for the sport in Australia to take a giant leap forward, and we were probably as gullible as anyone else, as to how FIFA really operated. We would find out later that year, when Australia's bid garnered just one vote.

Filling the half hour show every day meantime, could be tricky. We had highlights of the games – news access as it is called for non-rights holders – which, in the early stages of the competition, took up most of the show. But as the teams thinned out, we had to garner more and more material, which meant we were working long days, trying to ferret out stories. So, when we had an offer from the One Goal initiative (of which Steph was an ambassador), to go and film one of their projects in Soweto, I grabbed at it, figuring we could get 'something in the can' for later.

The little school in the township was to be one of the beneficiaries of the One Goal money – aimed at helping to provide proper nutrition for underprivileged children. The kids at the school were beautiful, even for a non-kid-loving person like me, and friendly to the extent that once they took hold of your hand, it was a trial to get them to loosen their grip!

The One Goal team – including my old mate from Burkina Faso, Martin Davies – had brought along a few celebrities of course, which was an additional 'hook' for the media. They included Andy Cole, the ex-Manchester United striker, his former teammate, Quinton Fortune (for the South African press especially), and best of all, the legendary Socrates.

Socrates had been one of those wonderful Brazilians the world had enjoyed watching at the 1982 World Cup in Spain. Tall and elegant on the park, he'd worked as a doctor prior to becoming a footballer, even though he'd famously smoked a pack of cigarettes per day.

A t-shirt company in the UK, Toff's, had spotted a gap in the nostalgia market in the 2000s, when guys like me had started wistfully harking back to the days of their youth, eulogising the stars of yesteryear. They'd made shirts emblazoned with names such as Lev Yashin, George Best, and Socrates. They made a lot of money from those shirts, I'm sure – the start of the football hipster movement perhaps?

Steph had purchased one of these t-shirts for me featuring the Brazilian great. On it, were the words 'Socrates – smoked a packet of fags a day!' I'd brought it with me for him to sign. As I produced it, he looked at the t-shirt, and not speaking much English, asked his assistant for a translation into his native Portuguese. When she provided it, he frowned, and shook his head at me, before saying in English 'No, two!' (packs). What a legend.

As I marvelled at my meeting with such an icon of the game, Steph came up with the line that perhaps only a wife could at that particular moment. 'His feet are too small for his body. Didn't you notice?'

On 19 June, the Socceroos faced their day of destiny against Ghana. The venue, Rustenburg, was just about close enough to drive, so we all piled into Dudley's minibus and set off for the Royal Bafokeng Stadium. Actually, I was only going halfway, before being dropped off to perform my NAB duties at a beautiful retreat just off the main highway. The NAB team would then deliver me to the stadium with them.

The build-up to the Ghana game had been tense. Some of the Socceroos, stung by the vicious criticism after the Germany defeat, had reverted to type, and were blanking the media in response to the harsh assessment of their limp display. My old colleague, Andrew Orsatti, was following the Australians around in his new role with ESPN, and it wasn't long before he fell out with one of the players, Jason Culina.

Orsatti had asked Culina a rather routine question at the 'all-in' press conference, where the players had to walk through an impromptu mixed zone. Culina had reacted furiously; ironic really, given Orsatti had championed Culina's inclusion in the Socceroos squad many years previously. This led to Orsatti issuing an official complaint to the FFA's new head of media, Rod Allen. Allen – who tragically died only a few years later – had, in our opinion, gone the way of many an FFA media officer down the years. He'd started off promisingly, assuring the main players in the media game that things would be different under his watch. But he'd then reverted to type, and gone 'native,' siding with the players in every dispute, and acting more like a security guard than a press officer.

He'd even taken to turning up in an official Socceroos tracksuit, a sure sign that he was part of the 'team', rather than a go-between twixt FFA and the press. So, Orsatti's beef was always going to be given short shrift – and that's exactly what happened.

I had my own issues to deal with when it came to Rod Allen. At one training session, I'd spotted Tim Cahill with his leg heavily bandaged. When he failed to complete the session, I duly reported it was a 'potential' injury scare, although no-one, of course, would confirm or deny that information. My instincts told me Cahill was carrying some sort of a knock, even if it was only a minor one. Tim of course, wasn't due to be involved against Ghana courtesy of his red card against the Germans, so I hardly thought it was something likely to upset him, particularly as I'd had a good, even close, working relationship with him in the past; but I was wrong.

The next day, Cahill appeared at the latest 'all-in' presser, and point blank refused to speak to either me, or anyone at Fox Sports. Quickly seeking out Rod, I asked him to intervene, promising Tim the chance to set the record straight, if he thought I'd been out of line. Rod refused to even ask the question. He didn't want to get involved. Later, he called me and promised to try and get the two of us together to sort it out, but it never happened.

Tim's 'ban' on speaking to me lasted until the end of the World Cup, when he approached me at the airport departure lounge. I said if I'd been wrong, then I was happy to apologise. Tim responded by saying only that I'd 'put him under pressure'.

Cahill of course is, without question, Australia's greatest-ever player. What he has done for football in the country will take a long time to be equalled. He's given me some of my best commentating moments, and joy unbridled for millions watching at home. I have immense respect for him, and most of the time, he is ultra-professional, diligent in his work, and happy to fulfil his duties with the media. But on occasion, he can get riled, especially if he feels his reputation is being besmirched. Brand Cahill is super important to Tim, and it's probably one of the reasons why he's become such a success in both football and outside.

At that time, Cahill, Harry Kewell, Lucas Neill, Mark Schwarzer and Tim all seemed to be competing for 'top-dog' status with the national team, and perhaps that played a part in this particular situation too.

Kewell was another who got wound up by the media during that World Cup, with an article written by Mike Cockerill after the Germany game (querying the player's fitness and commitment to the national side), properly irritating him.

Kewell was central to the story that unfolded in Rustenburg of course. After being an unused sub against the Germans, Pim Verbeek chose to unleash him against the Ghanaians, but his afternoon lasted just 24 minutes. A rather dubious red card for handball meant Kewell's World Cup was finished; he would never grace the finals again.

Australia had actually started brightly, and took the lead through Brett Holman, but playing a man short for the best part of 70 minutes, meant a draw was always the best possible outcome after Asamoah Gyan had scored the resultant penalty. And that's the way it turned out.

That meant a win over Serbia in the final group game was the only scenario left open to the Australians, IF they were to maintain their interest in the World Cup. Not only that, but they needed a favour from the Germans, who would also need to defeat Ghana by a decent margin. Not beyond the realms of possibility, you might have thought – even though the Germans had followed up that brilliant win over Australia by losing to Serbia.

We had a difficult night putting the show together that evening. Robbie Slater was due to be my guest, but he was wilting under the constant travel, and he had a bit of a fallout with Murray over his inclusion. As the two of them fumed after a tense phone call, I asked Paul Trimboli if he'd stand in, and he was happy to do so. An hour or two before the show, Robbie and Murray sorted out their differences, but I had already set things in train with Trimmers, and so it was me and Murray's turn to have a bit of a blue. World Cups can do that to you, they can be a real slog.

Australia saved their best performance for their final group game, defeating the Serbs 2–1 in Nelspruit, a real beauty spot near the Kruger National Park. The Mbombela Stadium even paid homage to the local wildlife, with its roof supports arranged into the shape of giraffes, while the seats were patterned into stripes resembling those of a zebra.

My abiding memory of that game is speaking to David Carney in the mixed zone afterwards. Australia had put in a hell of a performance to win, but Germany had only narrowly defeated Ghana, meaning the Socceroos were heading home. Carney however, had a very tough night at left back, losing his man, the zippy Miloš Krasić, time and again.

I saw (the always amenable) Carney, and as he sauntered over for a chat, his first words to me were, 'Who was that lad I was marking? He was a bit good wasn't he?'

in his strange Aussie/Scouse hybrid accent. Well, it was the World Cup Carns, they were supposed to be good!

Verbeek, of course, was castigated. While I could understand the anger at the performance against Germany, the truth of the matter was, Australia had recovered well, earning four points – the same total as under Guus Hiddink four years earlier. This time however, goal difference had not been their friend, unlike in Germany. Pim would leave unlamented, which I thought a shame for a thoroughly decent man.

Not many shared those sentiments, even some among the playing staff. Josh Kennedy gave us an interview at the airport the following day before the squad headed home, and he made it plain that he felt he'd been under-utilised by Verbeek.

We, however, were going nowhere. We had our programme to present, right the way through until the final. Fox were making a fair bit of cash from the sponsors, and they wanted their money's worth. Once the 'Roos had departed however, the buzz naturally disappeared back home, and the daily process of finding material for the show became a real grind.

Without official accreditation (non-rights holders had been excluded from gaining the precious media passes by FIFA, keen to limit media numbers, and more likely to increase revenues through broadcast rights at the world's biggest sporting event), gaining access to players and administrators was like trying to get access to Fort Knox.

Getting interviews with the Socceroos hadn't been a problem – the FFA ensured we always got at least something, thanks to the ongoing broadcast partnership back in Australia – but the other nations of course, had no such responsibilities. Occasionally, Murray Shaw would attempt to gain access to a training session involving one of the other countries, but normally it was a futile exercise – no pass, no entry was the usual rule.

So, when sponsors or FIFA put up ex-stars (normally to front some charity initiative or business promotion), we had little option but to jump on board with the massed ranks of the world's non-accredited media, working the same beat at us, and try to forage for scraps.

Even then, this process could be hugely frustrating. Case in point was one press conference, organised in Sandton (nice and handy for us), featuring none other than Roger Milla, the legendary Cameroon striker who'd played at the World Cup Finals well into his forties.

After helping our cameraman (Lennon Cooper) with his equipment into a packed media hall, we waited for over an hour for Milla to show. Journalists wanting to ask questions had to raise their hand, and wait their turn. I knew I had only one shot at getting a decent quote from Milla, so I wanted to make sure the question was a good one.

After Australia had departed, the buzz around the Aussie media was that Paul Le Guen was favourite to get the national team coaching job. Le Guen had coached Cameroon at this particular World Cup, so I reasoned that Milla would be just the man to offer us an insight as to his qualities, and whether he'd be the right man for the Aussies. After waiting half an hour for my turn, I got to ask my question. Milla's response?

'It's not really for me to say.'

And that was it. Next question. An entire half day wasted, waiting for a decent quote that never came. That can be the reality of journalism – and that's before you have to explain your failure to your bosses.

On other occasions, the opposite is true. Sometimes, you stumble upon a pot of gold unexpectedly. One day, we were hanging around the International Broadcast Centre (we weren't allowed inside – no passes), waiting for delivery of some broadcast equipment, when lo and behold, Hristo Stoichkov came strolling towards us, unmolested by any media or hangers-on. Immediately, I told Lennon to get his camera out, and I approached the Bulgarian legend, asking him would he mind giving me a couple of minutes of his time?

Stoichkov agreed, and after asking us which country we were from, proceeded to give us several minutes (in broken English) of gold on his career, and how, eventually, he would like to coach in Australia, as it was a country he liked. That was a good day.

One positive about Australia's early exit, was that it gave us the chance to have the odd excursion to see some of the other games. Paul Trimboli and I took that opportunity with both hands, as he secured tickets for England's Round of 16 clash with Germany.

I hadn't watched England play a full international since the European Championships in 2000, when they had lost to Romania in Charleroi, so I eagerly grabbed the chance to watch my country of birth against the old enemy. Dudley drove us down – a fair old hike of about five hours to Bloemfontein – and while Trimmers took up his seat in neutral territory, I was in among the England fans, at the end where Frank Lampard scored the infamous 'ghost' goal. It had been a long time since I'd been able to watch football among 'my' people, and it felt good. Not for long though.

Although the Lampard moment left a sour taste in the mouth, the truth is, England were battered by a German team that were everything we weren't. They were mobile, we were slow. They were creative, we were predictable. They were lethal, we were wasteful. The 4–1 result was probably no more than England deserved, and Fabio Capello's reign was coming to an end.

Afterwards, Trimmers and his brother (who'd also come on the trip) taunted me by waving a German flag as we made our rendezvous near Dudley's minibus, but I wasn't much in the mood for piss-take. I tried my best to put on a brave face on the show later on, but in truth, I was hugely disappointed, not to mention tired. The broadcast point was on a roadside a kilometre or so from the stadium on another freezing night. With cars whizzing past, honking their horns so loud it made the talkback from the Sydney studio almost unintelligible, I was spent. It was left to my pundit, ex–Perth Glory coach, Mich D'Avray, to deliver the withering assessment. He didn't hold back, saying it was symptomatic of the decline of English football. He was right.

The following day, we were at Ellis Park to witness Brazil's 3–0 demolition of Chile, where I sat next to Kelly Cross, one of FFA's coaching gurus. Kelly is a Londoner by birth, and has that innate Cockney wit. Many years ago, I was on a coaching course led by him while filming a story for SBS, and he had mocked me mercilessly (and rightly!) for my poor touches, and general lack of fitness on a boiling hot day at Valentine Park. Now was my time for a little revenge.

Kelly, who was doing some work for the FIFA Technical Committee at this tournament, had his notebooks with him as usual, so, when I saw him scribbling something at half-time (with Brazil already 2–0 up), I leaned over and took a peek. His notebook said the following: 'Brazil good at retaining the ball.'

I giggled, and said to Kelly, 'Blimey, no wonder you are the guru pal! That's genius!'

But by the time the final came around on 11 July, we were all ready for home. We had been in South Africa for almost two months. I was in the stands for my second World Cup Final in a row, wearing the colours of the Dutch, in homage to my new family – but it didn't do much good, as Spain deservedly won the trophy, defeating the Netherlands 1–0.

The World Cup was over, the Verbeek reign was over, and it was time – surely – for the national team to be revamped. But who was the man to do it?

That man turned out to be Holger Osieck, the feisty German who had enjoyed decent success with the Canadian national team (winning the CONCACAF Gold

Cup – leading to the team moniker 'Holger's Heroes'), and at club level with Urawa Red Diamonds, claiming the Asian Champions League in 2007.

For a host broadcaster, a good relationship with the national team coach is imperative; after all, in a country like Australia, where football coverage is scant, Fox was/is an important partner for FFA, and vice versa. So, when Osieck arrived in Australia, Murray Shaw thought it would be a good idea to take Holger and his wife, Elizabeth, out for dinner, along with myself and Andy Harper. Steph, and Murray's wife came along too, perhaps to facilitate small talk with Elizabeth, in case the football chat all got a bit heavy.

Our first impressions of Holger weren't overly positive. Not that he was poor company – on the contrary, Holger could be jovial, and great conversation. He also had a very sharp sense of humour but it was old school, and he was a product of his generation.

But right from the off, Holger told us that he wasn't interested in the media side of things. Already, he'd got the hump with the new FFA Head of Media (my old SBS colleague, Kyle Patterson), who'd offered the suggestion that the national team embrace the media a little more than under the Verbeek reign.

Osieck wasn't keen, to put it mildly. He reckoned that the media were an unnecessary distraction, and that he would only fulfil the bare minimum of his duties in that regard.

Osieck's first games in charge were two friendly matches against Switzerland and Poland in September 2010. We travelled over to cover both matches, spending a couple of days in the beautiful Swiss town of St Gallen ahead of the first game against the Swiss.

Here was our first introduction into the Osieck way of doing things. We were the only Australian media on that trip, but that didn't stop Osieck from barring us from training after just 15 minutes, after obtaining the obligatory warm-up shots. Given this session was conducted on what was, essentially, an open field (with vantage points all around on the nearby slopes), we thought this was particularly ridiculous, and our producer, Geoff Bullock, was properly irritated. FFA constantly stressed to us the need for proper coverage of the national team, yet their coach was going out of his way to obstruct us. In protest, we retreated a safe distance, and then filmed surreptitiously through a line of bushes, pointing our camera through the gap, with me providing narration as if I were David Attenborough, spying on mating gorillas!

Press Officer Adam Mark, of course, spotted us. He came sprinting over, wagging his finger as we giggled at the stupidity of it all. This was a friendly game, to be broadcast in the middle of the night back in Australia!

Australia drew that game 0–0, and we then moved on to Krakow for the game with Poland. If St Gallen was pretty in a rural sort of way, then Krakow was something else. The town square was like something out of a novel, all ornate gothic buildings, cobbled streets and horse-drawn carriages. It was spectacular.

We even fitted in a short trip to the infamous death camp at Auschwitz, just 40 kilometres down the road in Oświęcim. Another training session, with the now obligatory 15-minute filming window, cut short that excursion, for what amounted to, essentially, sod all.

In fairness to Holger, his team performed really well at the home of Wisla Krakow, winning 2–1. Meantime, Andy and I enjoyed a commentary first, calling the game from a half-built stand, which was undergoing refurbishment. We were the only people allowed into what was a building site – and we called the game wearing hard hats!

After the dour football under Pim Verbeek, the public quickly warmed to Holger. His tactics were certainly more proactive, and with the Asian Cup looming in January 2011, optimism was high that the Socceroos could win a trophy.

However, the sour taste of the World Cup wasn't about to disappear just yet, and we at Fox were partly to blame. Robbie Slater had written a column in the *Daily Telegraph,* echoing Mike Cockerill's thoughts from earlier in the year, saying it was time for Harry Kewell to retire from international football post-South Africa. He quoted an unnamed source from within the Socceroos camp, as saying that even some of the players were of the same opinion. This, as you can imagine, didn't go down well with Kewell's feisty manager, Bernie Mandic. Bernie was rarely slow in contacting the press if he believed he, or his client, had been slighted.

Bernie called me one night, asking for the right of reply on that particular week's Fox Sports FC. He said Harry wanted to defend himself personally. If we agreed to have him on the show, Harry would call us, direct from Turkey, where he was playing for Galatasaray. The rider was, that Robbie had to be on the show too; in effect, a showdown.

I wasn't sure. This would be potential fireworks, and I was putting a colleague right in the firing line. I ran it past my producer, Geoff Bullock, and Soames.

Both were keen to go ahead, and Robbie, after some initial reluctance, agreed to it too. In hindsight, it should never have been broadcast. Harry tore into Robbie, who gave a good account of himself, it must be said, but by the end, it was clear Robbie felt as though he was being used as a punching bag by his own network. It was a shameless grab for ratings, which worked, incidentally. That episode, and particularly the repeat, after much press coverage, rated its socks off. Robbie felt he'd been let down, and when Senior Executive Producer, Adam Cox, texted me later to tell me he thought it had been 'car crash' television, I could only agree. A lesson learned.

Back to events on the park, and even a 3–0 loss to Egypt in November couldn't dent the feeling of euphoria for Australia as they headed towards the Asian Cup. It was a match in which Osieck handed Sasa Ognenovski – mysteriously ignored by Pim Verbeek, despite a stellar season in Korea with Seongnam – his debut. We were all set to travel to Cairo, with our passports stamped with the required visa. But at the last moment, the trip was cancelled, when the local broadcaster failed to provide the necessary guarantees regarding our facilities. Shortly afterwards, Egypt, indeed the whole region, was in tumult as the Arab Spring took hold.

In December, I was due to travel to Zurich for the announcement of the World Cup hosting rights for 2018 and 2022. In the event, I wasn't able to go. A recurrence of my sinus problems left me in need of another operation to correct a deviated septum and the removal of further nasal polyps. The op was routine, but it ruled me out, and so instead, Nick McArdle travelled with Andy Harper and Murray Shaw to Switzerland, for one of the most infamous nights in FIFA's long history.

Even before the votes had been cast, there were rumours that Qatar had somehow won the 2022 race. A phone call with Andy confirmed what many suspected.

I had been asked to attend a 'celebration' in Sydney's Circular Quay that night – local organisers having tentatively booked out an area, complete with a big screen next to the city's iconic waterfront, in the hope of capturing historic pictures of Australian fans, celebrating a successful bid.

Australia never had a chance of course. Neither did any of the other bidding nations for 2022. What later transpired was a web of deceit, corruption and deals, to ensure Qatar got over the line. None of us could believe it – then, or now. I remember doing an interview for Fox Sports News, and saying that there 'were no good reasons to hand Qatar the World Cup'. I was immediately accused of sour grapes by some in the football community, but I knew something wasn't right – many people did. Those views have since been vindicated many times over.

But what has been forgotten by many, is that Australia's bid had question marks against it too. Many people refuse to believe FFA would engage in the dark arts, but I have regularly called for a full, independent enquiry into the Australian bid. Yet it is only recently that those calls have been echoed by others, in the wake of the FFA money that ended up in the pocket of the disgraced Jack Warner.

I maintain that every dollar spent should be accounted for, publicly. After all, if we are to preach from the pulpit, then we need to ensure our own backyard is clean first. No-one however, seems prepared – or able – to do this. It reflects badly on our game that FFA consistently says it has no case to answer, despite being heavily criticised in the infamous Garcia report. If there is nothing untoward, and clearly, I hope that's the case, then why not have an enquiry, prove it, and shut people like me up?

In a pure football sense, it is so sad that Australia didn't get the chance to host the World Cup. As the nation proved at the 2015 Asian Cup, the public would have supported the event in their droves, and the boost to the game here would have been enormous. That is surely what taking the game to new markets should be all about?

As it is, it will go to Qatar, a tiny country that has plenty of money, but a domestic league that leaves the locals cold. The average attendance of the Qatar Stars League in 2009/10 (the season before they were awarded the Cup) was 4200, that despite the local clubs spending pots of cash to attract top overseas talent. The 2022 tournament has even been moved from the traditional summer slot to November–December because of the unrelenting heat in the Gulf in June–July. Those conditions were well known to the Executive Committee at the time of the vote, which in my opinion, made the decision null and void, as a June–July World Cup was what they were voting for.

CHAPTER FIFTEEN 15

DUSTY DOHA & THE COWARD'S CORNER

As luck would have it, we were on our way to Qatar, just a few weeks after the vote was taken. The Middle Eastern nation was the host of the 2011 Asian Cup, and after a few days in the UAE (where Australia played out a goalless draw with the Emirati's in Al Ain), we headed for Doha, the throbbing capital of Qatar.

Actually, I'm being facetious. Doha throbbed about as much as your toenail does after you've trimmed it. The facade, as viewed from the air or the sea, is impressive, but that is all it is, a facade. When you tour the streets of downtown Doha, you see the buildings for what they actually are – beautifully constructed, and mostly empty.

The local marina, on the extremity of the 'Pearl', Doha's answer to Dubai's 'Palm', has a similar feel – it has plenty of expensive shops and restaurants, but few people to actually act as consumers. It's one of the weirdest places on the planet. It almost feels like a thoroughly modern city was constructed the day after a nuclear holocaust, when nearly all the people were wiped out.

The one area that did have a bit of a 'vibe' was the souk in downtown Doha. No wonder really, this market place was the oldest part of the city, and we chose this as the location to film our daily highlights show.

The hosting of that show meant a very busy month. In addition to the nightly programme, which required me to write links and facilitate chat segments with Andy as the chief pundit, we had a hectic schedule of games to commentate, virtually one per day throughout the group phase. Robbie Thomson and ex–Perth Glory coach,

Bernd Stange, were the other commentary team, who would take care of the rest.

In the days building up to the tournament opener, it became evident to us how, and why, Qatar had won hosting rights to the World Cup in 2022. Every day, the local English language paper, the *Qatar Tribune*, had a front-page lead, acclaiming a new gas or oil deal, signed between Qatar and various other countries. You could almost tally the nations with the nationalities of the various members of the FIFA Executive Committee. This was a World Cup won through business. You almost had to admire the Qatari's chutzpah – it was brutal economics, and they had the cash to back it up.

The tournament got underway on 7 January 2011. Qatar, feeling the weight of expectation from a large crowd, succumbed 2–0 to an experienced Uzbekistan side – Odil Ahmedov getting the Cup off to a flier with a screamer from long range. Server Djeparov made the final scoreline comfortable for the Uzbeks, who would go on to meet Australia, deep into the tournament.

The one positive about Qatar hosting major football tournaments is that the distance between venues is miniscule. The furthest stadium from Doha was in Al-Rayyan, a mere 20-minute drive from the centre. But the venue for our next game, Japan v Jordan, was even closer. The Qatar Sports Club Stadium was within spitting distance of the sky scrapers of Doha, and Jordan very nearly lifted the roof off those buildings with a spirited display. Only an injury-time goal from Maya Yoshida spared Japanese blushes in a 1–1 draw.

Australia's opening game was against India at Al-Sadd's home ground, the Jassim Bin Hammad. The venue had a revolutionary new system of cooling (even though this wasn't needed in the Gulf winter), and was a very smartly appointed stadium – but we had to laugh when we saw it described as a 'mini Old Trafford'. Unless they'd rebuilt Manchester United's famous home ground in the time I'd been away in Australia, this was about as akin to the Theatre of Dreams as the old Maine Road was to the new Wembley!

Still, the presence of India ensured a bumper crowd. Little wonder AFC is so keen to revitalise Indian football, the potential among a country of over 1 billion people is enormous. In Qatar of course, many from South Asia are employed, virtually as slave labourers, in the various construction projects, many surviving in appalling conditions and on meagre wages. I suspect, although it was never confirmed, that many were given free tickets to swell the crowd; I'm not sure they could have afforded the entrance price otherwise.

Australia were far too good of course. Goals from Tim Cahill (2), Harry Kewell and Brett Holman eased Holger Osieck's team to a 4–0 win, and a decent start in pursuit of the Asian Cup.

A day later, we were back at the Qatar Sports Club for one of the sterner tests of my commentary career. I was familiar enough with the UAE team (having called their friendly with Australia a week or so prior), so they weren't necessarily the problem. But North Korea?

Preparing to call the Hermit Kingdom play international football is surely one of the commentator's great challenges. Information is not merely sparse – it's almost non-existent. To make matters worse, the North Koreans had two players with EXACTLY the same name, playing in different positions – Pak Nam-Chol.

We'd already encountered – I can't really say met – some of the North Korean fans, who were staying at our hotel. They looked less like supporters, and more like bureaucrats, which I presume is exactly what they were. When the game kicked off, the North Korean 'fans' were all seated in two blocks, all identically dressed in white shirt, black tie and trousers, and they had a cheerleader, leading choreographed chants, stood in front of them. They didn't miss a word, or a beat. Each had a North Korean flag, which they waved rhythmically. They were mesmerising.

Sadly, their game wasn't quite as in synch as the fans – the North Koreans' isolation from the world was all too apparent, as they played a virtually prehistoric brand of football, featuring five defenders. It finished 0–0, leaving North Korea without a goal at the Asian Cup since 1980.

Back in Group A, Qatar redeemed themselves with a much more aggressive display to see off China in the Khalifa International Stadium. A young striker named Yusef Ahmed scored both goals in a 2–0 win, and we thought we were witnessing the rise of a potential star of Asian football. Yusef's story however, is typical of many in West Asia especially. After that two-goal salvo, capping a performance that was full of skill, pace, power, and exquisite finishing, Yusef virtually disappeared. He was reportedly offered a contract by Standard Liege in Belgium, but 'turned it down'. In other words, his club, Al-Sadd, turned it down for him, no doubt offering him enough money not to worry about Europe.

Yusef has since suffered with injuries, and at 28, there may still be time for him to make his mark – but so few from that part of the world achieve their full potential, and yet the nations concerned wonder why they can't qualify for World Cups?

Australia's next game was the big group showdown against South Korea. The game ended 1–1 at the home of Al-Gharafa, and was notable for an injury suffered by Jason Culina, necessitating his withdrawal at half-time. Culina would suffer recurrent problems after that, and would never play for his country again.

Holger Osieck's team then saw off Bahrain to top the group, and favourites Japan joined them after demolishing a dispirited looking Saudi Arabian team 5–0 in front of a crowd of just 2022 in Al Rayyan.

After overcoming stern resistance from Iraq, then dealing with a more compliant Uzbekistan, the Socceroos were in the final, against old foes Japan. With Osieck having coached Urawa Red Diamonds to Asian Champions League success in 2007, there were plenty of cross-references for us media types to enjoy in the build-up.

For Socceroos fans, the prospect of a major trophy meant thousands decided to book last-minute trips to Doha, which presented the organisers with a problem. An empty stadium for the final wasn't going to be a good look for the watching world (particularly with 2022 now a reality), and so the local organising committee had handed out free tickets to many of the South Asian workers employed on the construction sites.

When the ticketed Australian fans arrived, they found their seats already occupied, leading to chaotic scenes both inside and outside the stadium, as Aussies were either turfed out, or not allowed in. This is what happens when you hold big football tournaments in countries where there isn't much of a culture of support at the ground – and the contingency plan had backfired spectacularly.

We of course, had no such problems.

But I didn't have the best night behind the microphone. The winning goal in the final came in extra time, and whether it was tiredness or the fact that the scorer – Japan's Tadanari Lee – wasn't an overly familiar name, I didn't pick him quickly enough, and one of my 'money shot' moments in commentary was somewhat spoiled as a result. Had it been an Australian winner, no doubt I'd have heard much more about it, but because the 'Roos had lost, little was said. Such is the shallowness of sports broadcasting sometimes.

But if that was disappointing, then the presentation ceremony was torture. The handing over of the Asian Cup trophy to Japan took a full 45 minutes, during which time we had a procession of Princes, Sheikhs, VIPs, non-entities and hangers-on take to the field – all of whom were virtually unidentifiable.

Each time as a camera panned in to some member of an Arab royal family, I pressed the talkback button to ask 'Who is this guy?' Each time, I had the same response from our French DA (director's assistant): 'I don't know!'

Finally, the Australian team were called up, having been forced to wait around for three quarters of an hour to get their losers medals – or in this case, mini replicas of the trophy. On and on the procession went: players, coaches, support staff. Andy Harper turned to me and whispered in desperation 'Who's next – the media officers?'

Sure enough, two minutes later, up stepped Adam Mark (FFA press officer) to receive his gong, with Andy throwing his headphones on the table in utter disgust!

Around the time of that Asian Cup in 2011, a new phenomenon had come into all our lives. While the internet had revolutionised the journalistic profession, mainly for the good, the advent of social media was a whole new world, and not always for the better in my opinion.

In late 2010, I'd been asked by Fox to set up a Twitter account, to help promote our broadcasts, but even in those early days, I was very much a sceptic. I could see the potential pitfalls ahead, and as a relatively private person, being contactable, even through a relatively impersonal mechanism, didn't thrill me. Still, I agreed to give it a go, on the proviso that the moment people became abusive, I would be gone. I lasted three weeks.

That was plenty long enough to see that while Twitter had many useful facets, not least offering instant news and analysis, the trade-off was the sheer volume of abuse people in the public eye (and I was relatively low profile) have to put up with.

In my three weeks, I had someone label me an anti-Semite, had every word of my commentary analysed for 'bias' and was told to fuck off or called a 'cunt' on countless occasions. Part of the job? That seems to be the opinion of many, but I doubt they'd put up with total strangers hurling that sort of abuse at them on a daily basis. I didn't see why I should have to put up with it. I decided my coping mechanism would be to get rid of the account and ignore it.

Why I am I writing about Twitter, and sites like it? Because it has changed the media industry, and call me old-fashioned, but I don't think the benefits necessarily outweigh the disadvantages. The instant feedback offered by Twitter has become an easy way for bosses to gauge 'success or failure' or even the popularity of presenters, or commentators, even though it's hardly a scientific sample survey. The majority of the population remain only occasional users of Twitter, and so most areas of discourse regarding issues have become the preserve of the noisy few. Worse, TV promotes Twitter like there's no tomorrow, even though it has no financial stake in it. Advertising that other companies would have to pay thousands to obtain.

It works both ways of course. If you're so inclined, you can use sites like Twitter to 'promote your brand' which is why TV networks value it so much. In some ways, Twitter has become like a dick-swinging contest for those front of camera too, measuring how many 'followers' you have against the next person, in a bid to prove your popularity. You can even 'buy' followers, thus proving how unscientific it really is.

New media will eventually kill off mainstream jobs, because people are getting very used to acquiring their media for free. We're already seeing the long, slow decline of newspapers, and with the advent of Netflix, and the development of better technology for mobiles, iPads and tablets, traditional television is struggling to keep pace too, and is shedding both viewers, and the advertisers that help pay for their services.

I think it's a crying shame that we seem – eventually – to be destined to go the same way as the Blockbuster video chain, but whether people care is a different matter. In many ways, traditional media hasn't done a particularly good job of valuing itself, so why should we expect the public to clamour for our retention? I'm thankful in that regard, that I started my career when I did – if I'm lucky, I might just get through to the end of my working life, before jobs like mine become totally obsolete.

Social media has also changed the commentary industry. Prior to Twitter's arrival, you were only occasionally aware that people liked or disliked your work. Back in the pre-internet days, complaints and/or abuse came via the handwritten letter or phone call, something that took time and effort.

Today? Instant abuse is available to dispense to a public audience in 140 characters, and the sheer amount of vitriol people in the public eye have to put up with is staggering.

I've weaned myself off the 'ego surf' these days, but for a few years, this weekly hate-fest was difficult to ignore. Broadcasting is an insecure profession at the best of times, and I couldn't help but look at what people were saying about my call of a particular match. More often than not, it didn't make for pretty reading, and probably still doesn't. You have to have a very thick skin to be able to deal with that stuff on a daily basis, and clearly I'm not cut out for it, particularly in the hours after a game, when your brain is still operating on that 'disconnected from reality' level.

It's even more disappointing when the abuse comes from people within the media industry itself, as it often does. The public's views are one thing, but those from inside your own circle of expertise? If I'm critical of fellow media personalities (and I often am, this book being a prime example), then I make sure I do it in clear sight – not hidden away in the coward's corner of Twitter.

Twitter (or the 'great human graffiti wall' as Michael Parkinson memorably labelled it), wasn't the only development that changed the landscape in Australia in 2011. Brisbane Roar, under Ange Postecoglou, were embarking upon an incredible 36-game unbeaten run that not only smashed football records, but had purists licking their lips at the quality of their football.

I was, and am, a big fan of Ange. After his much-publicised row on SBS, he'd gone away to try and reinvent himself by coaching overseas. He'd been supplementing his income by doing some analysis on Fox Sports as he continued his recuperation, and he told me once that he felt he'd become 'unemployable' because of that SBS interview – a line I found incredible, given he'd won two national titles with South Melbourne in the NSL, and was clearly an erudite communicator, and student of the game. But Brisbane gave him a chance, and he repaid them in spades.

Occasionally, I thought they overdid things in their possession-obsessed game, but no-one can deny they were good to watch. The 36-game unbeaten run would have been back-page news for weeks had it come in the NRL or AFL, it was truly a phenomenal achievement. As it was, only football aficionados really understood, and football's lack of cut-through was evident the day Roar finally succumbed, losing to Sydney FC 2–0 at Kogarah Oval.

That day I was chatting to Ange in the apron of the tunnel pre-game, when a woman came running up to the dividing fence looking rather flustered, and with a trail of young kids behind her. Tapping Ange on the shoulder, she said, 'Can you direct me to where the ball boys have to go – nobody seems to be able to tell me?'

She had no idea she was talking to a man who'd just broken all Australian sporting records, and while we had a giggle about the ridiculousness of it all, Ange – jokingly – hit the nail on the head, when he said, 'You reckon Sir Alex Ferguson has to put up with this sort of stuff?!'

By the end of 2010/11, Roar had won the Premiership, and were in the Grand Final for the first time, up against Graham Arnold's Central Coast Mariners. Arnie had done a great job in Gosford too, albeit with a slightly more pragmatic style – and the final didn't disappoint. In fact, that's an understatement. It was by far the best Grand Final I've had the privilege of calling – I could even forgive myself for going off a little early when Olly Bozanic scored to put the Mariners 2–0 up in extra time, saying he'd 'surely' won the Grand Final for the Central Coast. I don't think I was the only person in Australia thinking that!

Suncorp Stadium however (if you'll allow me to digress for a moment), hasn't always been kind to me.

Twelve months on from that initial success, and Roar were back for the big showdown again, this time against Perth Glory, and after Roar had triumphed once more, thanks to a rather controversial late penalty, I was scheduled to host the post-match awards, pitchside.

With only minutes to compose myself to host a live ceremony after a commentary, my brain was probably tired. But while I'm not excusing what happened next, I wasn't helped by FFA's events company, Great Big Events.

As I hurriedly rushed down to the bowels of the stadium (fighting past thousands of fans in the process), I had no time to check the script I was handed as I raced into the players' tunnel. The stage was already set, and Fox was waiting for me to appear, in order to throw down to me 'live' in front of 50,000 people in the stadium.

The first hint of a problem came when I read out the list of victorious Brisbane players who were to come up to the stage to receive their winner's medals. After completing the list, I began to move on to the next part of the ceremony, but only got a few words out before my attention was attracted by Matt Smith (the Roar captain), furiously shouting at me that Roar winger, Nick Fitzgerald, was still waiting to be called up. His name had inexplicably been left off my list. That was embarrassing, but what came next went down in A-League folklore, sadly for me.

I moved on to the winner of the Joe Marston Medal – the man of the match award. This medal is decided by a collective vote from the assembled media, and the votes are normally gathered by an FFA person who then delivers the result to the organisers of the ceremony. The name of the winner is understandably left blank on the script, until his identity is known.

The problem in this instance was, no-one had remembered to write the name of the winner in. So, as my eyes scanned from line to line, reading out the prepared script, I became aware that there was no name to read out. Panic.

What to do? I couldn't exactly walk off stage to find the floor manager – I was live on stage, in front of 50,000 and a nationwide TV audience. I got to the words 'And the winner is' before looking along the line of assembled dignitaries to plead for help. At the end of the line was Lyall Gorman, then head of the A-League – surely he'd know?

'Who is it?' I mouthed to Lyall. 'What?' he mouthed back, almost as panicked as I was.

'Who won the medal?' I mouthed again, more furiously this time. In response, he mouthed what I thought was the word 'Broich' to me. I may have been mistaken – there were 50,000 making a din in front of me, in fairness – but that's what I believed he'd said, and so I announced that Thomas Broich was to be the recipient.

Cue huge roars of approval from the home faithful, and up came Thomas, genial as ever, to take his prize and offer a few short words of thanks to the fans. It was only later I learned that, in fact, Jacob Burns was the correct winner. Jacob wasn't best pleased, and the Glory owner Tony Sage (never on the best of terms with FFA) was furious. I was utterly mortified. Burns was presented with his medal in the dressing rooms later, after Broich was gracious enough to hand it over – a nightmare for all concerned.

The day after, I sent Jacob a text to apologise – and to his credit, he was great about the whole thing. But I have never been invited back to host the post-game function again. In any case, it's probably the wisest decision – you are in no healthy frame of mind to host a ceremony just moments after you have called a Grand Final.

CHAPTER SIXTEEN 16

BACK TO BOYHOOD, BEIRUT & BEYOND

Back in 2011, the end of the A-League season meant I could head back over to England, and finally fulfil a lifelong dream of seeing my team win a major trophy. Manchester City, thanks to the backing of Arab money, had been threatening to make the breakthrough for a year or two, but a semifinal meeting in the FA Cup with United presented a formidable obstacle to hopes of a first piece of silverware since Dennis Tueart was wearing sock tags, and I was wearing short pants.

Still, I just had to be there. My dad – bless him – came to the rescue again, queuing up to get me a ticket for Wembley, and Steph (by now a converted City fan – not that she had much choice) was desperate to come too. I purchased a ticket for her via a ticketing site (probably not strictly legal) at extortionate cost, and off we went to London.

Even that day, I was unable to escape being on television. My seat (one of the best in the house, almost directly behind one of the goals), was smack bang in front of a camera, and I was blissfully unaware of its location, being absorbed in a tense game, which ended with City winning, thanks to a Yaya Touré goal. But during the match, my phone began going off at a rate of knots, with people saying they were getting prime shots of me looking extremely nervous, every time the director cut to a shot of the crowd.

That day was one of the happiest of my football-supporting life – even though we hadn't yet won a trophy, it was difficult to escape the feeling City had finally made the big leap forward. United were still viewed as the stronger of the two Manchester teams, so to finally get one over on them in such a big game was huge, and I left Wembley feeling euphoric that the long wait was about to be over.

Steph had to return to Australia the day after the semi, and I'd been due to return with her but she knew there was no way I was coming home. If City were going to lift a trophy, I simply had to be there to witness it.

So, in May 2011, the coronation finally came. After 35 years of hurt, City duly saw off Stoke City to win the FA Cup, and I'd even managed to return the favour to Dad, purchasing him a ticket in the Wembley Club area. I have to say, the final itself was a huge anticlimax after the semi – there was almost a sense of inevitability that we'd beat Stoke, although they certainly fought hard.

I didn't quite shed a tear at the full-time whistle, but I do remember mentally leafing back through all the years of pain City had put us through, and thinking I'd never live to see the day when we became successful again.

City's rise had come on the back of huge investment by the City Football Group, which leads onto an interesting conundrum, one that perhaps lies at the very heart of one of the great mysteries of football, namely, why does a football-mad, money-saturated nation like England continue to fail so badly at international level?

One of the reasons, in my opinion, is that fans are obsessed with their clubs over the national team. It's almost the exact opposite in Australia (although that is changing), and the domestic focus has brought with it a whole set of problems.

For example, the 'selling' of the family silver, the clubs themselves, means that the Premier League, for all its shiny veneer as an 'English' success story (and commercially that is undeniably true), is in effect, run by foreigners, coached by foreigners and played by foreigners. The only thing English that exists in regard to the Premier League in reality, is the fans.

With the huge financial penalties for failure, coaches can't afford to blood young English talent unless they are very special, so instead, they buy cheaper, off-the-peg foreigners, already developed and ready for the rigours of a title tilt or relegation battle.

Talented English youngsters – and there are some – don't get much of a chance. But here's where the insularity of the English game takes over. The best course of action for such youngsters would be to head overseas, and learn their trade a different way, but too many opt to stay at home because culturally it is easier, and crucially, the money on offer is still too good. Thus, many end up dropping down the divisions, playing out their career in the lower leagues of England, wasting their talent, or else, sitting on a bench week in, week out, picking up great wages, but never quite fulfilling their potential.

The CFG takeover caused me a conflict of interest too. I can't deny that they have brought great joy to the club of my childhood, and I have – as I already explained – bathed in the reflected glory Emirati money has bought City, via championships and cups. When the takeover was announced in 2008, I'd been en route to the Netherlands to cover a friendly between the Dutch and Australia. I hurriedly penned a piece for the Fox website entitled 'City 'til I Buy', in which I extolled the virtues of the takeover – yet in the piece were a few words which reflected my inner turmoil at the news.

'It's all rather absurd, but this is what the Premier League has become post-Roman Abramovich – a world league in everything but name…This is the new reality in football. I don't have to like it – in truth, I don't much care for it at all – but post-Abramovich, what is the alternative, for clubs that want to compete?'

I still think that's a fairly accurate description of what has transpired. David Conn's excellent book *Richer than God* went much further than I did. Conn, also a lifelong City fan, has almost completely lost his passion for the club following the takeover, which didn't happen to me (my connection runs too deep), but I can empathise with his dilemma.

Perhaps what best sums up the situation for me, is a quote from a fan in Conn's tome. In a nutshell, the fan says that while wealthy foreign owners aren't really desirable, 'if we have to have them, then CFG are the best possible outcome.'

CFG have been responsible owners, not only restoring the club's fortunes on the pitch, but building impressive infrastructure off it, and being very good neighbours to the people of Manchester, investing in projects that have brought jobs and wealth to a very poor part of the city.

I have been fortunate enough to get to know one of their number, Simon Pearce, who is based in Australia, and who is now heavily involved in their sister club, Melbourne City. Simon is likeable, knowledgeable, and generous with his time. He also did me a huge favour in 2012, setting me up with a ticket to watch the (otherwise totally sold out) derby on 30 April of that year, as the two Manchester clubs battled it out for the title. Again, I knew I just had to be there.

Vincent Kompany's goal won the game, and took City top of the table on goal difference with just two matches left to play. As had been the case 12 months previously, I knew that with the club's first championship since 1968 within touching distance, there was no way I was going back to Australia until it was all over.

I travelled up to Newcastle with my Fox colleague, Daniel Garb, who kindly got me a press pass so I could watch the penultimate game (City's away allocation having been entirely exhausted). In scenes reminiscent of Sydney in November 2005, Dan had to hold my hands together to stop me celebrating Yaya Touré's late goals that sealed a 2–0 win.

That took City to the brink of the title. I secured my ticket for the final game against QPR by paying an online agency close to $2000 – a lot of money, but I didn't care. I could have gone back to CFG and asked for a ticket again of course, but I didn't want to push my luck, and anyway, this was a day to be in the stands with the fans, not the corporate boxes.

As the world now knows, that game was the most incredible finale to a Premier League season ever. I'd describe it as one of the best – and worst – days of my life, all rolled into one. To see the title slipping through your club's hands, minute-by-minute, was agony. I remember sitting, head in hands, wondering how I'd ever live it down. Especially as United were about to be the beneficiaries of City's propensity to win 'Cups for cock-ups' as Francis Lee once put it.

Then, miraculously, fate intervened. QPR learned they were safe from relegation late on in the game while leading 2–1. Did they relax? Maybe. Edin Dzeko equalised, and then after 94 minutes, 20 seconds (I have it immortalised on my Fox Sports business card), Sergio Aguero ended 44 years of pain for City fans everywhere. A moment best summed up by Martin Tyler's disbelieving call of 'Agueerooooooo' that trailed off into the realms of 'Is this really happening?'

I lost count of the radio interviews I did for Australian stations that night. As the one (perhaps the only?) City fan that people knew Down Under, everyone wanted to know how it felt. Pretty damn good was the answer. My club, champions of England – was it really true? Just 13 years after I'd watched them lose to York City in the third tier?

Yet as grateful as I was to CFG and Simon for getting me that derby ticket, he knows the commercial influence doesn't always sit easily with me. He jokes about my miserable 'glass half-empty' approach towards big modern-day football projects such as his, and I can't argue with his assessment. CFG bring huge wealth into football, and I can't complain about the benefits – witness the state-of-the-art facility they have built as a training ground for Melbourne City for example – but is it a price worth paying for the integrity of football? I'm still not sure.

I first met Simon through a mutual contact just after CFG had taken over at City. We had breakfast in Manly, and Pearce was a total unknown to me – I had to google his name, just to make sure he was actually part of the CFG project. That day, Simon talked about 'holistic' projects, and big picture stuff they were planning at City. I confess, I thought it was pie in the sky corporate bullshit, the type of which Mancs like me would never swallow.

Yet as the years have gone by, I can recognise that they have delivered much of what they set out to achieve. It's not just the playing side, or facilities either. CFG do small things such as the revamp of the exterior of Etihad Stadium (replete with pre-match entertainment) very, very well. Other things, like the reduction in ticket prices for pensioners go down a treat with longstanding fans, but don't necessarily make for sexy headlines.

But what is the end game? Is the acquisition of clubs around the world such as New York City and Melbourne City part of a plan for global domination? Is it just a business proposition? Or a ruse to circumvent financial fair play? I can't say for sure – perhaps the truth is a combination of all of the above? It certainly seems the whole football world is heading that way, with more and more clubs handing ownership over to wealthy foreign investors.

Whatever the truth, journalistically, my contacts within CFG have certainly given me access to some good stories, none more so than when I (along with Tom Smithies of *The Daily Telegraph*), managed to snag the exclusive on CFG's takeover of the (then) Melbourne Heart in January, 2014.

I had heard on the grapevine that Brian Marwood, Manchester City's Head of Football, was due to visit Melbourne in late 2013. That pricked my ears up, as I had heard CFG had been toying with the idea of investing in the A-League some months previously. The rumour was they were after Sydney FC, but that particular trail appeared to have gone cold.

I texted Simon, and half-jokingly asked him whether the reason for Marwood's visit was to 'buy Heart?' Simon replied in similarly jocular fashion, but refused to confirm or deny my assumption. But when I learned that Marwood was staying for longer than expected, my journalistic antennae sharpened again, and I repeated the question to Simon via another text. This time there was no response. Hmm.

One sunny January morning, I was out walking my dog when I got an unexpected call from Simon. He informed me that my hunch had been correct. They were about to do a deal with the Heart owners to buy the club, along with a consortium headed by local businessman, Bart Campbell. If I could get a camera crew to a Sydney hotel that night, he had all the big Man City hitters in town – Marwood, CEO Ferran Soriano and his offsider, the former Barcelona player Txiki Begiristain – and I could bag the exclusive.

Simon also invited Tom Smithies, of the *Daily Telegraph* along, so we could have a double whammy for News Ltd via print and television – it was the exclusive of a lifetime! I quickly phoned Tom, who was on holiday down on the south coast of New South Wales. He wasn't about to pass up this opportunity however, so he quickly made plans to head north, and all was set.

Simon had impressed upon me the need for total secrecy, until CFG gave me the go ahead to release the story. FFA had only a vague idea of the identities involved in the takeover, and CFG wanted to give them a nice surprise at their Monday afternoon meeting; we could release the story early on Tuesday morning, once the go-ahead had been given for the takeover. I said he had my word, and the only people I needed to tell were my producers at Fox, who would need to give the okay to book a cameraman.

At 6 pm, I went to the agreed hotel, and conducted interviews with all the main players, returning to Fox to put together a package that would run the following morning. I then wrote up a piece for the Fox website, and waited. That was to be one of the longest nights of my career. When you have an exclusive as big as that, there is always the danger of it leaking out elsewhere. Invariably in the modern age of Twitter, Facebook and instant messaging, someone, somewhere, gets a sniff. For hours, I sat trawling through social media sites, football forums – nothing. If we were lucky, we would have our big splash the following day.

At 9 am the following morning, I was in the Fox studios, waiting to go live to talk on set on the back of my exclusive package revealing news of the takeover. David Gallop, the new FFA CEO, had been lined up too, and at exactly 10 am, I got the text from Simon to confirm that we could go ahead and break the story to Australia.

The news caused a sensation. The back pages were full of the potential ramifications for the Australian game the next day, and Tom and I received many calls over the next 24 hours, congratulating us on getting the scoop of the year.

Have CFG lived up to those early expectations? It's difficult to say. In some ways, I think they have done a decent job. Certainly their training facility is magnificent, and in season 2015/16, they played the best football in the A-League by far. But have they kicked the club on to new heights? I think the jury is out. Crowds remain average, and their 'cut-through' in commercial terms remains limited in Melbourne. With the cash behind them, I certainly think they could have done more with marquee players, although the arrival of Tim Cahill was a good move in that direction. Perhaps their best is yet to come, and they've certainly made a start by lifting the FFA Cup in November 2016.

Sydney FC are one club which has tried to stimulate the Australian market through judicious use of marquees, and the arrival of Alessandro del Piero, ahead of the 2012/13 season (along with Shinji Ono at the newly-constituted Wanderers, and Emile Heskey at the Jets), gave the new season some real impetus. While this was pleasing, it also showed the immaturity of the Aussie market, and proved just how far we still have to go as a football nation. I truly believe that if Sydney signed David Beckham, even today at the age of 42, they'd sell out ANZ Stadium, at least for a time.

That sort of buzz certainly happened with del Piero, as over 35,000 rocked up to watch his home debut against Newcastle (with Heskey in the Jets line-up) at the outset of 2012/13. In truth, Sydney had endured a disjointed build-up to the campaign, and I also knew Ian Crook (the Sky Blues' new coach), had been presented with a bit of a fait accompli regarding the del Piero signing.

Not that Crooky didn't want him of course – who wouldn't want a talent like del Piero in their team? But Crooky confided in me, saying 'I signed Kruno Lovrek to play the number 10 role. Where can I play him now?'

In the event, Crook tried to utilise Lovrek as a number 9, but it didn't really work, and although del Piero put bums on seats everywhere he went in that first season, the Sky Blues were nothing more than a mediocre outfit, trying to accommodate a world superstar. Still, del Piero gave me a nice moment in commentary as he scored a cracking free-kick in that home opener against the Jets. Here was my call of his strike:

> Del Pierooooo…that's what they came to see! That's why Sydney FC paid the money, that is the measure of the man.

Del Piero then scored the winner in the first-ever Sydney derby – a welcome inclusion into the Australian landscape after the success of its Melbourne equivalent. With two relatively new clubs, not everyone was sure this fixture would live up to its billing as a proper 'derby' but the spice has been there right from the off. It's given us a real marquee fixture to add to the Melbourne version, and the Big Blue (Sydney v Melbourne Victory).

But Sydney were to miss the finals that season (2012/13), and the use of marquee players has divided opinion ever since.

Just before that particular season started however, we had another fascinating trip into a part of West Asia we hadn't yet visited. Australia were due to play a World Cup qualifier in Jordan, and as preparation, they had arranged a friendly against Lebanon in Beirut. This was at the time when the war in Syria was just beginning, in the aftermath of the Arab Spring in 2011, and I have to confess, I was a little nervous about travelling to this notorious trouble spot.

But Beirut was a pleasant, if occasionally unnerving surprise. The Christian part of the city (in which we were staying) was a typical western city, full of cafes, bars, bustling nightlife, and glorious architecture. We were told this was the only place in the Middle East where the mosque stood next to the church, and on the face of it, it seemed a relatively harmonious place. But scratch beneath the surface, and the tension was all too evident – every street corner had a heavily-armed soldier stationed on it, and at night, tanks patrolled the streets, their guns cocked menacingly, ready for the first hint of trouble.

The clue as to the real state of play in a country where the different communities exist only in a fragile peace, came when we were informed that the game had been suddenly moved from the capital to the port city of Saida, some two hours down the Mediterranean coastline. Officially, this was because the stadium had fallen victim to a 'grass virus' which had killed the turf – but I suspect that was a cover story. The real reason, I believe, is that intelligence suspected an imminent attack – a suspicion that sadly became reality a month after we left when a huge car bomb killed several people in the centre of the city. Even outside the capital, the country was on red alert, borne out by the fact that our taxi driver had to take a hasty diversion when in sight of Saida, due to the security services having found a suspicious device on the main road south.

Along the way, our cabbie made for compelling listening, as he outlined which of the villages on the hilltops had been obliterated, due to various battle between the Muslim and Christian factions. It was a sobering journey, particularly as our driver had to weave his way through the notorious 'green line' in Beirut, full of pockmarked buildings, just to get us out of the capital itself.

Things were tense in Saida too. The soldiers and tanks vastly outnumbered the spectators – the locals weren't taking any chances with a team such as Australia in town, and we even had a conversation with the head of security, whose job it was to ensure the safety of the Socceroos during their stay. We were open-mouthed at the massive army presence, but he was almost blasé – probably all in a day's work for him, in fairness. We tried to sneak a photo of the heavy artillery in the environs of the stadium, but that's where the nonchalance stopped, as we were politely, but firmly, told to put our cameras away.

Just 30 kilometres or so down the road lay Israel, which had reportedly been flying drones over southern Lebanon, as they scoured the countryside for evidence of a (reported) invasion from the north, given the tension in Syria. And if all that wasn't bad enough, the plumes of smoke from a fire, accidentally started at a rubbish dump south of Saida, started to billow over the stadium as kick-off approached. It was a surreal backdrop to a football game, which Australia won comfortably, and then got the hell out of dodge. On our way back, we had another diversion to contend with, as a gun battle had apparently erupted, just south of the capital. In 2013, the Lebanese army were involved in proper military action against Sunni militants in the Battle of Sidon (the English word for Saida), which killed over 60 people.

From Beirut, we flew the short distance to Amman, capital of Jordan, where another fascinating experience lay in wait.

Jordan is one of the more stable Gulf nations, although the country's demographics have been destabilised by heavy immigration from the Palestinian territories, just over the border. The national team are a mixture of immigrants and locals, and the passion they have for their team (in my opinion), is unsurpassed in the Middle East, 'Al-Nashama' perhaps being one of the few tangible entities that unites the tribes.

Before the game however, we took a trip to Petra, one of the Seven Wonders of the World and then, on the morning of the game, Tom Smithies and I hired a taxi to drive us to the Dead Sea. I remember thinking back to rainy days in Manchester in preparation for a game, as we floated on our backs in the salty brine, reading newspapers and glancing up occasionally to view the distant sight of Jerusalem over the mountains, one of the ancient birthplaces of civilisation. What a job we have!

After enjoying the restorative powers of the Dead Sea (very good for the skin apparently), we headed for the stadium, which was a seething hotbed of Jordanian passion. They chanted, sung and intimidated the Australians to such an extent, that the home team made off with a famous 2–1 win; disappointing for us visitors, but manna from heaven for the locals.

On our way back to the hotel, our taxi became gridlocked in a tunnel underpass, and the noise was deafening, as delirious Jordanians honked their horns and danced between the cars in celebration at a famous win for their nation. Some vehicles even had Jordanian flags tied to their windscreen wipers, which were extended outwards to wave vigorously, to and fro, on fast speed – this was football providing untold pleasure for the masses, and underlined why the game remains the biggest sport on the planet. None of the celebrations were intimidating, nor hostile, this was just pure joy, brought about by football. I loved it.

But that loss to Jordan was perhaps the end of the honeymoon for Holger Osieck. Before the game, he'd been tetchy in the press conference, when our Fox microphones had inadvertently picked up a rather caustic remark about the locals, made under his breath to his captain, Lucas Neill. Holger had never made any secret of his dislike of trips to the Middle East – whether it was the hot weather, the unfamiliar conditions, or the rather stilted questioning (through interpreters) at such conferences.

By the time Australia played Jordan again in the return game in 2013, Osieck was lucky to still be in a job. A home game against Oman had gone horribly wrong, with only two late goals salvaging a 2–all draw in Sydney; Frank Lowy had reportedly been all for dismissing the German, there and then. But he hung on, and I was again commentating on the night when Australia clinched a third successive World Cup qualification, by edging out Iraq 1–0 at Stadium Australia in Sydney (that venue again), in May 2013.

In truth, it was a nervy display, and when Osieck substituted Tim Cahill late on, replacing him with Josh Kennedy, it was arguably Holger's biggest call of his time in charge of the Socceroos and I said so during the call on Fox. But it paid off, as Kennedy headed home the winner with just seven minutes to go. The 'Roos were off to Brazil, and Osieck had saved his skin, for now.

But pressure was building on the German, and things weren't about to get any easier. In preparation for the 2014 World Cup, FFA had arranged two of the toughest friendlies imaginable – away to Brazil and France. By the time he named his squad for the two matches, I knew (and so did everyone else) that unless he pulled off something remarkable, he was on borrowed time.

Now, despite his rather gruff manner, I'd grown to almost like Holger. One on one, he was amiable enough, and I felt he was being set up for a fall. Whether or not he was the long-term answer for Australia, I wasn't sure, but he'd qualified the nation for the World Cup, and to my mind, that was enough to prolong his stay to Brazil at least. I soon learned that wasn't an opinion shared by many.

Osieck's dogmatic and old-fashioned approach to media conferences (not helped by a poorly executed 'joke' regarding a woman's place being in the kitchen), had put him offside with many. Results had tapered off, the playing style had reverted to a rather basic 'get it to Timmy [Cahill]' and his over-reliance on the golden generation had started to mirror the approach of his predecessor, Pim Verbeek. Still, I felt duty bound at least to warn him that the knives were out – particularly as he'd been very generous with his time with me some months before, when I'd written a piece about his football career in a series called 'My Football Journey' for the Fox Sports website.

So I asked to meet him for coffee, near his Manly apartment, and he agreed. During our hour together, I tried to warn him that moves were afoot to oust him from his position but true to form, Holger said he didn't care, didn't read the papers, and didn't take much notice of what went on around him. His focus, he said, was on the World Cup.

Twenty-four hours after our little tete-a-tete, Osieck sat in a press conference to announce his squad for the two friendlies. What he wouldn't have known, is that someone from the FFA had purposely asked me to pose a provocative question, designed to catch Osieck off guard, and heap further pressure on him. What the FFA guy didn't know was I'd forewarned Holger this question was coming from me (although I didn't reveal who had told me to ask the question), so at the very least, he was prepared for it. He answered it smoothly enough, and lived to fight another day – though not many more.

Was I right to have done this? In hindsight, I'm not sure. But it was my gut instinct that the forces were being aligned against the national team coach, and the FFA were trying to use the media to do their dirty work for them – the same FFA remember, some of whom were only too happy to obstruct the media when it suited them. Whatever the rights and wrongs of Osieck's tenure (and he got plenty wrong in my opinion), I didn't like those tactics; if FFA wanted him out, they had the power to sack him, with or without the media's help. Maybe they were hoping he'd be forced to resign if he answered my question poorly?

Eventually of course, results in Brazil and France did the job for them. Two 6–0 drubbings convinced the governing body that Osieck wasn't the man to lead the team at the World Cup, and he was dismissed.

The clamour for a local-born coach was understandable after the years of overseas appointments, and personally, I was delighted to see Ange Postecoglou complete his transformation from unemployable coach, to national team supremo. To me, he was the outstanding candidate, and that has been proven many times since.

Postecoglou's appointment signalled the changing of the guard. Some, like Mark Schwarzer and Brett Holman, saw the writing on the wall, and quit. Others, like Lucas Neill, hung around, hoping to be part of the new breed. Lucas's involvement in Postecoglou's first friendly, against Costa Rica, became a bone of contention among the public and media, and, after Ange had – only belatedly – named him captain for the game, it was clear there was going to be no free ride to Brazil, for a player who had served his country fantastically, for well over a decade.

At the time, Lucas wasn't playing regularly at club level, and many supporters felt his time was up. But among the media, it was more about the culture surrounding the national team. Under Holger Osieck, Lucas's spot had been almost guaranteed, and his demeanour seemed to be increasingly dismissive of anyone who dared to ask a question about his continued involvement.

Personally, I felt that so long as Lucas continued to perform well for the Socceroos, then it was up to the national coach of the day to make any decision, but he couldn't be immune from questions or criticism, as he (and some others) seemed to believe was the case, by virtue of what they had done for the jersey in the past.

So it was fascinating to read the body language of Postecoglou and Neill as they sat, side by side, at the pre-game press conference, ahead of Ange's debut as coach in Sydney. We'd become accustomed to Lucas slouching in his chair, being somewhat disinterested in proceedings, and whispering asides to Osieck, but on this particular day, he was sat upright, attentive, and very much on message. He knew what was at stake...the winds of change were blowing through the FFA, with Postecoglou leading the charge.

Lucas never played again for Australia after the Costa Rica game, when strangely, he actually played quite well. The catalyst was a section of the Sydney crowd, who booed the skipper throughout the game. Neill, unwisely, reacted by flicking two fingers at his accusers.

Later, in 2014, I bumped into Lucas at Manchester City's title-winning game against West Ham in Manchester. I'd been catching up with English broadcasting legend, Martin Tyler, when Lucas suddenly appeared, eager to chat – and clearly still upset at the way he'd been treated.

I had – and have – sympathy for players like Lucas. He was a great servant to the green and gold, and probably didn't deserve such a dramatic fall from grace. But did he fail to read the signs? He could have bowed out on his own terms (like Schwarzer and Holman) and left with his reputation intact. As it is, he is now a figure that divides opinion, and I think that's sad, because he deserved better. He seems to have disappeared since his playing days drew to a close, which is also a pity; he surely has a part to play in Australian football's future.

Ange's way certainly made life easier for us journalists. Acutely aware of how much the Socceroos 'brand' had suffered under the Osieck and Verbeek years, training sessions suddenly became events where the media weren't just welcome, but actively encouraged to attend. The departure of Gary Moretti, eased tensions further, as Ange sought to build relationships – relationships which, as I've already explained, are far more important in Australia, given the games relatively low profile.

In June 2014, the 'Roos – and we – headed off to Brazil for the World Cup. This was my fifth consecutive attendance at football's greatest event (if you include going as a fan to Korea/Japan in 2002).

Right up until June, my attendance in Brazil was in doubt. I had to fight my corner with the head of Fox Sports News to get a spot on the plane as a reporter, to be based out of Rio de Janeiro, covering the 'other' games and teams in the tournament. The bulk of the team were to be based with the Socceroos at their training camp in Vitoria. We were billeted at a beautiful apartment in Ipanema, and saw several games, including Australia's opening day 3–1 loss to Chile (in which they really took the game to the South Americans), on a stinking hot day in Cuiaba. Murray Shaw also got us tickets to watch Argentina defeat Bosnia at the legendary Maracana, on a night when the Brazilians in the crowd had a wonderful (verbal) battle with their Argentine foes – I won't repeat some of the translations of the songs they were singing, but they were hilarious!

But two incidents in Brazil left a sour taste in the mouth. The first came before the tournament had even started. We were in Salvador, for Australia's friendly with Croatia, a game we (Fox) were broadcasting live as part of our ongoing deal (outside the World Cup itself) with FFA.

A big sprawling city, home to many of African heritage due to its location on the north-east coast of the country, Salvador had built a brand new stadium, Arena Fonte Nova, in preparation for the World Cup, but that venue was being saved for the big event itself. Instead, we were at the rather more basic Estádio de Pituaçu, and because of security concerns, we were deposited at the stadium very early (which turned out to be a good thing, as I was able to snag a quick chat with Davor Šuker, the legendary Croatian striker, turned President of the Croatian Federation).

In charge of the technical side of things for our broadcast that night was an English guy, whose name I simply cannot remember. He didn't have a particularly good evening.

Whatever could go wrong with the broadcast, did – our one shot at televising a game in Brazil had floundered because of something out of our control. I had no sympathy for the bloke in that sense, but it was a good job he wasn't within range of an FFA staffer, who, upon hearing of our tale of woe, proceeded to say the following, 'When will the world realise that it needs less of these chinless Pommy cunts?'

This was yet another example of the 'anything goes' attitude towards the English. The guy may well have been useless, but what the hell did his nationality have to do with it?

Similarly, and to prove that I'm not just pro-British in this regard, let me state on record that the National Club Identification Policy, implemented by FFA in 2014, should have no place in a modern day nation's sporting landscape. For those of you unaware, the NCIP states that no new Australian club is allowed to carry an 'ethnic' or nationalistic name or logo. Yet, when Melbourne Heart changed to Melbourne City in the same year, the new badge contained the ship (signifying the Manchester ship canal) that also features on the Manchester City equivalent!

The wording of the NCIP was such that clubs were supposed to be left in no doubt that only 'references to the broader geographic area in which the club is located' were allowed. Clearly a case of double standards – and indicative of Australia's struggle in general with the issue of identity, and what multiculturalism actually means.

If you'll allow me to digress again, I tried to bring this issue into even sharper focus with a column for the Fox Sports website. In it, I had a crack at Peter FitzSimons (among others), after he'd used the words 'their coach' when talking about Holger Osieck in his weekly *Sydney Morning Herald* column, as opposed to 'our coach'. This to me, encapsulated how football was still being viewed as 'foreign' to the average Aussie.

FitzSimons, the head of the Australian Republican movement, demands the removal of the Union Jack from the Australian flag, to represent a more inclusive version of a country made up of many different nationalities. Fair enough, too. Yet he considered the most inclusive, multicultural sporting team in the country (the Socceroos) to be 'them' and not 'us'? I found that sort of argument typical of many. They loved to eat pizza, but weren't prepared to admit it was Italian.

Back at the World Cup, the second incident in Brazil was a little more frightening. In fact, it was downright scary.

One day back in Ipanema, we'd decided to go with the Green & Gold Army on a tour of one of the favelas, the notorious shantytowns that dot the hillsides around Rio, providing a stark contrast between the wealth and poverty of Brazil's most famous city. I'd actually been on a favela tour once before, many years earlier, when I'd been holidaying in Rio, so I wasn't too concerned, despite their fearsome reputation. We had guides with us, we were plenty in number, and so long as we stuck to the beaten track, we didn't expect any problems. I thought it would be a nice piece to do visually, and a good chance to get some interviews with Aussie fans at the same time.

The day started peacefully enough as we climbed through the rickety streets of Rocinha, the city's largest favela, towards a vantage point which is often used for tourists, offering beautiful panoramic views of downtown Rio from high up on the hillside. As we all snapped away with our cameras however, we became aware of a disturbance beneath us. Raised voices, and then a blur of movement, as soldiers raced through the narrow lanes below. A few seconds later, we heard the 'pop pop' sound of gunfire, and a kindly Brazilian lady leaned out of a window above us, and told us in no uncertain (Portuguese) terms, to take cover!

I have to say that, even at this point, I wasn't unduly concerned. My cameraman Tim Moran had got some of the gunshots on film from a distance, and with 30 or so Australians now crouching for cover, I figured this was going to make a decent part of my story, so I quickly did a 'piece to camera' outlining our sudden predicament.

After a few minutes, we were told it was safe to go, and we wandered back down the hill, laughing and joking about this 'crazy' experience. Suddenly however, the SWAT team we'd seen below appeared all around us, rifles pointing, ready for action. The commander barked out orders in Portuguese to us, quickly translated by a very flustered tour guide. Apparently, we had wandered right into the middle of the gun battle between the authorities and the local drug gangs. As the soldiers hadn't yet seen their enemy at close quarters, they were concerned that some of our group might have been infiltrated, and so we were ordered to stand up against a wall, and lift our jerseys (even the women), to confirm that none of us were carrying weapons. We were ordered to put down our cameras and stand still. This was no longer a joke, we were bang in the middle of some serious shit.

After satisfying themselves that none of us were part of the drug gang, we were herded into a local cake shop, and told we had to stay there until further notice. Outside, a burly soldier stood guard outside the door, his eyes trained on the streets above. It was a full 20 minutes before we were allowed out, and it was quite a nervous time, I can tell you. The only person allowed (or capable) to speak to the guard was our guide. I asked the guide whether we were being held inside for our own protection. He smiled wanly, and said, 'Not really. More like human shields. The drug gangs don't like shooting at soldiers if there are tourists around. It makes things worse for them if they hit a tourist!' Wow.

Eventually of course, we were released. But that was the end of the tour; no-one felt like staying longer, and we beat a hasty retreat back to our van, and back down to our digs in Ipanema. I got a very good story out of it, however. Although we'd all been told to put down our cameras, one of the Green & Gold Army members had a miniature GoPro that he'd somehow kept running throughout the drama, so after a little negotiation, I persuaded him to give us the footage to form part of our yarn. Back in the safer areas of Rio, I interviewed several fans about their experiences, and the story had quite an impact back in Australia.

Although what happened to us in Brazil wasn't particularly pleasant, travelling to far-off lands is one of the great joys of being involved in football. As I said earlier in the book, football provides an education – not just about sport – and offers opportunities that other sports just don't provide.

Early in my Australian career, I remember one or two people asking me whether I'd eventually 'move on' to work in Rugby League, Aussie Rules or cricket, as if football was merely a stepping stone to 'bigger' things. This, sadly, is typical of the way the other codes skew people's opinions Down Under. Not only could I never work on those sports anyway (due to my lack of knowledge), but why on earth would I want to?

I often think being involved in League, or Aussie Rules in particular, must be one of the most mundane and repetitive jobs in sport. With most of the clubs based in one city, no international aspect to speak of, few foreign players to give a different 'flavour' and no promotion/relegation/Cup competitions, I can't understand how the reporters don't retire through boredom! By contrast, football is an ever-changing, ever-challenging environment.

For example, just a month or so after being at the Maracana on a hot sticky night in Rio, I was in sub-zero temperatures at the most southerly football ground I have ever visited, the Forsyth Barr Stadium in Dunedin for the Carlsberg Football United Tournament, involving Wellington Phoenix and Premier League giants, Newcastle United and West Ham.

The mini-competition also took in games in Wellington and Auckland, and I called all the game alongside ex-Millwall (and Wellington Phoenix) winger, Paul Ifill. Steph flew over to join me for a mini-break in between the games, and we drove almost the entire length of the north island to get to the capital from Auckland via the incredible Rotorua, notable for its geothermal activity. New Zealand is undoubtedly one of my favourite countries, its natural beauty is staggering.

Three days on from windy Wellington, and I was back on commentary duty at the rather unlikely surrounds of Magic Park in Newcastle, as the first-ever FFA Cup opened its doors.

The Cup has been a brilliant addition to the football calendar, and even researching the two teams that night – Broadmeadow Magic and Brisbane Strikers – was a real test. I even enjoyed the old-fashioned 'open-air' experience of a commentary position based on a gantry, just like I used to do, back in my UK days. The Cup has opened up the top level of the game to the grass roots in Australia, and I'm of the opinion that it should only be the start. Promotion/relegation has to come sooner or later, or else we run the risk of aping the other codes. Closed competitions with the same old clubs, going round and round for years on end.

I know all the arguments regarding finance, history and geography, and there's no doubt Australia has some pretty unique problems in opening its football market up to a second-tier. But that doesn't mean it's impossible. I think it's the game changer for football Down Under, and the sooner it happens the better, but I have my doubts as to whether we'll see it in my lifetime.

The reason? FFA is an inherently cautious organisation, as, in fairness, such governing bodies are prone to be. While I'm full of admiration for what they've achieved since 2004, I've had many fallouts with them over the years, and such disagreements only intensified as 2015 loomed into view. The catalyst was the impending retirement of Chairman, Frank Lowy, and more pertinently, the identity of his successor. As early as 2013, we were hearing noises that his son, Steven, was going to be taking over when the elections took place, as far away as November 2015. I didn't – and don't – have a problem with Steven personally. He is a very capable businessman, he's a football fan, and on an individual basis, he's very approachable. But what I did have a problem with, was the system. To me, the process was engineered to deliver a certain result – in this case, Steven's election to the senior post, with several other 'hand-picked' candidates to sit on his board.

I wrote several articles on the topic as the months went by, as did my journalistic colleagues, Tom Smithies, and Mick Lynch. But we were lone voices. No-one in football wanted, or at least was prepared to, challenge the status quo. In December 2014, I wrote the following on the Fox Sports website – prescient words as it turned out: 'As we've seen with FIFA, paying lip service to proper governance can lead to major problems down the line. That's the last thing we need here.'

In the event of course, Steven 'won' the vote. His was the only name put forward for the job of Chairman, and several other candidates, mainly unknown to the public, were elected into their roles without any meaningful discussion (at least publicly), at all.

That would never happen in Rugby League or Aussie Rules, but football's still relatively low profile allowed such a process, and the game just wasn't strong enough to demand a debate. Many believe that Lowy Senior's record meant we media types shouldn't even have questioned him, but I disagree, despite the brilliant job Frank did. I used the example of Sir Alex Ferguson, who brought untold glory to Manchester United, but who was then allowed to choose David Moyes as his successor.

Furthermore, if the media fails to ask proper questions, then it becomes complicit in crucial decisions that affect the game, and people's livelihoods.

As I write this, almost two years into his tenure, there is no grand over-arching strategy to drive the game forward, save for the rather woolly 'Whole of Football' plan, released by FFA prior to his election.

The moment that summed everything up for me, came a day or two before the election in November 2015. Repeated requests to interview Steven during the process had fallen on deaf ears, but finally, a hand-picked number of journalists (of which I was one), were invited to Westfield to speak to the 'new Chairman' – BEFORE the official vote.

Steven wasn't keen on my rather direct line of questioning regarding the process, though we have had a good professional relationship since. His father didn't like my rather pointed questions either, when I interviewed him a week or two later, as part of what was, essentially, a valedictory tour to celebrate his achievements. Lowy Senior bridled at my suggestion that the Australian World Cup bid had been less than clean. Part of his reasoning was the 'nominations committee', which he claimed meant he was outside the process. I pointed out that the committee had no constitutional basis, at which point he totally lost his rag.

'Constitution, schmonstitution!' he roared in his Aussie-European hybrid accent.

It had already been a momentous year, with Australia winning the 2015 Asian Cup on home soil, the biggest football achievement since I'd emigrated back in 2003.

Andy Harper and I spent most of the early part of the tournament in Melbourne, covering the group matches at AAMI Park. Prior to the event, there had been lots of negative press speculation regarding the tournament, with many (mainly non-football) people predicting empty stands. Instead, Aussie football fans turned up in incredible numbers. When 12,000 show up to watch Uzbekistan and North Korea, you know the potential the game has Down Under. Michael Brown and his Local Organising Committee did a super job in selling the competition, and the final average attendance of 22,000 was a credit to him and his team. To put it into context, four years earlier in Qatar, that figure was 12,000, and the fact the Australian event made a big profit, was further reason to celebrate.

The Asian Cup was another endurance test for a commentator – as we knew would be the case, having covered the previous two editions. Fourteen games in 22 days (sometimes with travel in between) is tough work, particularly mentally, as you try to keep your mind fresh. Fox co-commentator, Robbie Slater, doing his own onerous shift in Brisbane, summed it up during one game at the tournament, when his offsider, Brenton Speed, queried one of the phrases he'd used to describe a passage of play, 'So many games, so many words to find!'

The final in Sydney was a brilliant occasion, but, as in 2011, I didn't have the greatest game behind the microphone. The mistake I made (I believe) was getting too hyped-up before the game, encouraged by Murray (Shaw), who had told Andy and me to be as 'parochial as we wanted to be' during the call.

Now, I had no problem with getting excited over a possible Australian success, if that's the way it turned out. I'd been in the country long enough to identify with the Socceroos quite closely, so that wasn't the issue. But really, I should have ignored the 'parochial' part of the advice, and just commentated in my normal way. Instead, I took it too literally, and at times was probably a little too partisan. This strikes at the heart of one of the major problems with being involved in football in Australia. Are we reporters OF the game, or promoters FOR the game? In my opinion, in a country such as Australia, you have to be both to a certain extent, but occasionally you can misread the situation, which is what I did that night in Sydney.

For every Aussie fan cheering on the team, there was another – perhaps not as committed, or interested in football – who was irritated by the rather parochial nature of the call. Afterwards, in the cold light of day, I could recognise my mistake, but at the time, I believed I was merely fulfilling my brief. The problem of course, is that you have to live with what goes out on air for years afterwards.

To be fair, I called the goal scorers correctly (so one big improvement on 2011), and because the result went Australia's way, I probably got away with that call, just as Craig Foster had done in 2005.

I've been incredibly lucky to have been associated with the Socceroos for so many years. I've formed a close bond with the national team, which hasn't always been easy when you're still trying to maintain a professional distance. But after calling over a hundred of their games, it's become impossible not to want them to do well, especially as they remain the greatest promoter of the sport, in a country which is still lukewarm towards 'soccer'.

Ahead of a game in 2013, Mark Schwarzer even presented me with a signed jersey to commemorate my 100th game with the 'Roos. I still haven't forgotten those words of Paul Williams in 2003, when he said calling the national team was a 'privilege' – wise words, and I think they can also be applied to every day I've spent working in football broadcasting.

I've been the luckiest guy in the world, and even at the age of almost 50, I'm still having new experiences through football – such as our 2015 trip to Kyrgyzstan, where the Socceroos played at a stadium that had one of the most beautiful backdrops I'd ever seen, the Ala-Too mountain range, and where people were so desperate to see the game, they crawled over the walls like ants. Our commentary position was on a rickety wooden platform, nailed onto ancient looking seats at the back of the main stand. Our OB director – Russian as I remember – asked us if we moved around a lot during commentary. I said 'No. Why?' His response was that the platform would probably give way if we did. Andy and I remained largely motionless throughout the entire 90 minutes!

Then later in the same year, we visited another of the Stans – Tajikistan – where our trip was only confirmed just before take-off, due to an Islamic insurgency that had reportedly claimed the lives of many policemen just days before our arrival. The game was also the first time the Tajiks had ever broadcast a game of football internationally. Todd Procter was again along for the ride, and was literally teaching his crew how to do their jobs as the game was progressing – all out of the back of an OB Truck that was, in effect, no more than a small van.

In 2017, we made it to Iran, where the politics of the AFC almost killed our broadcast of the Iraq–Australia game completely. We'd been designated to sit in the one area of cover in the outdated PAS Stadium, but were placed in the same room as the governing body's Refereeing Assessor and the Match Commissioner. Neither of whom wanted a commentary team spoiling their peace. With 10 minutes to go before kick-off, they were still attempting to kick us out – not ideal preparation for commentary. Nor was the fact the wrong team sheet had been issued, which showed the Iraqi captain, Ala'a Abdul-Zahra, lining up at number 10. It was only when my eyes scanned across the Iraqi team during the national anthems I realised there WAS no number 10 in the line-up. Then it was a case of working out who had replaced him – and why.

These are the tests that are sometimes put before you in unfamiliar, even hostile environments – but what incredible experiences, and they are only possible through football.

I'm still ambitious, and as my presenting career has declined, so my writing career has enjoyed a resurgence – as one door closes, another one opens, as the old saying goes. I've been fortunate enough to have been taken on as the Australian correspondent by the globally renowned *World Soccer* magazine – a real privilege, as it's a magazine I've loved reading for years. I write a weekly column for the Fox Sports website, and often, those stories or opinion pieces find their way onto the pages of the *Daily Telegraph*, so I've almost come full circle from those days with the *Portsmouth Evening News.*

Domestically, my hardline stance in favour of football (and often, its fans), has earned me regular slots on radio shows in Sydney, Melbourne and Adelaide – the latter two are even generous enough to pay me for my time, and my thoughts. I find I'm never more popular than when the A-League has endured a night of trouble in the stands. This is when people like me are forced to man the barricades, to defend the sport against the usual tirades from the 'Sheilas, Wogs and Poofters' brigade.

Case in point, in late 2015, we had perhaps the bitterest dispute involving football fans and the media, one that escalated into a full-blown boycott of A-League matches, on the back of David Gallop's rather cack-handed response to a report in the *Sunday Telegraph* by the late Rebecca Wilson.

Wilson's report painted the usual picture of a game beset by violent fans and inept administrators. Not much of it was true, although there is a small element among the Western Sydney Wanderers fan base that do us no favours, that's for sure. It's a similar story in Melbourne with a minority of Victory fans. But they don't in any way reflect the regular A-League experience, and when Gallop failed to defend the well-behaved majority, I penned a strongly-worded article the following day for the Fox website, lambasting Gallop's weak display as 'appeasement of Neville Chamberlain proportions'.

Two days later, and a second conference was held, with new Chairman, Steven Lowy, there to offer moral support to Gallop. But the damage was already done, and the fans found their voice to demand a proper appeals process for banned supporters, by staying away from matches the following weekend.

Mark Bosnich later brokered a meeting between the governing body and the supporters, and invited me to play a part in proceedings, but I decided that's where I needed to draw the journalistic line. Once you stop reporting on the story, and become part of it, you lose your way. Those sort of moments happen often in football in Australia; we're always treading that fine line, because overall, the game remains too small.

That little exchange damaged my otherwise good relationship with Gallop for a time, but unfortunately, that is part of the job. I've heard it said that David feels he was 'torpedoed' by the football media over the issue, and that may be true, but I felt he totally misread the fury of the supporters. As journalists, and football fans ourselves, we had to reflect that.

Gallop is the latest in a long line of CEOs at FFA who don't have football backgrounds, and while in most cases that shouldn't matter, when it comes to emotive issues, I sometimes feel that the lack of 'feel' for the game shines through. Football is a pretty unique game when it comes to fan culture, and if you haven't experienced that in your formative years, you are starting at a major disadvantage. It's the same with the longer-term strategy and global nature – many seem unable to think outside their 'traditional Australian sport' box, and football suffers as a result.

My written work in 2015 earned me a rare individual award, the Footy Fans Down Under Digital Writer of the Year, which was a pleasant surprise. Journalists cop a lot of abuse for what they write and say, so occasionally it's nice to receive some recognition. Much of that work in 2015 concerned the politics of the game, and the shenanigans at FIFA in particular. The rise of the Gulf power brokers has left the game balancing on a knife edge in my opinion – teetering between the old football establishment, and its new business-savvy paymasters. New money versus old football perhaps?

Talking of which, as we move forward to the current day (2017), the game of football in Australia appears to have come full circle too. With the major parties squabbling over the make-up of the new FFA Congress, the sport is once again hamstrung by politics, just as it seemed to be when I arrived Down Under in 2003. The only difference today is that it's not the old Anglo/Ethnic fault lines driving the splits, but money. Progress of a sort perhaps.

The other codes of football don't have this problem, yet their monoculture brings its own issues, of racism, of sexism, of parochialism. Little wonder the AFL in particular, has used 2017 to try and break out of its provincial enclave – although inaugurating a women's league (after 150 years), and playing a game overseas are hardly as ground-breaking as they'd like to make out. Football has been doing both for years.

Football still holds a significant advantage for the future. It has no boundaries to play (size, shape, gender), it has a genuinely global outlook, it is the richest and most popular sport on the planet, and has Australia's demographic trends (along with globalisation) on its side. The challenge for the game is harnessing those advantages, and converting them into bums on seats at A-League grounds, and eyeballs watching on TV. Twas ever thus.

As I write the closing words to this book, it is midway through 2017, and I am preparing for yet another season in the A-League, in my twenty-sixth year as a sports journalist. I remain as obsessed with football as I was when I was six, heading off to watch my beloved Manchester City. It's not just what I love, or what I do, it's more than that – it's who I am.

The game, and the industry, has changed beyond recognition since I watched my first game in 1973 – and so have I. I carry a bit more weight and many more grey hairs these days, and as I head towards 50, I have no idea how long I will be allowed to continue in broadcasting, or in journalism.

My previous contract ran out in June 2017, and for some time I thought it might be time to head back to England. My parents are now in their early eighties, and naturally, showing signs of slowing down. But what to do if I went? Certainly, I would not be able to walk into a top job, such as the one I hold in Australia. There is also family to consider, with Steph's youngest child still to complete her schooling. So, when Fox offered me another three years, I was happy to accept.

Do I feel completely at home in Australia after all I've talked about? The honest answer is, no. I'm not sure that will ever be the case, but then, when I return to England these days, I'm not sure I feel I belong there either. My good friend, Ricardo Piccioni, now employed by FFA to try and improve relations with state and federal governments, has a similar feeling, and calls it living in 'limbo-land' – I think it's a good description.

When I came to Australia, I had all the usual expectations of living the Australian 'lifestyle' with the job (in my eyes) being the conduit for that. Instead, I unwittingly timed my arrival with the exponential growth of the game, elevating my career onto an entirely different level, for which I'm hugely grateful.

It's been a fascinating journey, and when I look back on my quarter century in journalism and broadcasting, I feel immense satisfaction. I travelled the globe, reporting on football on every continent. I earned a good living, met some fabulous people (even if I fell out with a lot of them along the way), and moved to a great country, meeting a beautiful girl who later became my wife.

I've been very blessed, and if I don't know where my real home is, I do know I feel at home when surrounded by football. Not a bad place to be, for someone who is still, and will always be, just a gob on a stick.

ACKNOWLEDGEMENTS

This book wouldn't have been possible without the love and efforts of my long-suffering wife, Stephanie, who has been through the manuscript with me time and again, pointing out errors or corrections that needed to be made. She probably won't read the book, but she could certainly recite it back to me. Thanks my soulmate.

My thanks to Leo Karis, my long-time manager, agent, voice of reason and friend. He believed in this project, and made it possible.

To my parents, who've been through many traumas in their lives, and even though we live far away from each other these days, I know they are immensely proud of what I've been able to do. Thank you for bringing me up as a proper northerner – argumentative, glass half-empty, but with a very keen sense of right and wrong.

To the hard-working staff at New Holland, in particular, Victor Yoog, Alan Whiticker and Liz Hardy, who saw potential in the book, worked around my insecurities, and tempered my abrasive language – thank you.

My thanks to Tim Cahill, who not only provided the foreword without hesitation, but personally called me to thank me for asking. That's the measure of the man. I hope I'm calling your goals for a year or two yet.

Thank you to England for nurturing my love of football, for shaping me, and to Australia for embracing me, and giving me hitherto undreamt of opportunities to pursue my dreams.

Thanks to Led Zeppelin, Deep Purple, AC/DC, Hawkwind, Saxon, Motorhead, Iron Maiden, Black Sabbath and countless others, for making sure my life isn't totally one-dimensional.

Finally, my thanks to Manchester City Football Club. You don't know it, and you probably don't even care, but you're to blame for all of this.

First published in 2017 by New Holland Publishers
London • Sydney • Auckland

The Chandlery, 50 Westminster Bridge Road, London SE1 7QY, United Kingdom
1/66 Gibbes Street, Chatswood, NSW, 2067, Australia
5/39 Woodside Ave, Northcote, Auckland, 0627, New Zealand

newhollandpublishers.com

A record of this book is held at the British Library and the National Library of Australia.

ISBN 9781742579726

Group Managing Director: Fiona Schultz
Publisher: Alan Whiticker
Project Editor: Liz Hardy
Designer: Andrew Quinlan
Production Director: James Mills-Hicks
Front Cover Image: Ben Symons
Printer: HangTai Printing Company Limited

10 9 8 7 6 5 4 3 2 1